__Third Edition__

Coaching the Defensive Line: By the Experts

Edited by
Earl Browning

ISBN: 978-1-60679-147-9
Library of Congress Control Number: 2010942980
Cover design: Brenden Murphy
Text design: Brenden Murphy
Front cover photo: Jeff Golden/Getty Images

Coaches Choice
P.O. Box 1828
Monterey, CA 93942
www.coacheschoice.com

Contents

1

Defensive Line Techniques and Drills

Tom Adams
University of Kentucky
2000

It is a pleasure being here today representing the University of Kentucky. Kentucky is a great place to coach. I'm an Army brat and have been around the world. But, Kentucky is a great place to make a home.

I'm going to go completely off my film and show you the drills we use in developing defensive linemen. We shot this film during our spring practice last year. There is about one shot of each drill. Sometimes, it is a humbling experience to get what we teach in drills to show up on the field. That has to do with coaching and communicating with your kids.

The first two years at Kentucky, I coached the defensive ends. Last year, I had the defensive tackles and ends. Next year, I will coach the defensive tackles.

The first thing I want to talk about is stance. On our practice field, we have some posts set into the ground. We use them as shiver boards. You could use a flat wall. Jon Tenuta at Ohio State was my defensive coordinator at SMU. He kept asking me about hitting an immovable object. That's what gave me the idea about putting something in the ground. I had used a wall, but at Kentucky our field is surrounded by hedges. To get to a wall, I would have to run across two practice fields. I decided to put these posts into the ground.

When we come out for practice, we use these posts for punch boards. The posts are nine inches wide. They are eight by eight posts, with three feet above the ground. They have the same amount in the ground as you see above the ground. They are wrapped with natural fiber rope, which makes them nine inches wide. It is better than working on a wall because it allows flexion in the wrist. We are working the punch with the palms of the hand. It allows us to get into the drill quicker, because we are not working the wrist so much. We work from the knees to start with. We deliver 12 quick shots to the post. They do this on their own. We are watching for eye and hand movement with a nice flat back. We want them to get good punch from the hips. This is a quick-hands drill.

Figure 1-1. Post drill

After that, we put them in a stance. We punch on the post from the stance. We don't try to knock the post out of the ground. We are working on stance. I tell them that the post is going to catch them when they punch. I don't want them to get hurt going too hard at the post. I have seen some of our guys get too wide with the hands and really carom off the posts.

In their stance, we want their hips slightly higher than their shoulders. We want the feet about armpit-width apart. We are going to crowd the football in our stance. We are so close to the ball that they will have to back their face mask off their hands a couple of inches. In our stance, we always play with our inside hand down to the football. As I get down in my stance, I want my hand in front of my stagger foot, not in the center of my stance. That lets me keep my hips and shoulders even.

In the stance, we want a concave effect to their backs. We want a bit of a shallow area in their back. When I don't see that, I think that is weakness in the stance. I like the other hand down so, as he gets off and attacks the "V" in the neck of the offensive lineman, his hand is ready to get into the target area. On a passing situation, he might cock his other hand in the pass rush. I want his pads back so we can explode like he is coming out of starting blocks. Those are the things we address in the stance and punch on the post drill.

We take six shots with the right hand and six with the left hand. A lot of times, we don't let them take a step. The thing that is going to deliver the blow is the hip action as he rolls his hips. I want this guy to generate a lot of force out of his hips and put it on a spot of the offensive lineman. I think we can overwhelm anyone that we meet if we put our force on a spot on half the man. We want to turn the offensive lineman. We don't attack all his body. We work on half his body.

The thumbs should be up. That insures the elbows will be in. If the elbows get turned out, you have some big problems. The offensive lineman could collapse the arms and get into the body.

Twenty years ago, I did not think much about stance, but now I coach the hell out of it. That is the one basic place you start the football play from. If you are messed up there and don't know how to get out of your stance, you are useless as a football player.

When we get into a pass rush stance, we narrow the feet down. They are less than armpit-width apart. We still crowd the ball. We want the forward foot in the stance to be within five inches of the down hand. We want all of the weight balanced between the down hand and up foot. The hips are higher than in the regular run stance. There is a bigger stagger in the stance. The back leg straightens a bit to get the hips up further. We back out the opposite hand and cock it so we can get a hell of a jump.

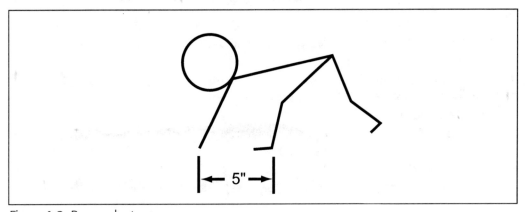

Figure 1-2. Pass rush stance

We tell our defensive line and show them on film how we want them to come off. What I am looking for is all four of our defensive linemen moving off the ball at the same time. When the center moves the ball, I want everyone off. If we want to check the get-off, we put the tape on slow motion, watch the ball, and check the movement of the hands of the defensive lineman with the ball.

I like to use the two-man Crowther sled. We teach a six-point explosion drill on this sled. To get in the six-point stance, the points on the ground are the knees, hands, and toes. We can get good teaching on hand use in this drill. This spring, since I am going to coach the tackles only, I am going to teach hands and face into the sled. The thing to emphasize in the six-point stance is to get the toes into the turf. Sometimes, the kids want to get up and stand on their feet. That takes away from the hip roll.

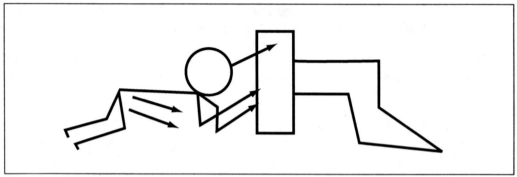

Figure 1-3. Six-point stance

The next thing we do is get into the three-point stance against the sled. We work on explosion, drive, and escape. We explode like the six-point drill. We drive with the feet and press away. Then, we execute an escape and rip through. We want the eyes on the level with our hands and dip in the hips. After the explosion and drive, I blow a whistle. On the whistle, the guy on the sled locks out and continues to push the sled back. After that, we execute the escape by ripping through.

The next thing I want to get into is tackling. At the University of Kentucky, we do not tackle body on body. We tackle with apparatus only. If we get an injury, it will occur on a game day. We use the one-man sled a lot in our tackling drills. We lock up on the dummy and lift. We punch our hips and put our face on the jersey. We lock up with the forearms and try to break the ribs. We take on running backs and wide receivers high on the shoulder pads above the numbers, grab cloth, and pull down, as we pull our hips through. We keep our feet alive all the way through the tackle. The thing defensive linemen want to do is use their bodies in tackling. We don't want to be dragging people down with our hands. We get the body on them and arms over them in a real nice wrap. If the lineman is just reaching, he won't make many tackles.

The next drill is a simple *board drill*. This helps the tackle because he is working in a confined area. The board is 15 inches by 15 feet. This is not like running the speed ladder or running ropes. The wood is very unforgiving. If you don't do what you are supposed to do, it will put you down. In the seven years I've been using this, I haven't had any ankle injuries (I have not had any and neither have my kids, ha, ha). We use a number of movements over the board. We make a stab step and cross the board like we are going across the face of an offensive lineman. We work lateral steps across the board. We work crossover steps across the board. We emphasis staying on the ball of the feet and not touching the board. It becomes challenging. If anyone steps on the wood, the whole line rides him out for being clumsy. They work their butts off not to touch the wood. We don't want one noise coming from the wood.

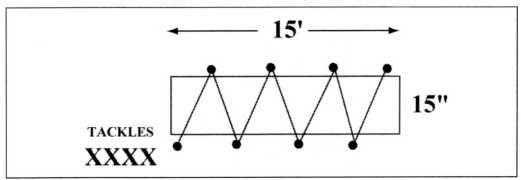

Figure 1-4. Running boards

We don't practice very long, so what we do in our drills is done quickly. We do a *line drill* to teach pursuit. We align and get off. We attack the offensive lineman, flatten him out, and turn his shoulders. This is basically working on getting off blocks. We get off, key the head of the offensive blocker, and flatten him out down the line of scrimmage by turning his shoulders. If the offensive lineman can't get upfield, he can cut you off.

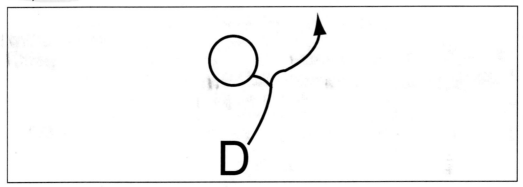

Figure 1-5. Flatten and turn

The next drill we do is called a *turn-and-run drill*. This is a pass-rush drill. We align the defensive linemen on the line. They get off and rush the passes. They come in on the passer and get their hands up. The ball is thrown out, and they chase the flight of the ball together. This is drill work for screens. Also, I will take the ball back, pull it down, and move forward. This gives them a draw key. They stop, shout, "Draw," plant the outside foot, turn to the inside, and retrace their steps to the ball.

We are a basic 4-3 defense. We play a lot of even defense with our tackles. They are always moving. They are always moving to the set or away in some scheme. They are getting upfield into minimum assignment with a lot of penetration. When we move our tackle, we don't lateral step on the line of scrimmage. Our defensive coordinator doesn't want anything lateral at the line of scrimmage. He wants to reset the line of scrimmage. He wants to move up the field and take ground.

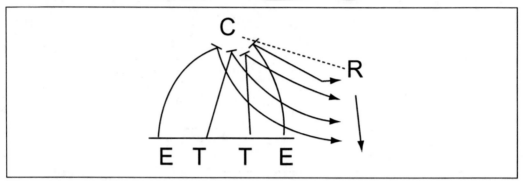

Figure 1-6. Turn-and-run

This type of movement with our defensive tackle is what we call *ears technique*. If we are going right, we step off to the right at a 45-degree angle. That removes part of the body from the contact. To get the rest of the body through, he has to put his *ear* into the body of the offensive blocker and rip through with the outside arm so he can clear the second step. He has to get his shoulder blades into the blocker and keep his pads down.

If we are going toward the strength of the set, that is called *go*. If he is going away from the strength, it is called *whip*. What they have to understand is the gap they are going into is going to move right or left. It is not going to stay there. He has to keep his head and eyes up to see which direction the gap is moving. Once they recognize which way the gap is moving, they don't have to stay square to the line. They can turn their shoulder and attack like hell in the direction of the play, flat down the line of scrimmage. The first thing the tackle should see is the offensive lineman and then the direction of the play.

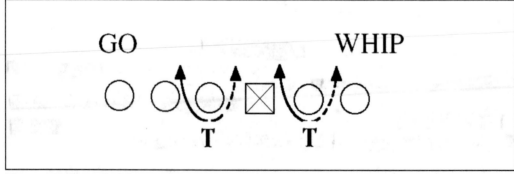

Figure 1-7. Go and whip

Defensive linemen think, when they break the line of scrimmage, they are going to make a tackle for a loss. What they need to do is pursue to the spot where the ball is going to cross the line of scrimmage. We want them to attack without hesitation down the line of scrimmage. If the ball is going away from them, we want them to stay square until they know the ball is not coming back. What we are trying to do is create things so the tackles can play faster.

The defensive tackle has to understand that the offensive lineman is not going to lie to him. The backfield will try to fake you out. When the center blocks back and the guard and tackle pull across the center, the tackles have to recognize that. When the tackle sees the center blocking back on the other tackle, he has to know he's got to get his inside foot down on the ground and get upfield with penetration. We want him to knock down some of the blockers. The counter is a recognition play. You have to rep that until your guys know what is coming.

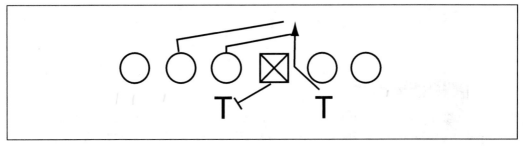

Figure 1-8. Counter

What I'm trying to do is get these guys to gain confidence that what they see is going to take them to the play. The zone play is a big play today. When we see the zone, recognition is important. As you watch this film, you see our tackle actually attacking the guy he is aligned on. That is not right. He is stepping left and should be attacking the guy in the next gap. He might have to attack the guy he is aligned on, but we want to try to get over to the far side of the gap.

The next thing we work on is the trap. We have to play the down or veer trap. The first thing I tell our tackle is, any time we get a down block from the guard, we want to get our hands on him and dump him on the center. There are only three things that can happen to him. It is veer dive, play away, or trap. We try to spill the trap block. We get our shoulder pads down under the block of the trapper. We want to wrong shoulder the blocker and see if we can't get upfield.

The next block we work on is the double-team. The double-team starts as a base block. We have to destroy the base block portion of this block. We want to turn our shoulder blades and hips into the double-team. I don't want to touch the ground. If you get in trouble on the double-team, the defensive tackle may have to touch his knee to his gap responsibility. The whole time he is touching his knee, he has to play with his hands and try to get them locked out. He drops his hips down and tries to get his hat down to hip level of the offensive blocker. If the offensive blockers get their shoulders together, it is hard to beat the block. He has to keep his feet alive.

The reason I don't want my guys dropping to the ground is we don't see the straight double-team anymore. All the double-teaming now is the start of a combination block. We see two types of combination blocks. The first example is the defensive tackle in the center-guard gap. The center can't reach the tackle. The guard comes down on the tackle to keep him from penetrating. The center comes off on the tackle. The guard stays on the tackle until the center can get leverage. The guard comes off on the linebacker, and the center secures his reach.

Figure 1-9. Combination block

The second type of combination is one like Syracuse used on us. That is the center blocking back on the defensive tackle. The off guard comes under the center block onto the tackle, and the center comes off on the linebacker.

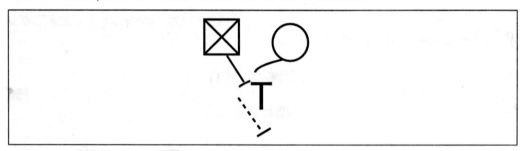

Figure 1-10. Combination block

If the offensive linemen see the tackle drop to the ground to hold the double-team, chances are both of them will go up on the linebacker. That is one thing we don't want to happen. That is why we don't go to the ground on the double-team. He has to hold his ground knowing that one of the blockers has to release him to get to the linebacker. When that happens, he has to explode upfield.

The next thing we have to recognize is a pull inside. When the defensive tackle gets an inside pull, he cannot hesitate. He goes directly on the line he wants to take. The point of attack is in the C gap away from him. He can't allow the center to dictate what path he takes. Forget the center. If the center happens to get into the tackle's face, cross his face. If he gets into the hip or butt area, use the rip and go around him. If the center pins the tackle, he can't get wasted. He squeezes until he can find a way off the block. The most important thing is to *eliminate hesitation*.

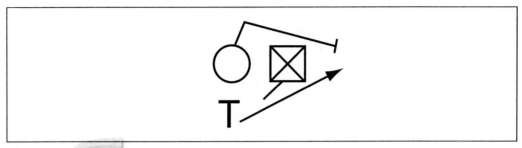

Figure 1-11. Pull inside

These next drills are pass-rush drills. This drill is called the *close drill*. We want the defensive tackle to get into the offensive lineman before he gets comfortably set. If I am a defensive end, I want to attack the "V" of the neck. The farther I want to go across his body with my inside hand is the tackle's sternum. The reason I don't go any further is so I can protect the outside shoulder from the offensive lineman. Once he puts his hand on the shoulder and shoves me away from the quarterback, that is the end of the defensive end's rush.

The outside hand is shoved into the armpit of the offensive lineman. Then, I can use whatever move I have been taught. I can use the club or uppercut, rip or swim, or whatever moves you want to teach. We attack edges of linemen, never down the middle. We want to attack one half of the body to see if we can get him turned or off balance.

When we work on the close drill, the key things are to *break leverage and rip*. Sometimes, our people think that breaking leverage is bull rushing. I want to exert so much pressure into a spot that the offensive lineman crumbles. It is that immovable object. Once I bust him, I want to get into my pass rush. A move we use in our pass rush is called *flip*. All I am trying to do is grab cloth and pull the offensive tackle toward the line of scrimmage. He then flips his hips past the offensive blocker.

This next drill is called *scramble*. The defensive line has rush lanes to the passer. The two inside guys will attack the numbers of the offensive linemen they are lined up on. They attack the inside edge to the outside edge of the numbers. The defensive ends attack the outside edges of the numbers to the middle of the shoulder. If the quarterback moves in the pocket, we want the rush lanes to change with him. Everyone is responsible for contain. If the quarterback moves left in the pocket, the defensive tackle should move laterally to maintain his contain shoulder. If the quarterback crosses the rusher's face, he wants to move to stay in his lane. If he doesn't, you have two rushers in the same lane.

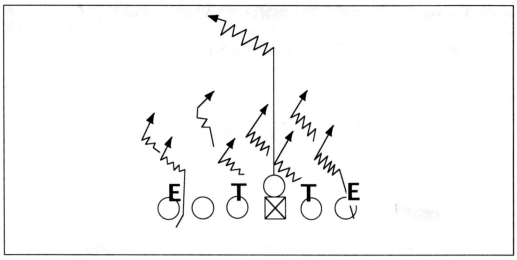

Figure 1-12. Contain the scramble

If there is a stunt, the guys work together if pass shows. The tackle comes down and picks the center. He tries to knock him in behind the guard. The nose guard takes a lead step upfield. If the guard shows high hat, the nose should be able to come up field free. If the guard closes down with the movement of the tackle, I want the nose guard to bull rush over the guard. I don't want the nose to attack wide. I don't want the quarterback to be able to step up and throw without someone in his face. If the nose goes wide, the throwing lane is created.

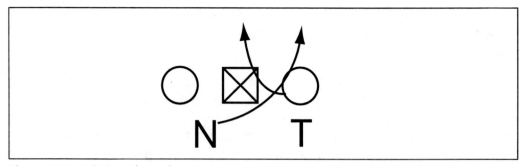

Figure 1-13. Twist into the rush

We use a *trail technique drill* to stop the cutback run. The tackle closes down. As he goes down, he wants to key the mesh area. That means he wants to see the football. If he doesn't see the football, he attacks the naked. When we play the naked bootleg, we attack straight upfield or vertical. Some people will turn and run to the sideline until they contain the quarterback.

Defensive ends should see the reverse coming. When they see it, they explode vertical to the goal post. They should see it quicker than the naked bootleg. We want no hesitation. This was a big play for us against LSU. They came out on the first play and tried to run the reverse. Our defensive end did a good job of closing and exploding straight upfield. He made the play and that gave us a big boost right off the bat.

A defensive lineman has to know who can block him. The man he is lined up on is the first threat. The off guard is the second threat. The fullback or the near back is the third threat. If the defensive lineman is playing a 5 technique and gets a down block, we want him closing to the inside leg of the guard to spill the play outside. When the lineman goes down inside on a close, the linebacker is going to exchange responsibility with him. When the defensive lineman spills the play outside, I want his body north and south. I don't want him turned perpendicular to the line. I want him to be more square.

I'm not saying that Kentucky is the best defense in the league, because that is not true. But, you don't see us getting manhandled or pancaked against some good offensive teams in a tough league.

2

The 4-3 Defensive Line Techniques

Jared Backus
Temple University
2008

It is a real honor to come back to lecture where I grew up. It is good to see friends I made over the years. It is an honor for me to speak to my peers in coaching. I feel very strongly about this point. I want you to know I have a tremendous amount of respect for the job the coaches in this area do in the schools and with the players. I have a great deal of respect for the job you do and for the way you are on-hands people. That is what it is all about in coaching. We want to try to change the culture of the program at our school. I am very humble to speak at this clinic.

My goal today is for you to get one thing from this lecture that will help you in your program. We won four games this year, and people came up to us and told our staff we had done a good job. I have never seen that in the other programs I have been associated with. This simply shows you the status of the program at Temple. When we beat Akron for our second win this year, it was the first time our players had won a road game. You talk about emotions; they were pumped.

I want to cover two points before we get into the X's and O's. Rules without relationships equal rebellion. If you are going to push a player to do his best every practice, you better have a relationship with those guys. Find ways to get closer to the players. The coach has to get his hands dirty and work with the players.

The second point I want to make is this: from a football-schematic standpoint, if you are going to be simple, you cannot be simplistic. We are going to talk about the 4-3 defense, and the over front with cover 2 behind the front. Being simple with the players and not having them confused is very important—but the players need to know everything about what you are doing. If you want a player to play a 1 technique, that players must know every reaction to that technique. You cannot be simple and be simplistic.

I want to start with some general points about playing defensive line. This could be used as an evaluation for the defensive linemen.
- Feet
- Flexibility
- Eyes
- Balance and body control
- Quickness
- Toughness
- Explosion
- Strain
- Speed
- Running
- Endurance
- Strength

The eyes are the most important thing you will train with the linemen. We want them to know their key progression. What are they looking for? We key man on to near back to backside pulling linemen. What is the player seeing with his eyes?

There are two points that are undercoached when we talk about running. This is what we talk about when we are pursuing the ball. We want them to move the arms and the upper body when they are running. We talk about being close to the play or making the play. We use one quote to illustrate these points: "Great defensive linemen play with their feet behind their hips."

What are we going to ask the players to do every day? We talk about flipping the switch. In the indoor program, when they come in the room we want them to flip that switch so they are ready to go. It is the same when the go to the classroom or study hall. They have to flip the switch and concentrate on what they are there for.

I want the players to flip the switch when they come into practice. We are talking about practice and procedures. We want them to give great effort and to improve each day. Here is what I am talking about. We want them to strive to improve. We want them to be aggressive, and we want them to be tough. We want them to intimidate the opponents. They must be dedicated to what we are trying to accomplish. We want them to be "six-second competitors." That means we want them to play hard for those six seconds in which a play is run. That is about the average time for a play.

We want the players to finish and to create takeaways. To us, the finish point is very big. The way we define finish is to beat your man to the ball. We grade this in games. Are you beating your man to the ball? We have improved on defense because we are running to the ball. We look at the video to grade the players to see if they are beating their man to the ball. We talk about having an 80-percent rating on beating their man to the ball. If they have an 80-percent rating on the finish, it is a winning effort. If it is less than that, they are not going to meet with the head coach on Sunday during the season.

Let me get to the X's and O's. We play a gap-control defense. This is a quick overview of our gaps and of our designations (Figure 2-1). We pay a lot of attention to splits and levels of offensive linemen.

A gap = OC – OG gap

B gap = OG – OT gap

C gap = OT – TE gap

D gap = Outside/imaginary TE gap

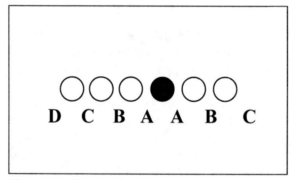

Figure 2-1. Gap designations

Next, we have our techniques. This is how we get lined up on defense (Figure 2-2). It is important for the defensive linemen to know where the linebackers are lined up.

0 = Head up on the center

1 = Split leg on center

2 = Split inside leg of guard

3 = Split outside leg of guard

4 = Split inside leg of tackle

5 = Split outside leg of tackle

7 = Split inside leg of tight end

6 = Head up on tight end

9 = Split outside leg of tight end

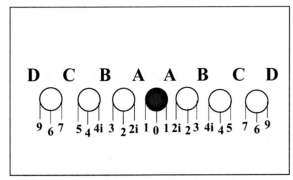

Figure 2-2. Techniques

Wide and *tight* are terms used to alter basic alignments. For example, we may call a "wide 9" or a "tight 5." *Ghost* is a term used to explain alignment to open end side. For example, we could call a "ghost 5."

The linebacker alignments are the same as line numbers except the defensive man is aligned off the line of scrimmage. For example, we could split outside the leg of the guard with a depth off the line of scrimmage, and that is a 30 technique to us.

We play with four down linemen, three linebackers, two deep safeties, and two corners. Our defense is a formational defense, so we get lined up to the formation. The way we get our front lined up is by role-playing the positions. We do not play a left or a right position. We flip-flop the defensive linemen, depending on the formations.

Our tackle and end are always going to line up on the tight-end side of the field, or the strongside of the formation. The linebacker makes a call as the offense breaks the huddle. The tackle and end go to the tight-end side of the formation. We can play an over alignment with the defensive end in a wide 9 technique (Figure 2-3).

The other defense we can play is the *switch* defense, which puts the defensive end in a 6 technique, which is a nose-to-nose alignment on the tight end (Figure 2-4).

On the over defense, the tackle plays a 3 technique. The nose plays a 1 technique. Our rush tackle will play a wide 5 technique. These are their base alignments against a pro set.

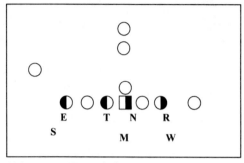

Figure 2-3. Over defense

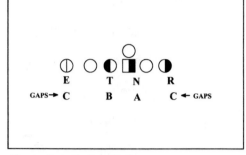

Figure 2-4. Switch Defense

Our linebackers line up in a 50-10-50 alignment. Our corners line up one yard outside and five yards deep on the wide receiver. The safeties are playing on the deep hash marks at a depth of about 12 yards.

We feel a four-man front with cover 2 behind the front is a good defense against the spread offense. It is a very simple defense, and it does not get the players hung up getting lined up. It is simple to adjust to the different offensive sets with this defense. If the tight end trades from one side to the other, we just check to a solid call. We bump everyone over.

Here is why I like this defense. It is very simple for the linebackers to line up against the one-back set. All the Sam and Will linebackers have to know is that they line up on the #2 receiver. If the #2 man is in the backfield, they play in a 50 alignment over the tackle. If the #2 receiver is detached from the formation, the linebacker plays an apex look, or halfway between the ball and the #2 receiver. The Mike linebacker picks up the #3 receiver. The alignment is very simple for the players.

I want to go over how we coach the defense. We start with the fundamentals. First is the stance. Our inside hand and foot are always down and back. We are in a three-and-a-half-point stance. We have the knees bent, and the back is flat. We want the hand behind the ball, and the helmet behind the hand. The toes are pointed straight ahead. We are approximately heel-toe stagger.

We must be exact in our alignment to ensure success. We call solid left or solid right to align our front. On the solid left, the tight end is lined up to that side of the formation. On the solid-right alignment, the tight end is on the right side.

The next step is the technique part of the progression. We want to play low and to attack the line of scrimmage. We want to play with our feet in the neutral zone. Here is how we describe the techniques.

Get off: Explode-step on ball movement. We are looking at the ball. When the ball moves, we want to know if our linemen are out of their stance. You can slow the film down and have the center stop the snap after he starts his snap to see if the players are moving on the ball. You must coach get-off. When the ball is snapped, we want the front four attacking using the run technique or pass-rush technique. They must move out of their stance. Get-off is an acquired skill.

Target: Step to the near shoulder of the blocker, striking through the proper V-neck. This is what we are looking at with our eyes. The inside players, that is the tackle and nose man, are looking inside at the side of the blocker's neck. We call it the V or the neck. If the end and rush are cocked on the outside, they are looking at the hip of the offensive man they are lined up on. That is where their eyes are.

The target is going to do one of three things. The target is coming at you, going away from you, or is going up and away from the blocker, giving him the high-hat move. All linemen know the three things and they work on attacking them. The target comes at the defense, or goes away from the defender, or goes up on the pass block. The players must work on getting good on that first step. When that target moves, we are going to try to strike it.

Cloth: Hands fit on inside breastplates with thumbs up.

Separation: Work to lock out elbows preparing to escape.

Escape: Release from blocker with violence.

We tell our players desire is the moment of truth. Three factors are involved here:
• Pursuit: Get proper angle to the ball. Punish the ballcarrier.
• Tackle: Execute temple tackle. Punish the ballcarrier.
• Excitement: Celebrate with the team.

We want to make sure the players know they must use maximum effort at all times. Effort plus desire equals success.

When we play a cocked technique with the end and rush, we cock them inside. The end is one-and-a-half feet outside the tight end. His hand is one-and-a-half feet outside the tight end's outside hip. The reason we do this is to force the offensive tackle to move his feet to block us when they are running a pass play.

While this may be simple to coaches, the players do not know all of this information. At times, the players do not know that they do not know what we want them to know, so we assume they know absolutely nothing.

The next thing we drill is cloth. We want to grab two fists of cloth of the lineman we are lined up on. The hands fit on the inside breast plates with the thumbs up. The aim points with the hands are the numbers to the top of the shoulders when we play out on the edge. They must be able to see what they want to hit. That is what cloth means.

If we have one hand on the chest plate and the other hand is on the outside of the body cylinder, it could be a trap play, or it could be an option play. It could be a backside play.

The other thing we are trying to do is to fight his near number with our hat and to get our hands on the chest plate. We refer to that as *hat and hands*. They must be able to feel what is going on during the block.

On the separation, we are trying to bench the man off us. We are trying to lock him out. We want to use the "power-hand/trail-hand" principle. We are trying to get the blocker turned, lock the gap arm out, push with it, and then push with the inside arm and pull with the trail arm. We want to turn the blocker. Once we get the man turned, we want to step at a 45-degree angle, and then escape the gap. We teach three escapes. We teach the rip, we teach the wipe, and we teach the cut.

The next thing we talk about is pursuit. We want to take a good angle to the ball. This includes the pass rush as well. Then we want to tackle. We must execute Temple tackles, and we must punish the ballcarrier. This is what we teach on tackling. "If we can get sock, we get sock. If we can get jock, we get jock. If we can get skin under our fingernails on the tackle, that is really good." We want the tackle to be violent. We are clubbing up through the rib cage of the offensive lineman, and we are holding on. We cannot teach all of the positions the linemen will be in position to make tackles up front. We have a couple of simple drills that we do, but this is basically what we talk about in tackling.

The other thing we talk about is setting a base on the rib cage of the ballcarrier. We want to attach our elbows to his rib cage. We want to squeeze the elbows and take the ballcarrier to the ground.

Here is the over defense. It is our solid left call (Figure 2-5). We have a couple of base line movements we use with this defense. You develop the movement package based on what the offense is running for that game. The movements are things you can do to help the defense. We call the defense over, and then we tag the movement we want to use. This would be our "over spike cover 2."

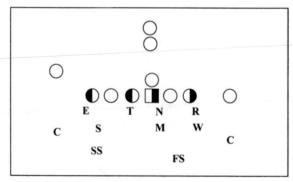

Figure 2-5. Over spike cover 2

The spike tells us the 3 technique is going to go from the B gap to the A gap. There are some techniques and fundamentals involved in these movements. The player's eyes must be coached, and he must know what to do on every reaction.

The way we coach the players that go from a shade technique to the 1 gap, or from the B gap to the A gap, is that we heavy-up on the man. He is going to aim for the middle of the A gap. The 3 technique will have his knee on the belly button of the guard. He is not head-up; he is heavy-up. He is looking at the guard. When the ball is snapped, he is stepping, and he is gaining ground as he steps. He is going to be violent with the arm and the leg. It is the same step as a T-board step for offensive linemen.

We know the blocker is going to do one of three things in the running game. Remember, we are going from the B gap to the A gap. The first thing he is going to do is to reach my level. On the first step, I know what he is doing. We call this *reach*. When he reaches, we want to step inside and shoot inside the hip to the A gap.

The second move is the base move. The blocker is blocking aggressive on our 3 technique. We step inside, use our hat and hips, and break it inside. The ball will be coming straight at the 3 technique.

The third thing the blocker will do is the veer. If the blocker goes down inside, we do not expect our 3 technique to cross the blocker's face inside. I do not think we can teach this move. If the blocker slants inside, I do not think we can expect the defender to get inside on the slant block.

When we see the veer block inside, we step to the blocker and turn the play into a squeeze move. We take the body of the blocker and stuff him in the A gap. A perfect veer read would be to take the blocker and stuff him inside to the A gap.

The second move we use is the rip movement (Figure 2-6). This is a move to the rush end. He is going to go from the C gap to the B gap. He is cocked wider. His aiming point is the crotch of the tackle to the B gap.

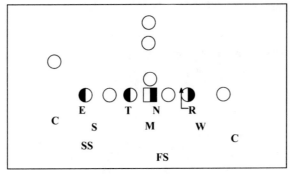

Figure 2-6. Over rip cover 2

If the offense runs a lead play, the rush is responsible to come underneath the tackle and fill the B gap. If he reads a hard inside release, he squeezes down the hole and comes down hard to the B gap.

The next movement is what we call the stick (Figure 2-7). This is a stunt for the 9-technique end. He is going from the D gap to the C gap. Remember, these are one-man movements. So we have spike, rip, and stick. These three moves fit into all of our pressure calls.

If we call tank, it is a stunt with the tackle and nose man (Figure 2-8). It is a pass rush between the 3 technique and the 1 technique. It is best against protection where the offensive guard is 1-on-1 with the 3 technique, and the center is turning to block the 1 technique.

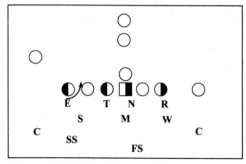

Figure 2-7. Over stick cover 2

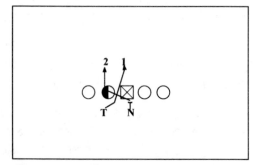

Figure 2-8. Tank stunt

The 3 technique penetrates the A gap on movement. He must get his helmet in the crease between the offensive guard and center. If the center sets away from the tackle, he "climbs his back." If the center sets to the tackle, he works across his face. He wants to narrow his body and keep his feet moving.

The job of the nose man is to attack the center to ensure that the center blocking him. If he goes too fast, the offensive guard will squeeze off the penetration. He must come tight off the hip of the offensive guard. We expect him to execute a pass-rush move on the offensive guard.

I want to show the video of these moves. I hope it will give you a better idea of what we are doing on defense with our linemen. Thank you. oves. I hope it will give you a better idea of what we are doing on defense with our linemen. Thank you.

3

Defensive Line One-Gap Techniques

John Banaszak
Robert Morris University
2005

First, I want to thank Nike for inviting me here to speak to you today. In addition, I want to thank Pete Dimperio, II, Earl Ceh, and the rest of the advisory board. My topic is "One Gap Techniques." This is an exciting subject, right? I have to talk over one hour on the 1 technique. Here is the secret: "Close on the down block and never get hooked!" Thank you! Do we have any questions?

I want to thank some other people before I get into the lecture. I want to thank Robert Morris University and head coach Joe Walton for giving me the opportunity to coach the defensive line. I also want to thank Dan Radakovich. I want to thank our other staff members for being here today. I have been a thrill for me to coach for Robert Morris University.

The first thing I talk about when I am working with the defensive linemen is expectations. I tell them this every single day. We must be better with every technique we use. I like to break things down to basics. That is how I learned to play the position. I had to do that. I had to be a technician. I was too slow, too small, and not quick enough to play the defensive line positions. I had to make sure my hand placement was where it had to be and I had to take the proper steps at the right times. I had to do that to play against the big, 280-pound offensive linemen.

I learned a great deal from George Perles. He taught me the things that have stayed with me as a football coach. I am tough, demanding, and I am intent. That is what I expect out of my players on every single rep of the football. They must improve everyday. When I walk off the football field, if I am not a better coach than I was when I walked on the field, then I did not have a good day. My players must feel the same way as I do in this regard. They have to be better football players when they walk off that field.

I have one rule and one rule only about practice. Practice is not punishment. Practice is preparation. I have to prepare the kids for every game they play. The only way I can be sure of that is to make sure we practice hard. I will never punish a player or team on the field. That is not the place for punishment. It is for preparation. I learned this a long time ago.

I was fortunate to play with the greatest defense that ever played the game of football. I played with the greatest defensive line that ever played the game of football. From those experiences, and from the coaching staff, it is the foundation of what I believe in today. My coaching philosophy is very simple: I want to prepare the football team for every challenge it faces and I will work as hard as I can to make sure that happens. I work with as much enthusiasm as possible, because that is how I played the game. That is the way I coach the game. I coach to win the game.

There is no doubt in my mind that one of the reasons I am here today is because of my experiences and because I have won. That is irreplaceable. You learn as you go along. Again, I like to break things down to the basics. I do not want to get too technical because then I get lost. If I get lost then my players are going to get lost. I learned a great deal from George Perles. I can remember the first thing George Perles told us in training camp in Latrobe in 1975. We were watching film of games from the previous year. The only players there were the rookies and the free agents.

The first play on the film, L.C. Greenwood took on a blocker, went around the blocker, and made a defensive play. George asked the group if anyone could do what L.C. Greenwood had just demonstrated on the film. He told us there was no one in the NFL that would do that. He told us not to even think about it. That is one of my "10 Commandments of 1-Gap Play," which I will talk about later. "Don't run around a block. You have to play through the blocker's head." That stuck with me all of these years.

In the middle of the season in my rookie year, we were playing Houston at Three Rivers Stadium. Dwight White had to miss the game because of an ankle injury. Steve Furness was his replacement. I was the only remaining defensive lineman on the sideline. Midway through the second quarter, L.C. Greenwood got his leg caught in a pile and hurt his knee. As the medical staff was administering to L.C. Greenwood, George Perles was administering to me.

George got up in my face and said, "You cannot get hooked. You cannot get reached! Oh my goodness, isn't there anyone else we can put in the game?" I was stunned a little. "You cannot get double-teamed. You cannot get blocked. Damn, there has to be someone else I can put in the game." I looked around and saw that we did not have anyone left to put in the game. I started out on the field. Before I got away from George, he grabbed me, looked me right in the eye, and said, "Don't blow it!" With that motivational message echoing in my helmet, I ran on the field. By the time I got to the defensive huddle, I realized he was right. I knew I could not blow my chance. I had a chance to prove I belonged in the NFL.

I did my job in the game. I did not blow the chance I got in that game. I proved several people wrong. I got in the huddle and to the left of me was Jack Ham, to the right of me was Mean Joe Greene. Ready to bark out the signals without any teeth was Jack Lambert. To me, everyone was at ease. How bad could I blow it? Three future Hall of Fame players surrounded me. I knew if they blocked ten yards off the ball, my teammates would still be there for me. I had confidence in my teammates. I did not blow it.

I am a Polish kid from Cleveland, Ohio and I understood where the Oilers were going to run the ball. Certainly, they were not going to run the ball at Joe Greene, they were going to run it at me. I knew that. I had that going for me. It was second down and seven for the Oilers. I threw the tackle aside and made the tackle on the play. I was starting to get excited. Now it was third down and long. Joe Greene said to me, "Do you want to win the game by yourself?" I said, "No, I just want to win the game."

On third down, I shot the gap and came free in the backfield. I sacked the quarterback for my first sack in the NFL. I jumped up in the air and started waving my hand in the air. I was elated. Now, when you see the modern day NFL players celebrating on the field, just remember this. I predated all of those other heroes that celebrate in the NFL. I started all of that activity when I got my first sack in the NFL in that game. If you get sick of all of the celebrating, you can blame it on me because I started it.

Let me talk about the 1 gap. Some people do not like the term 1 gap. What we try to do is to expand the 1-gap technique all over the football field. I see high school film of players that play the 1 gap. They secure the 1 gap but they are oblivious of anything else that is going on in the game. We do not want to stay in the 1-gap technique. The point is to be successful at the point of attack. You must stay in that gap and protect it because that is your responsibility. However, we have to understand we have the responsibility to pursue to the football. Once we take care of the 1 gap, we must get to the football. We do not want to make the 1 gap a tunnel vision.

You will not be a good defense if all that your players are worried about is their gap. If your linemen and linebackers are only worried about their gap, you will not be a good defense. We want them to expand their responsibility. We want a defense that can make plays all over the field. We tell our players they have to secure their gap, then run, and hit.

Defensive linemen have to realize that their initial gap responsibility lasts for only a split second. After that split second, the expansion begins. They have to be able to find the football. We want gap control established immediately and then we want them to be on the move. They cannot hesitate. He who hesitates is lost. They are responsible for those gaps. He who hesitates is beaten and cannot recover. Just to take care of one gap is not good enough. You must expand the gap no matter of what they do from sideline to sideline.

I like to breakdown the teaching process into basic areas. I start with the "Five Critical Steps of Defensive Line Play."

First is *stance*. (Demonstrator came up to assist.) If a player does it right one time, I expect them to do it right all of the time.

We want the toe to the instep on the stance. We have the feet slightly wider than shoulder width. Then we put the elbows on the knees. Then all the defender has to do is to roll forward. When we flip-flop to the other side, what do we do? We want the hand nearest the ball to be on the ground. This is especially true when we are in a shade technique on an offensive lineman. We want to be able to get the hand of that man as quickly as possible.

The second step is to *explode* off the football. We want a great takeoff. We work on a start drill every single day. We want to explode off the football. It is the only way to play the game. We want to beat the man across the line of scrimmage.

The third step is to *engage* the blocker. Then we want to control the blocker. After we gain control of the blocker, we want to separate from him. It should happen very fast. It comes with instinct and it should happen immediately. We need to understand where the ball is going instantly. We have to combine the engage, control, and separate into a quick, distinct move. That is because it happens so fast.

The fourth step is *escape*. At times we are going to get blocked. There is no doubt about that fact. Offensive linemen are going to block you. We must learn how to escape. We must learn how to get away from that block. We have to understand what is happening to us on that block. We have to be able to see that block, and we must feel the block, and we must have an instinct of how to escape the block.

The fifth step is to *make the play*. We have to be able to finish the play. Now comes the fun part. Get to the ball and make the play.

Looking at our stats from last year, I see that our fourth leading tackler was our defensive tackle. Our fifth leading tackler was the defensive end. Our seventh leading tackler was the other defensive tackle. We had production from our defensive linemen.

We are looking for defensive linemen. The defensive tackle can make a play on the opposite side of the field. We tell the players they had better take care of their gap and then they must be ready to run to the ball. "Go make that tackle." I love it when one of tackles makes a tackle on the opposite side of the ball on the opponent's sideline. "Where did he come from?" He is unaccountable. The offense does not have anyone assigned to block that backside tackle. We want our linemen to make tackles all over the field. Those are the five steps to great defensive line play.

I have broken down our defensive steps. Our defensive linemen only take two types of steps. First, is a *reaction step*. It is not a read step. It is a reaction step. We play with the eyes wide open. We want to be able to see the hand of the offensive lineman and his feet. When the hand moves, I know he is coming. We work on reacting to the types of blocks everyday in practice. We want our linemen to believe what they see. If the offensive lineman steps toward you, believe he is coming inside to block you. We tell our linemen to see it, believe it, and feel it. Once the defensive lineman can trust what he feels, he can make tackles all over the field.

The second type of step we take is a predetermined step. We are going to tell our linemen where to go on the play. We can call a slant, angle, loop, or anything we want to call. We are going to tell the lineman where to go. We are taking all of the guesswork out of the play. That is easy. The player better beat the offensive player in the gap. Now we have the advantage.

We teach our defensive linemen only those two steps. It is that simple. We teach them reaction and predetermined steps. We believe it is simple. That gets us to where we need to be at all times. Our linemen get excited when we let them move. For the most part, we are a four-stack, cover-2 football team. We play this alignment because our defensive linemen are very effective in this front.

This year we did not blitz as much as we did in the past. When your tackles can make the stop on first down, you do not have to blitz as much. Both of our tackles are 2-gap tackles on the guards. We have a 5 technique or a 7 technique. They offense should not be able to block them from those sets. We stack our linebackers in our 4-3 alignment.

I have had the opportunity to coach some outstanding players. My claim to fame is that I taught the great (but unfortunately, late) Reggie White the plug move. Our last year playing together was with the Memphis Showboats. Reggie White was the greatest defensive lineman I ever saw. One the first days of practice I saw him do the things he did and I said, "He is the greatest." You asked me about Joe Greene. What made Reggie

White so good was his size and his speed. He was 6′5″ and he could move. Not one player in the league could block him.

The first thing we do does not have anything to do with 1 gap. We feel this helps us in our defense. This is what we do. We do the 2-gap technique. We line up nose-to-nose on an offensive blocker. We play them nose-to-nose to see how tough they are. Let us see how good we are. It was how they played football when it originated. They played the game in the early days of football. They played nose-to-nose.

I tell our staff if George Perles can teach me to play 2 gap, then I can break it down and teach my players to play 2 gap. We have been able to do that over the years. We have two players here to demonstrate those steps. (Demonstration)

We work against these blocks everyday. We give each of our players an opportunity to work on these steps everyday.

We work against five basic blocks. Those five blocks are what we are going to see in the games.

- Drive block
- Double-team block
- Hook or reach block
- Seal block
- Down block

We may work on some other things during the year. I do not have the pull block listed because we do not have anyone here to demonstrate it. We need offensive linemen to show that technique. We work on the pass set depending on the type of blocking the offense uses. That is all game planning. We block on the five blocks above every single day.

We split the tackles and ends up and we work against the blocks. I take the tackles and another coach takes the ends. We want them to see the movement, feel the blocks, and know where the ball is going to be after contact. We want to engage, control, and separate. We put it all together in the drills.

We know defensive lineman get blocked at some point in the game. We must work on an escape when that happens. We have to work on this drill because we know it is going to happen in a game. Offensive line coaches do not teach blocking any more. They teach "holding." We must find some way for our defensive linemen to escape. Not only are they going to be blocked, they are going to be held. Therefore, we set up an escape drill to help them. We get into a "fit" position in a shade technique. He can be on one shoulder or the other. We want to feel the pressure, wrap the arms around the blocker, and push or pull to one side or the other and escape. We must keep the feet moving as we rip past the blocker.

Our opponents had more offensive holding penalties this year than they did the previous year. Our linemen come to me during the games complaining about the offense holding them. I tell them there is nothing I can do about that. I tell them this: "If we can get the shoulders turned, and get underneath the 'hold,' we have a chance." One of two things happens with our move. We break the "hold" and move on, or we have a chance to escape on the illegal block and have it called.

I mentioned earlier about the "Ten Commandments of 1-Gap Play."

Ten Commandments of 1-Gap Play

- Never, ever guess
- Never stay blocked; dig it out
- Never get hooked or reached
- Close on all down blockers and take a piece of the blocker
- Keep the outside arm free all of the time
- Never go around blocks; fight through the head
- Explode off the ball and reestablish the line of scrimmage
- Never look into the backfield. Players must trust what they have been taught
- Never quit fighting for your gap
- Always attach one half of the offensive blockers body

Guessing will get you in trouble every single time. If you guess, you are done. You really have to work hard to overcome that mistake.

We want our players to dig out of any block. We assign the players a gap and tell them it is their gap and they had better fight for it. They must be willing to win every single down. We do not stay blocked.

No one offensive man should ever hook or reach our defensive lineman. If we are in a shade technique or in a 5 technique, we can never be hooked. It is simple.

We want to close on all down blocks. We want to get a piece of the lineman when he comes off the ball. We want to keep the blockers off our linebackers. Linebackers love to run and hit. Unblocked linebackers end up being All-Americans. As great as linebacker Jack Lambert was, if he was blocked it was the fault of the defensive line because we did not keep them off him.

We want the outside arm free at all times for the inside men or the 5 technique. The 7 technique should keep his inside arm free.

We never go around a block. We fight through the head of the blocker. The easy way is to go around the block. You will not get there by going around the block.

We want to explode and reestablish the line of scrimmage. When we do that, many good things happen.

We never look into the backfield. They do not need to stand up and look into the backfield. "The ball will find you."

We attack one half of the blockers body. They must understand leverage. They must be able to execute the bull rush. We said going nose-to-nose was good. They must be able to use the proper leverage. It does not happen all of the time.

I want to talk a few minutes about pass rush. We attack the blocker by going for one half of the man. From a 1 or 3 technique, we are going to force that quarterback to have happy feet. He is going to feel the pressure and he is going to be on the move. We use the "speed rush" and get upfield. We are going to get outside. We may use the spin move, and then get back inside and get depth. We do the spin moves several times in a game.

We will fit and swim, fit and rip, and do all sorts of moves. We can work on those movers in the off-season. We do not have time to work on these moves during the season. When we get into the training camp to start the season in the fall, we do not have to go over the spin, rip, swim, or other moves.

4

Defensive End Techniques

Bill Conley
The Ohio State University
1996

First, I want to talk about the philosophy we go by at Ohio State as it relates to end play. Back when I played at Ohio State, we were a slant and angle defense. Almost everyone in the country was running this defense, especially in the Big Ten. Then, I coached the inside linebackers, and we ran basically a 50 defense. Now, we are a 4-3 team. Within the last few years, we became a stack 4-3 Team. Now, we have a little different philosophy. I learned one thing in coaching high school and college: there are certain things that do not change. I know this for sure: if you are coaching a four-man front as compared to a five-man front, you better be able to control things up front. If you go against a good two-back attack with a four-man front, you better have good people up front and some attacking linebackers. You are going to get the isolation and the sprint draw run down your throat all day long. So our philosophy, especially on defensive end play, is this. Number one, we are going to attack. To be a defensive end at Ohio State you better be physical. You better be ready to get after it. I am not saying you have to bench press the world or be one of the strongest players on the team. That comes as you develop in the weight program. The biggest difference in high school athletes coming into college is not always how fast they run, and it is not always the techniques. You can teach techniques in a short amount of time. You do have to become efficient at those techniques in college. The big thing, or difference, is the strength factor. You have to be strong to be physical.

The main thing is that you have to attack. Also, you have to give great effort to get to the football. The team must swarm to the football. The key to playing the 4-3 front is the fact that the whole front must attack. The second part of that is the defense must squeeze from the defensive end area. You can't play a read at the line of scrimmage with just four men. Teams can talk about read, but you must penetrate.

The next step is to react. You must learn to react on the run. What I am talking about is this. We call our end on the strongside our Leo. On the other side, we call him the end. We have our tackle and nose inside.

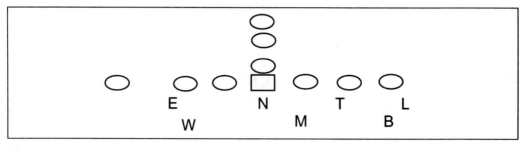

Figure 4-1

We must attack, and squeeze, forcing the ball to go east and west. The ends force the ball to go outside. If they try to run inside, we squeeze the hole. You have to play on their side of the ball. It is an attack defense. That is the key. Don't try to play a read defense with a four-man front or you will get beat every time.

It does not matter what level you play on, you must stop the run first. You have to get yourself in a position where the offense has a bad situation. You want it to be second-and-five or more. You do not want it to be second-and-two, or second-and-three. If you do that, you will be hurting for sure. Make sure you are forcing the situation to make the offense throw the ball or come up with something a little different or unique on second down. That is our basic philosophy behind our defensive end play at Ohio State.

Next, I want to show you the base technique. We will talk about three basic things. We only have two techniques for ends at Ohio State. One is a base technique, and the other is a rush technique. Everything comes off those two techniques. The key to any defense at any level is *repetition* and *keep it simple*. Keep it simple, so your players can be aggressive. The more you make them think, the more you increase the chance they will not be successful. If they have a lot to think about, they definitely will not be aggressive. This is especially true for your people up front, because things happen so much quicker. In the secondary, you can react to a lot of things. Up front, we want to keep it simple. All of our adjustments, with a few exceptions for our linebacker, are done with our secondary. We want to keep things basic and simple up front so our players can attack.

In our base technique, we will talk about stance and alignment, get off (key man), and reaction. Looking at the base block and down block first, our defensive ends are in a three-point stance. The inside hand is to the outside foot of the offensive man. When we get ready to line up, we want to line up on the split end side or the tight end side—it is all the same. They are interchangeable. The Leo lines up on the tight end, and the end lines up in a 5 technique on the split end side.

What happens is a lot of teams like to trade the tight end. They will start him off on one side and shift or move him to the other side of the line, after they line up. Instead of running our whole front around to the other side, we just wave at each other and switch spots, because the techniques are the same. As the end, I want my inside hand to the outside foot of the offensive man. It is elongated, with the inside foot back. It is not a square stance. We are not a read technique. We are an attacking front. Our elongated stance is determined, not by the stance of the offensive man, but more by the physical makeup of each end. The tall players have even more of an elongated stance. It is the feet spread from toe to heel, and most of them will be longer than that.

Next, the butt is slightly higher than the helmet, with the inside foot back. We are in a narrow three-point stance with the butt up in the air. Next, you see that we are slightly tilted with our aiming point, 1.5 yards behind the offensive man's inside hip. We want to crowd the ball. What we are saying is this. Just by the nature of our alignment on the offensive man, I am tilted inside in an attacking mode. We tell them they must penetrate to that 1.5 yard aiming point behind the man. No matter what happens, we have to get there.

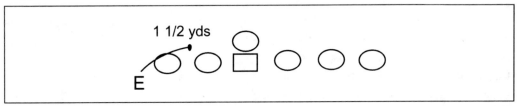

Figure 4-2

We will not be denied. If that man is in our way, we want to take him with us. We must do that.

We crowd the ball. We want to get as close to the ball as possible. The advantage we have in college is this. In high school if a defensive lineman jumps into the neutral zone, it is a penalty. That is not the case in college. If we jump into the neutral zone, we can get back and go again. When you look at the side angle, we may be lined up offsides at times. But, the officials do not call that a lot. Once in a while, officials will call it. We just back them up for a couple of plays and then go back where we started from.

We crowd the ball as much as possible. We are in a three-point stance with our butt up in the air. When that offensive man moves, we are going to attack through him. That is what we call the *get-off*. We want to get to that spot 1.5 yards deep. Both of our ends are coming at an angle. We are going to automatically squeeze the off-tackle hole. There is no off-tackle hole. By bringing our ends down at an angle, we knock the ball inside. The key is to have a nose and tackle that is knocking their man upfield. We want to knock the offensive line upfield enough to create a new line of scrimmage on the offensive side of the ball. The ends squeezing will force the ball to go east and west.

On the get-off, we key the man. A lot of teams key the ball. In the rush technique, we do key the ball. But, if it is a running situation, where it is 50-50 that they are going to run the ball, we are going to be in a base technique, lined up in a three-point stance, and we key the man. We have a lot of individual drills that we do in our individual periods where we will move a foot or move a hand to key the defender. If the offensive man twitches, we are going to attack. If you will think about it, if you come out in an elongated stance, you have a lot more power and momentum as you move. You have more power than someone that is in a wide, three-point base stance. This is because the first thing they have to do is to take a short jab step. As they take a short jab step, the offense attacks and gets into them.

We have the proper stance, and we are in the proper alignment. We are keying the man. The man moves. Boom! What happens next? Now, we are going to talk about the different types of blocks you will face. We see the following types of blocks: base, down, reach, overreach, pass protection, draw, and screen blocks. I will talk about what you will do as you attack the offense and they apply one of these blocks against the defense. I want to cover the reaction as you are attacked by these blocks.

First is the base block. This is the first thing you start off teaching. To the defensive man, what is the most aggressive thing the offensive man can do? It is to come off the ball and try to put his face mask in the defender's numbers and knock him off the ball. Coaching point: against the base block, we talk, coach, preach, and teach hand position. The biggest mistake the defensive man makes is to grab the blocker by the shoulder pads and fight with him. You can't do that. They let the offense hold so much today you can't fight with that man. Our hand position is very important.

As we are taking that first step, as we are replacing the hands, we are expecting the base block. We expect that above all. We want our hands to hit so the inside hand hits the base man's side number, and our outside hand hits the "V" right square where the arm pit is to the inside. As we make contact, we snap our hips and lock out. It has to be all one motion. So many players will lead with the chest and hand, and it gives the offensive man a chance to grab you. Some young players that are not as strong as some of our experienced players will make the mistake of letting the face mask get inside the same time the offensive blocker gets his hands inside. When contact is made, we want a big boom! The hips must snap, and the arms must lock out. The thumb on the hand on the number must be at one o'clock, and the thumb on the hand under the armpit must be at eleven o'clock.

As we make our move against the base block, our feet must keep moving. You cannot stop moving your feet. We want to lock out as we are attacking. Remember, where did we say we wanted to end up? We want to get 1.5 yards just inside the offensive man. The only way to get there is to keep moving your feet. Your feet have to be slightly in, and the weight on the inside balls of the feet. I heard a coach describe the stance like this: "It is just like pushing your car out of the mud." The power comes when you get on the inside balls of your feet. You have to be pushing and pushing. The same is true in football. That is where your power is. If the blocker tries to base block me, I want to create a new line of scrimmage by knocking him back off the line. Again, the advantage I have is the fact that I am coming off in a narrow, elongated stance. The blocker has to take a short jab step. By that time, boom! I want to be in his face. That is against the base block.

The next block we see is the down block. Here we have some real key coaching points. Our philosophy is to make the ball bounce east and west. If we get a down block, we are going to come running off the hip. But, we must make contact. This defense is not like the 50 defense, where we had to worry about keeping that man off the linebacker. That is not the way the 4-3 works. However, we must bump the blocker long enough so the linebacker can shuffle and get to where he is supposed to be. I said the first thing we are going to expect when that man comes off the ball is that he is going to base block me. As I attack the blocker, he tries to go down inside. Now, I have to come up fast and hard enough so I get a piece of the blocker. There is no way I can get both hands where I want them to be. My inside hand must get to the base of the inside number. I, at least, want to get that much of the man. Sometimes, we may only get a piece of the hip. You have to practice this technique. You must knock him off his course a little. So, you practice that first step with the hand coming up where you can get it in place with the thumb up. We use the quick draw drill to work on this. We say from the holster to the number. Boom! We want the thumbs up. We sprint off the butt. It is like the old roller derby, where they whip around the corner. That is what we want against the blocker.

We are going to attack anything off the hip. I start my line of vision from the center to the back. I am looking for anyone to trap or kick me out. If there is no one coming to trap or kick me out, my vision now goes to the near back. It may be the sprint draw or off-tackle play. Now, I am going to take on the fullback. The only exception to that is if I have an offset fullback. Then, my vision will go to him first. When the offensive lineman goes down inside, we are going to come running. There is no way we should ever get trapped or kicked outside by an offensive lineman. There should be an explosion taking place at the inside hip of the near guard, if the backside guard is pulling. We are checking his course as we are attacking to see if it is a boot course or a flat down-the-line kick-out. We are going to attack the guard.

Here is the coaching point. Most defensive ends take a piece of the down blocker and see the guard pulling on the trap. They want to go to the inside and boom! They say they took out the trap man. "I did my job." That is not good enough at Ohio State. You must do more at Ohio State. You don't just go underneath the block. If you coach just that technique, you should know that the ballcarrier has a downhill running lane. What is the philosophy? Squeeze the attack and make the ball go east and west. This is what we want the end to do against the pulling guard. We want to wrong arm and pry the man. It is just like the old can opener. You lift and pry. The rule is this: when you wrong arm and pry, you must take out two people. If you do not take out two people, you are not doing the job.

We want to get position on the guard and align with his ear hole and knock him up the field. Why? One of the biggest plays you see is the counter play. They may pull the backside guard and tackle. They may use the backside guard and fullback to block on the play. You want to make sure you make the ball go east and west. We do not want to just take out the lead blocker. We want to take out two people on the play. One of them may be the ballcarrier.

On the other side, you may get the fullback and I back coming at the Leo. As Leo comes off the hip of the blocker and sees the fullback starting to attack, he is the first man we see. We go up between the fullback, heavy. We go into him with the inside arm to the fullback. We use the same technique as we use on the pulling guard. We want to take out two men on the play. You really screw the ballcarrier up there because he cannot go inside. He is coached to go outside on that play, and there you are. That forces the ball east and west. With our two linebackers scrapping, we tackle the back for a loss. This is how we play the down block.

Let's go to the reach block. Now, the blocker tries to reach block the end. One of the things about the four-man front that is different than five-man front is this. On the five-man front against the toss sweep, you always wanted to keep your outside arm free. I think you have to do the same thing in most situations today. This is especially true in high school football. As a high school coach, I always had this philosophy. There were two ways you were not going to beat me in high school. You were not going to run the toss sweep or option down the field on me, and you were not going to throw the ball over my head. You would have to pound the ball inside all day long to beat me in high school. We did not want them to make the big play on us.

When you play the 4-3, because you are a man short on the front, the linebackers are there to help you out when the ball goes wide. What the line has to be more concerned about is getting off on the ball, attacking, and creating a new line of scrimmage. If the ball is outside, it is no big deal as long as it is going east and west. I am not saying that we want to get reached. We never want to get reached. The first thing you want to do to the tight end, if he is trying to reach you, is to knock him upfield. I want to keep my feet moving, and I want to lock the blocker out. The key is attacking when the ball is snapped. The ideal way to play the toss sweep is to knock the offensive end two yards deep on the snap of the ball. That is the key on the reach block.

The overreach block is the move by the blocker to get outside. Instead of taking a short jab step, they take a big lateral step and then cross over. They try to get to your inside number. They throw their hip into the block and try to hook you, and they actually hold you. They do this all along the line of scrimmage. Because of this zone-blocking scheme, the one-back offense is very successful. It is because of this scheme. Teams will even get back off the ball on the zone scheme. They get as far back off the ball as they can, so there is no way you can get into them to attack them.

The way we take care of the overreach is this. We are going to square up a little and loosen up a little. On the snap of the ball when the blocker tries to reach me, I attack up and end up in the same situation as I do on the reach block. We drop our inside hand to the blocker's hip and push him upfield. We are coming off low and hard and attacking. We drop that inside hand and push the man upfield.

The next block is the pass block. I want to talk about the little things we feel are important on the pass block. When it is first-and-ten or second-and-four, we are thinking of run. Teams will also show pass on these downs. There are a couple of different ways you are going to see the pass. You will see the three-step pass. This is where the offense will fire straight out and try to hammer you. Also, you will see the offense step back off the ball. First, against the three-step, as soon as you take that first step and the offensive man steps out to jab you, we want to throw our hands up. Our ends will swat the ball a lot on the three-step pass.

If the offense goes with the basic five- or seven-step drop, when the line comes off the ball, we have one key coaching point. When the blocker sets back off the ball, we immediately get to the edge and pass rush. Physically, we are not a good match against the big offensive linemen. We are going to attack one half of the blocker's body; now, we have an advantage and have a chance to win.

Next is the draw block. There are several ways to run the draw. The teams that run the draw the most effective against us are the teams that set up like the pass and then run the draw. We do not see that very often. Most of the time when offensive linemen are going to run the draw, they are going to open up, but they are going to keep their inside foot on the line of scrimmage. They want to take their hands and knock you upfield and then go out to block the linebacker. If it is a running situation, say a 50-50 run or pass situation, we want to keep it in a run technique. We want to squeeze the blocker and then retrace and come back down the line and make the play. We want to try to strip the ball.

Next is the screen block. We see three types of blocks against the screen pass. The offensive linemen will just drop back deep and try to pull you down. That is one technique. Another block is where they drop back off the line of scrimmage and try to cut you down. The other technique is when they drop back and try to knock you upfield and set the draw a little deeper. We are not really expected to make the play on the screen pass. We have to do either one or two things. If we can react quick enough by reading the offensive back, then we can react. They come way off the line and try to pull you down. There will be a back across your face, if it is going to be a screen. We will react to that type of play. If the back releases inside, we can read it quick enough and play it down the line. If we are past the back and recognize the screen late and we are going after the quarterback, we keep going after the quarterback. Our linebackers are keying those plays, and, hopefully, we will force the quarterback to throw the ball into a lot of traffic.

Finishing up on the run, let's talk about movement versus the run. We have three basic movements we use against the run. We use the echo/lance. They are the same, except echo means end and lance means Leo. They are the same technique; one to the tight end side, and one to the split end side. We also use a slant technique and a loop technique. When do you use movement if you want to stop a run? The basic philosophy is this. First, we use it as a change-up, instead of playing base technique. It is just a change-up. Second, if we get a big gap, we use movement. We may take a defender and just line him up in the gap. If you do not do that, the offense will split you out all day. The third thing we have to do is to bump the linebacker out into coverage. If they come out in an A set or motion someone to an A set, we adjust with the secondary, and we may have to bump a linebacker out in the coverage.

What do we do on these movements? First, on the echo and lance, here are some coaching points. First of all, anytime your ends are moving, you square up your stance slightly. There is no way the end can take a good inside step out of the elongated step. So, we will square our stance slightly. We do not square up enough that will allow the offensive man to read it. The second thing we are going to do is to back off the ball a couple of inches. This is where most people make their big mistake. When they go to slant inside, they cheat inside. That is the worse thing you can do. That gives your move away. They know right now if you are going inside. The key is this. Don't cheat inside; just back up a little and square up slightly. That gives you room to clear.

The next coaching point is a short jab step with the inside foot followed by penetrating up in the gap. We do not allow our ends to even look for the football until they have made that full move. Then, they can find the football. We do not find the football until we get to the hip of the blocker. We want to make our penetration first. If you do not do that, they will short step you, and you will end up a gap short.

Next, we want to key the inside offensive linemen and then react. If you are moving inside, your action no longer is on the man you lined up on. What is great about teaching this position is that everything is the same. If the blocker base blocks me, I will squeeze it back in the gap. If he blocks down, we come running off his hip. If he sets and shows pass, I will get over his outside shoulder and rush the quarterback. Everything is the same for us as a base technique. That is why it is so simple.

The other thing we do on the inside movement is to key the ball as compared to the man over us. We do not care what that man is doing. That is the echo and the lance.

Next is the slant technique. A lot of the things are the same as on the echo and lance. We use this in two basic situations. First, if it is short yardage and we expect a trap or dive. The other way is if we have linebackers coming up on the outside. Now, we are really concentrating on squeezing the inside gap. We square up slightly and come off the ball a little. Now, we step at the inside man's near hip. Now, we are attacking the hip instead of going up through the gap. We tell the end, if he has to get his helmet and face guard through that man's hip to knock him inside all the way to the center's hip, to do it. If the blocker is turning out and we have our end slanting down, we expect our end to end up on top of the pile. Our whole purpose on the slant is to restrict everything inside.

The next technique is the loop. We use the loop when we expect a team to run a play-action pass, or bootleg in a normal situation, and we go by tendencies. We line up as we do in base, except we square up a little so the offense can't detect it. Now, we want the end to step four to six inches laterally with the outside foot, followed by an upfield crossover step. You want to get to the hip of the blocker, and then you are reacting. It is the same as the inside step, except now we are stepping outside. This is how we work the drill. We have an old-fashioned cage. When we are working on movement by the end, we start them under the cage in practice. They have to go inside or outside. If they raise up, they hit their helmet on the cage. If you do not do that in practice, then in a game, they will take one step and try to find the ball. Don't let them find the ball until they have completed the technique. On the crossover, the arm and leg always come together.

Now, we are going to look at defensive end play versus the pass. Now, it is third-and-long, and we expect the offense to throw the ball. Now, our mind-set changes a little. One thing is still the same. We are still going to attack. The second thing is that we are going to rush the quarterback. We may not get to the quarterback, but we can get close enough so the quarterback has to get rid of the ball before he wants to. The next thing is to react as you are rushing the quarterback.

Let me go to the rush technique. We work on stance and alignment. We want to get-off or key the ball. Also, we work on our reactions against all of the same blocks. Here is the difference. First of all, we are in a three-point sprinter's stance. Now, that elongated stance is even more elongated. We are in a narrow stance. We align four to six inches outside the blocker's outside foot. Understand one thing. If it is a definite passing situation, that man across from you will be blocking you. We really are aiming at the outside hip of the offensive tackle. We will screw around with the tight end. Sometimes, we will line up inside the tight end; sometimes, head up with the tight end.

The offense does not know where we will line up. This will screw up the tight end's release. We do not want to go into a game and let the offense know where we are going to line up on their tight end.

At the same time, if we know it is a passing situation, we will take our end and line him up and make sure his aiming point is the outside hip of the tackle. It is a race to that point. Everything in practice is set up so we can get to the area beyond the blocker's hip. It is the same principle where we want our whole body on half of his body. It is a race to get to the spot behind the line of scrimmage. Those big offensive linemen have a hard time getting back there. That is one reason the offense likes to go from a two-point stance, so they can put the outside leg back. It is a passing situation, and we have a rush call on. We are keying the ball so we can get off in time.

I will go through the reactions against the different blocks very quickly, because we have covered these before. If they come out and try to base or reach block us or to attack us and it is a passing situation, the only difference is that we are squeezing with a hard outside arm conscious attitude. If they down block on us and we are lined up four to six inches outside the tackle, we are not going to touch him. If he down blocks inside and we come across and upfield and here comes the sprint draw, we will see it as we get to the hip of the offensive man. We turn and attack and squeeze it to the inside. Our secondary players are thinking pass, and they are back deep. We want to force the ball back inside.

The reach and overreach blocks are the same as before. We are a little more outside conscious now. When we have the man locked up, we will be skating a little more along the line of scrimmage.

What happens when that man shows pass? We are going to get to the outside edge and use a pass rush technique.

If it is a draw, we are going to retrace and come right back down the original line that I started on. We use the chop on the outside hand. If the blocker has his hands low, we use the swim technique. You can't do a swim technique if your hips are square. We want to slap and, boom! we slide the hips. Now, we are going to slap the man's butt as we come through to rush the quarterback. If his hands are high, we can use the old rip technique. We rip underneath the man's hands. If we are really good with our hands, we may use the karate chop with both hands. If the offense wants to set back and use both hands, we can come in and cross our inside hand and put our outside hand over the top of the inside hand in a chopping motion to knock the blocker's hands down when he goes to grab us. That is how we play the pass. We want to get our whole body on one half of the blocker's body and rush the quarterback.

A key coaching point on the draw: very rarely does a draw break straight ahead. Most of the time, when a team runs the draw, it starts in the backfield and then breaks to one side or the other. We are going upfield, rushing the quarterback, and we read draw. We better not read it too soon. We want to be past the hip of the blocker before we read the draw. It is a passing situation, and I am after the quarterback. I should not be on the line when I read the draw. I am not going to see the draw until after I have attacked. When we see it is the draw, we want to run back down the same line that I started from. I know the ball will break to the spot where I lined up. We do not teach the ends to tackle the man on the draw. We teach them to strip the ball. The running back does not expect anyone coming back from the outside edge. They are looking for the linebackers. The term we use is to retrace. We are not satisfied just to make the tackle. We want to cause the fumble.

On the screen, we react to the type of block the offensive man makes. He is going to try to pull you, or he is going to try to cut you, or he is going to flash and release. If it is a passing situation, you must know what type of screens the team runs from the scouting report. But, the key is the back. If you get a flare back, a team will use a certain type of screen pass, and you know what is going to happen.

I want to go over our pass rush stunts. First, I will talk about our two-man stunts. We run three two-man stunts: one, pic, two, pop, and, three, knife. We all come up with a lot of different terminology in football. Here, in the pic the "I" means we are trying to free the inside man. We are not saying the other man is not supposed to make the tackle. We want to do something special to free up the inside man. Pic means it is just a one-side stunt. When we call double pic, it means we are stunting on both sides. The pic means we want to free up the nose and the end. The nose and end are always together, and the tackle and Leo are always together. The end pulls the offensive tackle. The nose guard steps and flashes his hands at the offensive guard. Then, he reaches the outside hip of our end and comes around.

Let me go over both of those techniques real quick. If I am the end and it is a passing situation, we are four to six inches outside the tackle. I want to try to free up my buddy to the inside. On my first step, I step at the tackle and pull his outside shoulders inside. I will not release the tackle until I get his outside shoulder perpendicular to the line of scrimmage. At that point, the tackle has had enough time to come around the end. Now, the end must release and rip or swim and become the inside rusher. We do not want to get knocked past the ball. We want to stay in the pass rush lane where the nose guard started.

What does the inside man do? He is going to cheat a little inside to the A gap. We step at the guard, and he sets up for the pass block. The nose flashes his hands and takes an outside step and reaches for the outside hip of the defensive end. That forces him to make a move upfield. It is not a lateral step, it is up the field. We step, reach, and come so tight off the tail of the end, the quarterback will not see me as I come around. We are only going to pull the tackle if they are zone pass blocking. There is no reason to pull him if they are man blocking. If they are in man, the end comes down inside on the guard and knocks him inside. The tackle will try to pick up the end, and the nose becomes free. If they are man protecting, we do not pull anyone; we just run to the inside man.

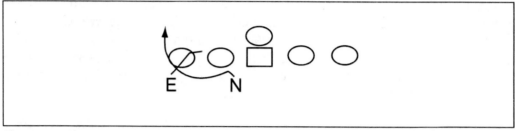

Figure 4-3. Pic

On the pop, we do just the opposite. Now, the nose guard is going to pull the guard. We are going to free the outside man.

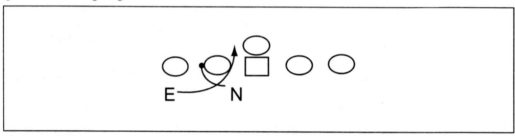

Figure 4-4. Pop

The end is going to step upfield and flash up and come off the butt of the nose guard. Understand something when you are rushing the quarterback. You have four men rushing, two on each side of the ball. If we have someone on the front four who is not a good pass rusher, we take them out of the game at that point.

In practice, we move the four down linemen around and let them work from each position. They are basically the same anyway.

Next, is the knife stunt. It is a little different. The end is lined up six to eight inches outside. That forces the tackle to really widen as he tries to get to the end. That is what we want. As soon as the tackle's shoulders go parallel, the end goes under him. There is no way a 330-pound tackle can get his feet going back to the inside once he starts outside on the block. If we start upfield and the tackle does not open his shoulders to the outside, the end can beat him with speed to the quarterback. The end can't be wrong. The call that is made between the end and nose guard is a read call. The nose is waiting to see what the end is going to do. He will power rush the offensive guard. He wants to get him coming off the line of scrimmage and get him squared up. He is not going to get his body into the blocker; he rushes with his hands. As the nose sees the end come inside—boom! the nose goes outside. It's an upfield pic.

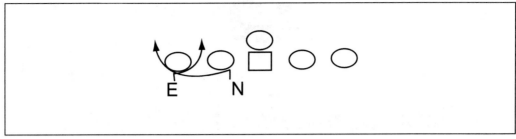

Figure 4-5. Knife

When does the end not come under the tackle? He will not come under if the tackle does not open his shoulders outside, or if the quarterback sprints away. We do not want the nose coming outside if the quarterback goes the other way. It is a timing thing, and it takes practice and practice. The nose knows, if the end has not made his inside move within a two count, he just keeps rushing.

Next, we will look at our four-man stunts. All we do is to double things up. We have a double pic, double pop, and double knife. Both sides are doing the same stunts.

Now, we have three special stunts. First is the flame. We are running a pic to the field and a pop to the boundary. We run two different stunts, one on each side. The man to the fieldside must be a good contain man.

Second, is the tango. It is a three-man stunt. We use this against a straight drop-back passing team. We do not expect any type of sprint out. We know the quarterback is going to drop back. Now, we do an automatic knife stunt. We must commit to the inside move. If the blocker's shoulders are square, we grab them and turn the man inside. The tackle goes inside, the nose guard flashes, then comes around for the contain. The end has an option. He can straight rush the play, or he can knife the play. We call this stunt into the boundary because we do not worry about containment on the dropback quarterback into the boundary. Leo is the contain on the fieldside of the formation.

The last stunt is Toledo. Teams like to area block inside with the guards and center and man block with the two tackles. Usually, they have two good blocking tackles when they use this scheme. They area block inside because the defense runs twist stunts inside. They lock the tackles on the outside rushers. Toledo screws the offense up. We give quick knifes to the outside. Now, this forces the offensive tackles to go inside. The inside blockers are sitting inside waiting to see who is going to come to them. All of a sudden, the nose guard comes around the end on the knife. Now, the two guards run into the offensive tackles coming inside on the outside rushers. The tackle is the contain man on one side, and the nose guard is the contain man on the other side.

5

Fundamentals of Defensive Line Play

Canute Curtis
Towson State University
2010

Thank you. I am excited to be here. I am going to talk about defensive line techniques and play. I want to get right into the talk. The basis for any line techniques goes back to the fundamentals of football.

The defensive line serves as the foundation of the overall defense. It is imperative that the line functions in the realm of their responsibility because, in order to have a sound defense, you must have a solid foundation; it all starts with the people up front. It takes a person with innate tenacity and aggressiveness to play defensive line. He must possess the size, strength, and power to go against, generally, the biggest players on the football field: the offensive line. But, he must also have speed and quickness to get off blocks, pursue and make tackles, and rush the passer. It takes a dedicated and determined individual to work constantly on the techniques that are necessary to become a defensive lineman.

MASTER OF RUN DEFENSE

We have six essentials that the defensive linemen must master in order to have a good run defense:
- Stance and alignment
- Key and initial movement
- Target

- Block recognition
- Separation and escape
- Pursuit and tackle

For a defensive lineman to play, he must have a good *stance*. I am not too particular about the stagger in the stance. I do not want him stretched out in his stance. I want a balanced stance with his feet under his body.

Stance and Alignment

The techniques for run defense are:
- Flat back with weight distributed between the balls of the feet and hands
- Feet shoulder-width apart, no more than a toe-to-heel relationship
- Shoulders parallel to the line of scrimmage
- Down hand is three inches in front of the head; off arm and hand are in a ready position; head is up in a bull-like body position cocked in a position ready to explode
- Proper bend in three great levers: knees, ankles, and hips
- Concentration

If he has too much stagger in his feet, I do not like that. If he spreads out wide, I do not like that. I want the lineman to be comfortable in his stance. If the lineman can take off and move from his stance, I will not change his technique.

We align in both right- and left-handed stances. When we get down, I want the inside hand on the ground. When the inside hand goes on the ground that means the inside foot is back in the stance. The off hand is not dangling or resting on the off knee—I want it cocked and ready to go.

When the lineman gets down in his stance, I want his cleats in the ground. I do not want him up on his toes. It is like a race car. They have big, wide tires on those cars. They have those types of tires to give the car better ground traction. I want the defensive lineman with his cleats in the ground so he can push off. The most important thing for the defensive lineman to do is get off the ball. Every drill, we work on takeoff. We have to work hard on the getoff in practice. I want the defensive lineman out of his stance and off the ball. That is the focus of the drills. I want to work on stance and start.

In our *alignment*, we have a vertical and horizontal alignment. In their vertical alignment, I want the defensive linemen as close to the ball as they can possibly get. I know you have all heard about being able to run a credit card through the defensive lineman's hand and the ball. That is what I strive for. We want to get as close to the ball as we can.

When I talk about *horizontal* alignment, I am talking about the alignment on an offensive blocker (Figure 5-1). We use the numbering system that has been in football forever. In our defensive scheme, we align in a shade on the center, 2i, 4i, and 6i techniques. Those are the inside positions on the guard, tackle, and end. The head-up positions are 2, 4, and 6 techniques. The shoulder positions are 3, 5, and 9 techniques. We replaced the 7 technique with the 6i technique. Those positions give us our horizontal alignments.

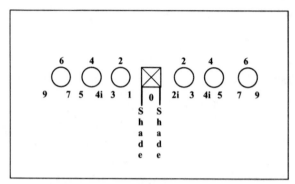

Figure 5-1. Horizontal alignment

When you work with a young lineman, you should back him off the ball. That gives him a chance to read the offensive lineman.

Key and Initial Movement

The next aspect of defensive line play is the *key*. Keying gives us a quick indication of what the play is. We will react to our primary key by making an initial reaction. A correct reaction to your primary key is a vital part of whether you can make the play or not. You should see and react to your primary for two steps while expanding your vision to your secondary key.

When I teach keys, I start with a key progression (Figure 5-2). The primary key for the defensive lineman is the offensive lineman he is aligning on. In the key

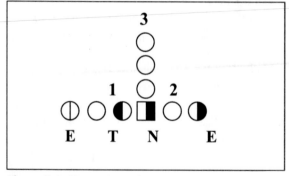

Figure 5-2. Key progression

progression, the defensive lineman has three keys that come from the primary read on the offensive lineman. If the offensive lineman fires out at the defender, we know we are near the point of attack and we play accordingly. We want to protect our gaps in that case.

If the offensive lineman goes away from the defender, he has to react in a different way. He has to make contact and look down the line of scrimmage for a trap. The third part of the key progression is to look into the backfield for an offensive blocker.

To play on the defensive line you must *move*. If you play on the defensive line, you must have quick hands, quick eyes, and quick feet. The defensive lineman must play with his hands. If he tries to play with his forearms, he cannot play defense. When I first look at a player, I want to see what he is doing. If he has a bad stance, he probably has bad feet.

With initial movement, a player must:
- Maintain peripheral vision on the football and move on ball movement
- React to ball movement, not sound (no gifts, and no mental errors on cadence)
- Attack his man with fast eyes, hands, and feet

Target

- Half of the man on
- Outside hand to near shoulder; inside hand to breastplate
- Tight hands, elbow tight
- Fast hands
- Get-Off
  - ✓ Power-pack step with the hips, not the feet
  - ✓ Shoot hand
  - ✓ Let feet follow

When we work against the offense in practice, we want to get a jump on the ball. If the quarterback calls the cadence and does not go on the first sound, we are going the next time he opens his mouth. He is not going to snap the ball on three. If the ball is not snapped on the first sound, we are going on the second sound. That gives us an advantage on the get-off. That is particularly true on third and long. We are going to get a good jump and go.

When the defensive lineman attacks the offensive lineman, he attacks half the man. When the defensive lineman comes off the ball, he wants his inside hand to be down the breastplate of the offensive blocker. He wants his outside hand on the near shoulder pad.

When he attacks, he wants to attack with tight elbows. As he attacks with his hands, he wants his thumbs up with his fingers flared outside. That brings the elbows inside. He wants to get his hands on the offensive blocker as fast as possible. The offensive blocker is going to try and get his hands on the defender. The one who gets his hand inside has control. If the offensive blocker's hands are outside the defender, he has no power or control over the defender.

When I was playing, the coaches taught us to take a six- to eight-inch power step. Every time I taught that type of movement, the player would stand up and play too high. I do not emphasize that anymore. What I emphasize now is to shoot the hands as fast as possible. If I can shoot my hands and get them on the offensive blocker, the feet will follow.

I want to shoot the hands and roll the hips. If I can do that, the feet will follow in the technique. I do not teach the six-inch power step. I teach shooting the hands, rolling the hips, and keeping the back flat.

We do a 1-on-1 drill every day which teaches everything I want the defensive linemen to do. We work with the bags and without the bags. We work from our knees to start with and shoot the hands into the linemen. We shoot the hands and bring the feet. We work on shooting the hands, bringing the feet, and shedding the blocker to one side or the other.

When we do this drill, I want the defender's hands above his eyes. The eyes have to see the target. The eyes cannot be looking for the football. They must see the target, shoot the hands, gain control, and then look for the football. When he shoots his hands, I want to see him grab cloth. I want his elbows in tight and the thumbs up. As he comes off, we want a good body lean into the offensive blocker.

When we play head-up an offensive blocker, both hands go to the breastplate of the lineman. If we play an odd or shoulder technique, the inside hand goes to the breastplate and the outside hand goes to the shoulder.

When we are working this drill, I want the defender to get his hips into the technique as much as he can. I do not want the hips lagging behind. I want him to get them rolled and into the offensive blocker.

Block Recognition

The defensive lineman must be able to recognize what type of block the offensive lineman is using. If the offensive lineman fires out on the defender and tries to cover him up, we know that is a *base* block (Figure 5-3). The first thing the defender wants to do is come off the ball, get his hands into the blocker, and get a vertical push. The thing he wants to do is stay square to the line of scrimmage. I do not want him to turn one way or the other. He has to have a two-way go once he recognizes where the ball is going.

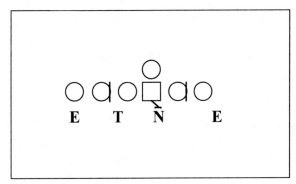

Figure 5-3. Base block

If the offensive blocker tries to reach the defensive lineman, I coach them not to run away from the reach (Figure 5-4). I do not want the defense to do what the offensive lineman wants him to do. I do not want to turn and run outside to keep from being reached. I want the defensive lineman to get in contact with the offensive lineman and get a vertical push into the backfield. If the offensive lineman reaches the defender, it will be three yards deep in the backfield, not on the line of scrimmage. If he gets penetration three yards into the backfield, he is allowed to get reached. The thing that kills the zone play and a reach block is *penetration*. On the reach block reaction, I do not want the defensive lineman to turn and run. I want him to keep his shoulder square to the line and work for depth.

If the offensive blocker *down blocks*, the defensive lineman's key goes away from him (Figure 5-5). The 3-technique defender is playing man-to-man defense on the guard. If he tries to go down and get up on the linebacker, the 3 technique is not going to let him get inside. He gets his hands on the guard, works flat down the line of scrimmage, and then he gets off and pursues. As he plays inside with the guard, he keeps his shoulder square to the line until he finds out what is happening or finds the ball.

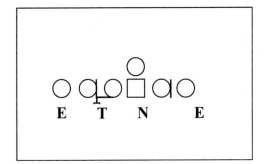

Figure 5-4. Reach block

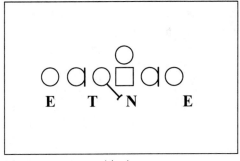

Figure 5-5. Down block

If the defender encounters a *double-team*, we want to split it (Figure 5-6). I was taught if we were double-teamed to fall on the ground and create a pile. We do not teach that technique. I emphasize splitting the double-team. The double-team will start out as a base block by the man the defender is aligned on. When he feels the double-team coming, the defender wants to beat the shoulder of the drive blocker and get a vertical push up the field. He should be starting the vertical push on the post man because that is the way we play the base block. When the guard comes down on the shade technique, he wants to get his hat in front of the shoulder and work for penetration up the field.

The next block we play is a *chip block* (Figure 5-7). That is a form of a double-team. The defender will encounter two blockers but be blocked by only one of them. In the chip block, someone other than the blocker the defender is aligned on will end up blocking or passing him off to another blocker. It could be the center trying to overtake the shade technique with the guard getting up to the linebacker. The defender attacks the center the same as he did on the base block. He wants to stay square to the line of scrimmage and dip his shoulder into the guard until the guard leaves. After the guard leaves to go to the second level, the defender reappears in his gap and does not let the center overtake the block on him.

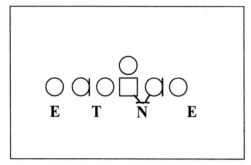

Figure 5-6. Double-team block

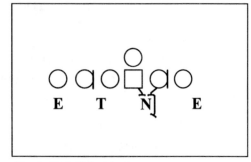

Figure 5-7. Chip block

The *slip block* is similar to the chip block (Figure 5-8). The offensive guard will try to push the shade-technique defender onto the center's block or hit him so the center can overtake the offensive guard's block. The guard's responsibility is someone on the next level, and he wants to slip after the hit. He is helping the center get a block on the shade-technique defender. The nose defender wants to make sure the guard cannot get to the next level. I coach the shade-technique defender to play the center and snatch the slip blocker. He grabs the slip blocker and prevents him from getting to the linebackers. We call that holding the *jump through*.

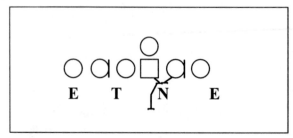

Figure 5-8. Slip block

We face the *power O* all the time. The offense will block down on the defenders and kick out at the point of attack. I coach the 3 technique to fight the pressure and get vertical. If he cannot get vertical, he fights the pressure and gets across the blocker's face. If the defender gets out into space, he can turn his shoulders and pursue. When he is playing blocks on the inside, he has to stay square and play the blocker. Some coaches teach the 3 technique to play from the backside of the block. I feel that 99 times out of a hundred, the defender will not get in a position to make a play.

The next type of block we have to recognize is the *turnout block*. When the offensive blocker turns out and tries to drive the defender to the outside, the defender squeezes down inside. I want him to squeeze but keep his shoulder square to the line of scrimmage. We want to get into the middle of the blocker and squeeze him down.

The *lead block* is like the turnout block in some ways. This becomes a spill technique for the defender. We want to wrong arm the blocker. The thing I do not want to do is run down the line of scrimmage. I want to spill the play as deep in the backfield as I can get. I want to go through the inside of the block but at the same time get up the field.

When we teach block recognition, we use 1-on-1 drills, including the mirror-read drill (Figure 5-9). In the 1-on-1 drills, we work on the base, reach, and cutoff blocks. In the 1-on-1 drill, we are working on mirroring the offensive blocker. The players align in three-point stances. The blocker squats down with his hands to his side. He lets the defender get his hand into the breastplate. The coach standing behind the defense will point to the defender's right or left shoulder or chest, or he'll show a pass set to direct the blocker as to what type of block to show. The coach gives the snap count to the blocker.

We go to a 2-on-1 drill (Figure 5-10) and work on the chip and slip blocks. After that, we go to a 3-on-1 drill and work on double-team, down, trap, and lead blocks. We can work on a scoop scheme in this drill. We want to work on schemes we will see in the game.

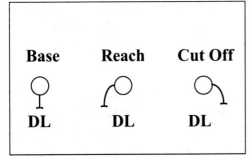

Figure 5-9. Mirror-read drill

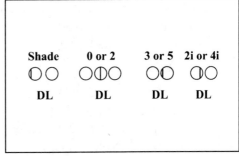

Figure 5-10. Key Read Drill (2-on-1 or 3-on-1)

Separation and Escape

Key Elements of Separation

- Get eyes into the V of the neck
- Hands into breastplate
- Elbows in, thumbs up
- Good bend into knees, ankles, and hips
- Be able to explode, hands above eyes, and hips in front of feet

Key Elements of Escape

- Push/Pull technique: Initially the gap hand is the power hand and the cover hand is the trail hand. Push with the power hand and pull with the trail hand.
- Arm over (swim)
- Underarm (rip)
- Shrug

After we recognize what the block is, we have to play it. In all cases, we want to try to get penetration. However, to make a tackle, we have to get off the blocks. We must learn how to separate from the block and escape. That goes back to using your hands. To get into position to separate, we must have our hands above our eyes and our hips in front of our feet. You cannot separate from a blocker if your hands are below your eyes.

To escape, one of the techniques we use is a *snatch and shrug*. We have to snatch and shrug at a 45-degree angle to the side. What happens many times is the defender will snatch the offensive block and, instead of pulling him at an angle, he will pull him right back onto himself. We want to shrug him to the side and escape at a 45-degree angle.

Besides the shrug, we use the *arm-over* or swim technique. We want to punch the offensive blocker, gain control, grab the outside shoulder, and bring the inside arm over and across the face of the blocker and outside shoulder. We also use the underarm rip technique. When we rip, it is important to get the inside arm as high as you can under the outside armpit and shoulder of the offensive blocker. If you do that, it allows the hips to stay in front. The higher the arm gets in the rip, the further the hips are in front of the blocker.

We also use a *push/pull technique.* The way I want to perform this technique is to push with the outside hand and pull with the inside hand. We attack the outside shoulder and push hard on it. When we pull with the inside hand, it turns the shoulder of the offensive blocker. You cannot escape from a block until you get control of the blocker. Using the push/pull technique lets us get control.

We can drill the push/pull technique. Fit two players in a pre-locked position with both players facing one another in a square position. The defender places his hand on the offensive blocker's shoulders while the blocker's hands are at his side. On the coach's command, the blocker takes a step to the right or left, simulating a reach or cutoff block. The defender power presses the shoulder of the blocker upfield while pulling the other shoulder in order to turn the blocker. Repeat the drill several times and then switch.

Another drill we use is a *separation-and-shed drill* (Figure 5-11). We fit two players in a pre-locked position with the offensive blocker's shoulder square to the line. On the coach's command, the blocker tries to reach block the defender. The defender locks out the upfield shoulder of the blocker and pulls the other shoulder in order to turn the blocker. After he has turned the shoulders, he uses one of the three escape moves:
- Underarm: Rip arm underneath the armpit and shoulder of the blocker.
- Over arm: Pull the outside shoulder down, and bring the inside arm over and across the blocker's face.
- Shrug: Use the blocker's momentum to jerk his body sideways. The coaching point is to never try to escape until you have control of the blocker.

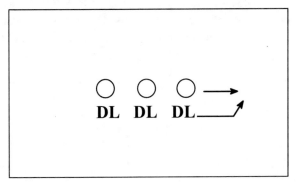

Figure 5-11. Escape

Once you get off the block, you have to pursue. We do pursuit drills all the time.

Pursuit and Tackle

Pursuit does the following things:
- Eliminates a long touchdown (the big play)
- Discourages your opponent (especially the ballcarrier)
- Helps to cover any possible mistakes in your defense (helps your teammate)
- Makes us the best defensive team in the country

What it takes to pursue:
- Pursuit, first, is a mental process (if you want to, you can)
- Visualize pursuing and making great plays (be a big-play guy)

- Physical condition is necessary so you can have great pursuit every play
- Speed (think fast and quick)
- Get-off blocks-get to the ball If on the ground, get off the ground quickly using only the hands and feet then proper pursuit angle

How to pursue:
- Play your responsibility
- Take correct course to ball (near hip of the ball), then adjust to the angle of the ball
- Wanting to get there (mental)

We do all kinds of pursuit drills to fit the scheme we have to face. One pursuit is a *sprint-to-the-receiver drill* (Figure 5-12). The purpose of the drill is to teach get-off, pass rush moves, sprint to the quarterback, then hustle to the receiver to make the tackle. The drill starts on the movement of the ball. The defender rushes the quarterback then sprints to the cone where the quarterback throws the ball. Set the cones to represent a swing pass to the back or a downfield pass to a receiver.

We work on *screen pursuit drills* (Figure 5-13). The defensive linemen align in their positions. We throw the ball to the outside as if there was a jailbreak screen. The defensive linemen get off the ball, go through their initial steps, and pursue to the ball. You create the pursuit drills that fit what you want from your defensive linemen.

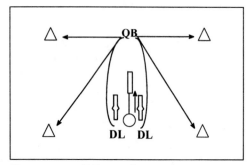

Figure 5-12. Sprint to the receiver

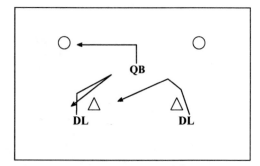

Figure 5-13. Screen pursuit drill

We have a *sight* and a *pressure* key. The pressure key is the man the defender is aligned on. The sight key is the offensive linemen to the inside of the pressure key. If the defender is aligned on his pressure key and goes to the inside, he does not want to be flattened and washed down the line of scrimmage. As he steps inside, he has to get his outside hip back to square and get a vertical push up the field. If he can get his hip turned square to the line of scrimmage, he can get up the field.

We drill the movement in a simple 1-on-1 drill (Figure 5-14). I put two trashcan barrels about five yards apart. I put the defender in front of the barrel. The blocker will be directly behind the barrel, slightly turned inside. On ball movement, the defender will slant, dip his shoulder, rip into the blocker, and get his hips going upfield. The blocker will try to push the defender flat down the line of scrimmage while the defender leans into him working his hips upfield. Put a cone five yards up the field between the two barrels. The defender does not want to be driven inside past the cone.

The next drill we do, slant and read (Figure 5-15), involves the sight key. The defender does the same thing he did in the slant drill. However, in this drill, he reads the sight key. If the sight key steps toward him, he gets vertical up the field. If the sight key moves away from him, he continues flat to the inside and locates the football. If the sight end shows a pass set, he gets vertical and rushes the passer.

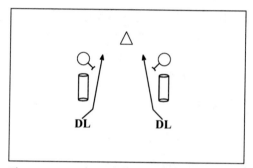

Figure 5-14. Slant drill (1-on-1)

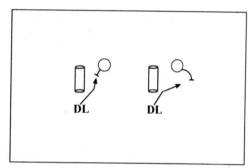

Figure 5-15. Slant-and-read drill

The next thing we do is expand the drill and add the second offensive lineman in the drill (Figure 5-16). We have the pressure key and the sight key in the drill. It is a repeat of the two drills. This time the defender is reacting to both his pressure key and his sight key. If he cuts inside the pressure key and he tries to block him, he gets vertical up the field. If the pressure key goes inside, he focuses on the sight key. He plays the technique the sight key gives him. If the sight key comes to him, he gets vertical. If the sight key goes away, he flattens, continues down the line, and locates the ball.

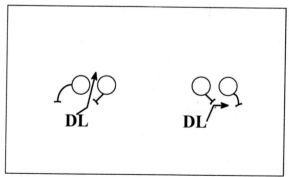

Figure 5-16. Two-man key drill

The coaching point to all these drills is to concentrate on the defender getting his hips square as he cuts inside. If he cannot get his hips square, he has no power. If his hips are going inside, he will continue inside, get flattened and washed down the line.

The next thing I want to cover is the *pass rush*. I do not teach pass rush moves anymore. If you spend all your time teaching a pass rush move and the player never uses it, you have wasted your time. What I teach now is the leverage side of the pass rush and the techniques of the pass rush. The defensive end lines up on the offensive tackle in a tight alignment. However, after the offensive tackle gets in his stance, the defensive end may widen his alignment. Those are the coaching points I help the defensive linemen with.

We run many defensive line games in our scheme. I have the defensive linemen fake moves before the ball is snapped. We fake as if we are going inside when we are really going up the field. It is like I told you earlier, if the ball is not snapped on one, we are going on the next sound. We have a pass rush progression.

PASS RUSH PROGRESSION

Have a Plan

Predetermine your move. Picture what you are going to do before the ball is snapped. That will aid your quickness. You should be:
- Confident
- Coiled
- Concentrating

Take-Off

Explode on the snap. Gain ground on each step. Keep good body angle until you make contact with the blocker. Get inside hand placement on the blocker as soon as possible by:
- Grabbing in a vice-like manner
- Having the eyes strike the chin simultaneously with the hands

I teach the defensive line a pass rush stance. In that stance, we want the lineman to narrow his base and get more weight on his hand. That means he gets his tail higher and increases his stagger. He looks like a track sprinter in his stance. The biggest advantage the defensive lineman can get in the pass rush is the take-off. We want to get on the offensive lineman before he can get set. We want him to be scrambling to get to his set-up point. We want to get our hands on the offensive blocker as quickly as possible.

The next thing I talk about is *hand placement*. The defensive lineman wants to get his hands on the blocker as *soon* as possible and keep them on him as *long* as possible. The one thing I tell the pass rushers is to move their hands and feet. If they stop their hands and feet, they will not be good pass rushers. They have to have busy hands and feet. If they stop their feet, they are dead as a pass rusher.

If the defensive lineman is a contain rusher, he contains the quarterback. He does not contain an offensive lineman. If the defender is supposed to contain, he needs to stay outside and contain. If he goes inside, he may look good, but everyone else will look bad when the quarterback escapes.

We contain the quarterback, but we do not rush past him. We are no good running behind the quarterback. We have two targets in our pass rush scheme. The targets are the front shoulder of the quarterback and the back shoulder of the quarterback. The contain rushers are targeting the back shoulder of the quarterback and the interior rushers are focusing on the front shoulder.

When you rush the quarterback, you do not have time for four or five moves. You have time for one move and a counter off that move. The pass rusher must have what he is going to do in his mind. His first move is not going to work all the time. He has to know what his counter move is going to be. If that does not work, he becomes a bull rusher to the quarterback. If he feels he cannot get home, he gets in front of the quarterback and gets his hands up. The pass rusher wants to use the offensive lineman's technique against him. We do the following things:
- Keep feet moving. Do not lunge.
- Stay in lanes. You need to keep a balanced rush on the quarterback; watch for draw.
- Contain rusher; force the quarterback up inside. Rushers force the quarterback back.
- Do not allow the quarterback to step up or roll out.
- If you can get no push, get your hands up.
- Do not rush behind the quarterback.

You have no more than three seconds to get to the quarterback. You do not have time for three or four moves.

Be undaunted. By a missed move, be ready for the counter move. Keep working, and get penetration.

Use His Technique Against Him

- If the blocker is giving ground, use a power move.
- If the blocker is meeting the defender on the line, use a quick move.
- If the blocker set takes your original move, counter with another.
- Move.
- Take advantage of anything the blocker gives you.

We use a number of drills to teach pass rush, and most of them emphasize the get-off. The first drill is a *see-and-touch hand drill* (Figure 5-17). Align two players facing each other one yard apart. The defender aligns in a three-point stance and the blocker is in a two-point stance leaning over at the waist. On the coach's command, the defender will come out of his stance toward the blocker. The blocker will move his hands in unison to various positions around his body as targets for the defender to touch with two hands. This makes the defender concentrate on where the blocker's hands are.

The next drill we use is a *close-the-cushion drill* (Figure 5-18). Have the blocker start two yards from defender within a 10-yard mark area. The defender will start on the line. The blocker will backpedal as quickly as he can to the 10-yard mark. The defender will get off on the blocker's movement and close the distance from the blocker as quickly as possible. The defender will try to touch the blocker's shoulders with both hands before he can reach five yards. The second time, have the blocker start at three yards, and the defender must touch him before he can reach seven yards deep.

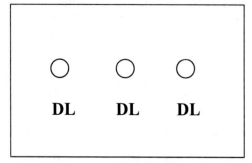

Figure 5-17. See-and-touch hand drill

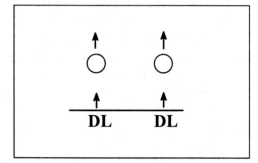

Figure 5-18. Close-the-cushion drill

The last drill I want to show you is the *lean drill* (Figure 5-19). This shows the ability to get off on the ball, to run and lean in non-parallel lines, and to burst and close on

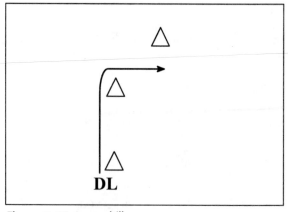

Figure 5-19. Lean drill

the quarterback (timed between 1.1 to 1.5 seconds). The defender aligns with his inside shoulder outside of the first cone. He gets off on the ball movement and sprints to the set point (second cone), then dips the inside shoulder, and sprints underneath the last cone, which simulates the quarterback. You can also add to the drill a towel on the ground inside the second cone so when the player turns around the second cone, he will pick up the towel to emphasize dipping the shoulder.

I have reached the end of my time. Do you have any questions? If you are good, I appreciate your attention.

6

Developing Defensive Linemen

Butch Davis
University of North Carolina
2009

I want to give you a brief history about myself. I grew up as a gym rat. My father was a high school football and basketball coach and later became an administrator. My first six years of coaching was spent in the high school ranks. I started out at a small school in Sand Springs, Oklahoma. I got a break in 1979 and was hired on Jimmy Johnson's first staff at Oklahoma State.

Throughout my career, I have coached a variety of different positions. At Oklahoma State, the first year on Coach Johnson's staff, I was a receiver and tight ends coach. I switched to the defensive line in 1983, when we went to Miami. I coached the defensive line at Miami from 1983 to 1989. In 1989, we went to the Dallas Cowboys and I coached the defensive line. I coached the defensive line there until the last two years when I became the defensive coordinator and coached the linebackers.

I have a passion for coaching the defensive line. In all the places I have coached, I had 25 players make it to the National Football League and nine of them were first-round draft picks. When you have the opportunity to speak at clinics, you need to talk about things that are applicable to the coaches to whom you are speaking. You want to talk about things that are going to help high school coaches. I started out as a high school coach, and I never wanted to go to a clinic and hear a coach talk about a scheme which was not applicable to the players I was coaching.

I will give you some drills, ideas, and mind-sets about coaching defensive linemen. I want to give you the role of the defensive line. I want to share what we expected of the defensive line when I was at Miami, the Cowboys, and North Carolina today.

GENERAL OVERVIEW

- Defensive line role
- Developing mentality
- Progressive teaching
- Basic fundamentals
- Practice time
- Video
- Q & A

The overview is an outline of what I am going to do today. Notice I want to save a little time at the end for questions and answers.

When you talk to your players, you must make them understand that no matter how talented or good they are, the defensive line sets the tempo for the entire football team. I have believed that all my life, and a lot of that belief is a byproduct of the things I learned from Jimmy Johnson. He coached the defensive line at Oklahoma when they had the Selman brothers. He coached Hugh Green and Rickey Jackson, who were great defensive linemen at the University of Pittsburgh. Every great team I have ever been around, the defensive line set the tempo for the mentality of the entire practice. That includes the national championship teams at Miami and the Super Bowl teams at Dallas.

If you cannot stop the run and pressure the quarterback, you will not win many football games. Go back and think about the history of football. There are reasons the defensive line groups are the ones that get legendary nicknames. You remember names like Doomsday, Purple People Eaters, Fearsome Foursome, and The Steel Curtain. Two years ago, the New York Giants were not given a chance to win the Super Bowl. Their defensive line totally dominated the entire playoffs.

If you look at the trends in college football, you will see defensive linemen flying off the board on NFL draft day. Exceptional defensive linemen can change the complexion of the game. The influence on developing the mentality of what your defensive linemen can do has become extremely important. The physical impact of your practices is controlled by the defensive line. They set the tempo for the entire defense.

We know it is a team game, and we need to have 11 players with great attitudes for practice. However, you cannot coach each player exactly the same. Some things are universal in coaching the defensive linemen. You coach the get-off and pursuit the same way with each player. However, there are some things that are fundamentally and uniquely different with each player.

At the Cowboys, we had Ed "Too-Tall" Jones who was 6'9". We later drafted Russell Maryland, who was 6'0". You cannot coach those two players to do the same thing from a pass rush or leverage standpoint. You may not have that extreme difference with the player you coach, but you may have a 5'10" noseguard and a 6'4" tackle. You must structure the way you teach those players.

At North Carolina, we have a defensive line role that we teach each player.

DEFENSIVE LINE ROLE

Your role with the team concept:
- Football is a team game—be a team player. You must be willing to make sacrifices to help the team. In doing so, you are ultimately helping yourself.
- Approach each phase with a positive attitude. Attitudes are contagious. A positive attitude will help the team win.
- Every player on the team has a role to play. As the season goes along, your role becomes clearer. It is your job to do everything mentally and physically to be successful within your role and the team concept.
- Applaud the accomplishments of your teammates.
- Each drill and practice is designed to help you improve. Practice with a purpose. There is a definite correlation between the way you practice and the way you perform in games. Practice at top speed.
- Always look for ways to improve.
- You must make a commitment to all areas: practice, weight room, film study, meetings, off-season conditioning, as well as games.
- Ask yourself:
  ✓ Am I committed?
  ✓ Am I sincere?
  ✓ Can I be trusted?

Every place I have been, we always ask the players the last three questions. We want to know if they are committed, sincere, and willing to make sacrifices to be special.

I believe the off-season is critical to the development of your entire football team. We have started to develop some role models for our players. In the past month, our coaching staff has downloaded 193 film clips of players we have seen in the NFL that looked like somebody on our football team. I did not say *play* like someone on our football team. We look for body type similarities. We have a running back on our team that looks like Brandon Jacobs of the Giants and one who looks like Adrian Peterson of the Vikings.

We put those clips on a computer and let our players come in and watch them. We hope that by watching these stars from the NFL play, it will give them a mind-set about how to make themselves better.

When we talk about developing the mentality of the defensive line, the first thing they must possess is great *desire*. They must have a willingness and burning passion to excel. I look at video tapes all the time. I have seen tapes of players in practice who make play after play. However, on the game tape they are making two or three of those types of plays. That is not good enough. You have to sell your young players on the fact they must have the desire and passion to get to the ballcarrier or passer on every single play.

They must obtain *physical toughness* by practicing tough and hard. This is a hard thing to do. I know none of us have enough players. However, I know if you do not practice physical, you will not play physical. That sounds stupid, but we won three Super Bowls in Dallas.

In practice, we actually tackled Emmitt Smith. Every Wednesday, we had a live inside drill. If he carried the ball, we knocked him to the ground. His plays were limited, and we never hit him low or took cheap shots, but we hit him like it was a game situation. Because we practiced physically and put an emphasis on being tough, we developed a tough mentality at Miami, Dallas, and North Carolina.

To play defensive football, you must know *assignments* so you can play confident, fast, and aggressive. You have to keep things simple for your players. When I listen to people talk at other clinics, I am amazed at how much they try to teach. They have hundreds of techniques and assignments. How can anyone master all that? I could not, and I do not know many players I have coached that could.

If you keep it simple for your players and let them know exactly what you expect out of them, they will have the confidence to play fast, cut loose, and become playmakers for you. If you are overcomplicated, they will overthink what they are supposed to do.

I know from experience and I'm guilty of trying to teach too many things. We taught pre-snap reads. We looked at the offensive linemen's alignment, splits, depth off the ball, pressure on the fingers, and running back positions. If you give the defensive lineman too many things to remember, the offense will snap the ball and the defensive line will be brain locked. Keeping everything simple allows the defense to be as aggressive as they possibly can be. Desire is the most important intangible in winning—desire will overcome some physical limitations.

The next point takes precedence over everything we do. We believe *conditioning precedes everything*. We lost five games this year and finished 8-5. We had a lead in the fourth quarter in four of those games. When the game is on the line, you have to stop the run and rush the quarterback in the last two minutes. You cannot have your best players tapping themselves out. You cannot have your best players standing on the sideline during that critical part of the game.

As part of our philosophy, we try to play seven or eight defensive linemen a game. However, it does not matter how many plays they play in a ball game, they must play every play as hard as they can. They have to fly around, make plays, and compete as hard as they can. If they cannot, they have to come out of the game.

This off-season is a crusade at Chapel Hill. We got away from the fast explosive defensive linemen we had with Dallas and Miami. We got bigger. We had a defensive lineman this year who was arguably the best defensive linemen in the nation. He did not get fat, but he got stronger and bigger. He was up to 328 pounds. We evaluated his performance during a drive which lasted eight or nine plays. In the first three or four plays, he was a monster. However, in the last three or four, he looked like just another defender on the team.

We are trying to get leaner and faster and make the entire defensive line better. If a player is in condition, it gives him a chance to play hard every play. It is necessary for mental toughness and maximizes his speed and quickness.

When I talk about keeping it simple, you have to make sure it is built into the packages you play on defense. It is important to not ask too much of your players. If you are too complicated players cannot be aggressive.

I want to use an example of two players we had at the University of Miami. In 1987, both these players were left defensive ends. The starter was almost robotic in everything he did. In his mind, he went through the checklist of steps for every technique he performed. In 25 plays, he might have one tackle, two assists, and maybe a quarterback pressure.

In 25 plays, the other player would jump offside one time, but would have two sacks, a forced fumble, a strip, and made plays all over the field. He was the backup player at left defensive end. We kept it simple for him so he could get into the game. We overcoached the other player so much he could not play. That is when the light came on for us. We want to make sure we are not overcoaching these players. Let their natural instincts and skills show.

Most of you will be able to appreciate this. I coached at Miami in two generations— once as an assistant coach under Jimmy Johnson and once as a head coach. College and high school coaches came to us and wanted to look at our cut-ups. We had 16mm film at that time. We had six cans of cut-ups and all of them were a 4-3 front and cover 2 in the secondary. We had two cans of stunts that we had run in our 12-game season and the other four cans were straight defense.

Our players could line up and know exactly how to play everything we ran. That allowed the coaches to focus on fundamentals. The players learned techniques, tackling, hustle, and effort. It eliminated confusion and thinking, and created reaction. People would look at us and would know what we were going to play on every down. Of course, our players knew what we were going to play on every down and that was the important thing.

We have a teaching progression for defensive linemen.

DEFENSIVE LINE TEACHING PROGRESSION

- Mental
  - ✓ Assignment
  - ✓ Alignment
  - ✓ Stance
- Technique
  - ✓ Get off
  - ✓ Head/hand placement
  - ✓ Read/react
  - ✓ Escape/rush
- Effort
  - ✓ Pursuit/chase
  - ✓ Tackle

The first part is somewhat technical. There is no compromise on the mental part of the progression. Every player on our team, regardless of his talent, speed, size, or who he is, has to learn his alignment, assignment, and stance. The third part is a no-compromise area also. Pursuing the football takes nothing but effort. Everyone must play with great effort regardless of his talent, speed, or size.

The second part of the progression separates the coaching aspect and the athletic ability of the players you have. We are a team that attacks the line of scrimmage when the offense snaps the ball. We want to play football on their side of the line of scrimmage. In this part of the progression, we teach hand pressure and leverage points. They must know the contact point and be able to dominate and control their visual key. The visual key for the 3-technique defender is the guard. The key for the 5-technique player is the tackle and the 9-technique defender's key is the tight end.

The read-and-react part is what is covered in the individual periods in coaching. That is where the player learns how to play defensive schemes. I believe consistency in what the defensive line coach calls "certain techniques" is extraordinarily important. The coach and player have to be on the same page. The player has to know what a reach block is. He has to know the difference between a reach block aimed at the outside armpit and a reach block that tries to gain control of two gaps.

The coach has to delineate what he is telling the player so they can converse when they come to the sideline. That allows the players and coach to accomplish something and make adjustments. It gives them a common language to describe what is happening on the field.

The last thing in the technique list is escape and rush. The biggest mistake I see players make is trying to escape from a block before they have control of the blocker. When we teach this, we put our linemen in a disadvantaged position and make them recover before they try to escape. It teaches them not to run behind the blocker and lets the linebacker exchange leverage opportunities.

Our ends and tackles use a three-point stance. We teach two types of stances at North Carolina. We play recognition or situational downs. In a running situation, we align in a basic stance. We want our players to be comfortable in their stance. You have to adjust the stance for the body differences of certain players. You cannot expect a tall player to align in the same stance as the shorter player. They have to make adjustments to become comfortable.

NORMAL STANCE

- Feet spread width of armpits with very little stagger
- Right hand down, right foot back, left hand down, left foot back
- Slight weight on hand, legs up under body
- Knees flexed no greater than 90 percent
- Heels slightly off ground
- Back parallel to ground (tail may be slightly higher than shoulders)
- Head and eyes up, weight equally distributed to balls of feet

This stance must permit powerful, explosive first steps. We use this stance primarily for rundown situations. There are so many players that cannot succeed because they cannot get into a proper stance.

The second variation is the *sprinter* stance. We use this stance in passing situations when we need to rush the passer.

SPRINTER STANCE

- Feet spread slightly tighter than armpits, exaggerated heal-to-toe stagger
- Hands and feet the same as above, more weight on hand
- Tail higher, legs cocked
- Free hand leading
- Eyes locked on the ball

In this stance, we are not worried about the control. We want to be aggressive and get up the field and into the guard and tackle as quickly as we can. A high percentage of effectiveness in defeating the blocker is who get their hands on the other player first. Getting the hands inside has a lot to do with who wins the battle.

The first couple of years I coached the defensive line, I fell into a bad habit of using verbal commands in teaching drills. You do not want the defensive line to listen to hard counts and cadence. The defense wants to read and react triggered by the movement of the ball. Movement triggers all the drills we do. We have a scout team player moving or a ball on the stick moving. When we do off-season conditioning drills, we have a coach using some type of movement to begin the repetition.

Moving on movement is the essence of the get-off. In our defensive alignments, the players on the right side of the defensive line will be in a left-handed stance. If they play on the left side of the line, they are in a right-handed stance. We teach both stances to everyone because you never know who will be injured. I know there are coaches that think it does not matter, however, after 35 years of doing this, I think it does.

Looking at the types of pass-rush moves and schemes you have to play, it is infinitely better to be in those kinds of stances. It goes back to the footwork. On the right side of the defensive line, the left foot is the power step and the first to move. If that foot is taken away by the charge of the offensive linemen, you must have the right foot free to recover your charge and keep the shoulders parallel to the line of scrimmage.

CHARGE AND GET OFF

- Explode on first movement of the ball or offensive linemen
- Explosion step (first step)—roll off ball of foot, bringing up rear for balance
- Balance step (second step)—bring parallel up to rear, parallel base as you charge, eyes forward on key for reach
- Read must be completed during balance step
- Next step will be reaction step

When we teach this part of the get-off drill, we back up the players. There is nothing more intimidating or confusing for a defensive lineman than to get multiple reads. We compensate for their mistakes by backing them up and giving them more time to read. The more experience they gain, the closer they play to the ball. What we are striving for is to take as much of the ball as we can get. We want to crowd the line of scrimmage and get as close to the offensive blocker as we can. We want to be into his face before he can react.

REACTION STEP

- The third step will be your reaction to your read.
- The better you become at reading and reacting, the closer you should crowd the ball.
- Make all steps as short and quick as possible. Never be so intent on "reading" that your charge is delayed or soft. Be aggressive, attack the line of scrimmage. Penetration is vital!

I want to talk a little about practice. The time allotted to the position coaches changes from day to day and week to week. The amount of time allotted is relative to the team you are playing. Passing teams require a different time allotment than running teams. If the opponent is a passing team, more time has to be spent on rush techniques than run assignments. However, I think you are making a tragic mistake if you do not devote a certain amount of individual time every day to certain things.

I believe that every position coach can improve the athletic ability of the players he coaches. If the coach will focus on that aspect of the skills required to play the position, the players will become better at those skills. You cannot coach defensive backs and not spend a significant amount of time on backpedaling drills. You must have drills that assimilate game situations. A certain amount of time in our drill is spent improving the athletic ability of our players.

DEFENSIVE LINE INDIVIDUAL PRACTICE

- Always have drills that reinforce fundamentals and technique.
- Have drills that emphasize execution of the game plan defensive scheme.
- Drills should build confidence through repetition.
- Do not make drills too elaborate (one or two aspects per drill). If they are easy to explain and set-up, the players get more reps.
- Only use drills that help you master your position.
- Incorporate conditioning and stamina into drills.

I have some pet peeves with drills. Do not try to teach too many things at one time. The players must see and know that the drill will make them become a better player.

The second peeve is a drill that is too complicated. If it takes too long to set up the drill, by the time you finish the drill, the players only get one rep apiece. In our coaches meetings, I continually tell our coaches to keep their drills simple, have some application to the game plan for that day, and do not make it too complicated.

When you do drills, one or two concepts are all you need. If you are doing a bag drill, having the players explode off the last bag into a finish is awesome. That is what the game looks like on Saturday. They are working on a fundamental drill and finishing with an explosion.

Do the drills that help your players master their position. If you use a fire zone blitz scheme, you have to practice tackles and end dropping off the line of scrimmage. However, if you are going to use the scheme twice in the game, do not spend 15 minutes doing something that will only occur once or twice. Make sure the things you practice are going to show up proportionally as to what your players are going to do in the game.

The last thing is for defensive line coaches to incorporate conditioning into their drills. If you come to our spring practices at North Carolina, you will find our drill periods extremely hard. We will go 30 minutes in our drill period. We will push them and they will be wringing wet because of the difficulty of the drills.

I have a script of drills that we do in our defensive line. There is a different emphasis placed on each set of drills. The first group of drills is devoted to developing athleticism.

- Bag
  - ✓ One foot in the hole
  - ✓ Two feet in the hole
  - ✓ Shuffle and redirect
  - ✓ Lateral
  - ✓ Redirect
- Ladder
  - ✓ Quick feet
  - ✓ Lateral run
- Change of direction drills
  - ✓ L drill
  - ✓ Pro agility
- Stance
  - ✓ Takeoff
  - ✓ Mat drill

During the stance period, we work on the two variations of the stance. In the normal stance, we have the ability to go sideways as well as straight ahead. In the sprint stance, we are not worried about sideways movement. The emphasis is on speed and penetration to the quarterback.

When we do the mat drill, we use a tumbling mat to break the fall of the players. They get into their stance and explode out onto the mat. They turn everything loose, explode off the ball, and dive into the mat. This teaches explosion without worrying about injury from the ground.

The second group of drills is classified as run drills. Emphasize head and hand placement in these drills.

- Versus
  ✓ Sleds
- Run reads
  ✓ 1-on-1 basic blocks
  ✓ 2-on-1 basic blocks
  ✓ Torque drill
  ✓ Torque drill from reached position
- Run escapes
  ✓ Tackling
  ✓ Bag tackle
  ✓ Bag redirect
  ✓ Tackle

The torque drills are used to make the defensive linemen work from a blocked situation. We put him in a disadvantaged situation and make him reestablish control of the blocker. We fit the defender in a position where he is reached and must recover from the block. That teaches him to recover control of the blocker before he tries to escape from the block.

We do all kinds of tackling drills. We tackle sleds, bags, dummies, and people. To become good tacklers you must tackle every day.

The third group of drills is devoted to pass rushing. In these drills, players should work on the technique that fits their body style.

- Pass rush 101
  ✓ Run curve
  ✓ Run curve with ball

- Pop-ups
  - ✓ Gauntlet
  - ✓ Tight gauntlet
  - ✓ Clup rip dip
  - ✓ Counter drill
- Hoops
  - ✓ Touch drill
  - ✓ Chase
  - ✓ Leverage drill
  - ✓ Two hands
  - ✓ Speed rip
  - ✓ Rip
  - ✓ Wipe
  - ✓ Counter club
  - ✓ Spin

PASS RUSH ESCAPES

You have to develop drills that fit your defensive scheme. I want to do drills to help my players become better athletes. Defensive linemen will always be playing in trash. There will always be bodies under their feet or someone trying to trip them. Develop drills that will help them develop the skills they need to play the game. Coaches should make a master list of the drills that will accomplish what they want to cover. From the master list of drills, they should develop a checklist of the drills they do.

I ask my coaches to make a list of all the things they plan to teach during the course of the season. I want them to list the drills they will use to teach those skills. As they go through the season, they should put check marks by the drills they do. That will tell you a tremendous amount about what you emphasize.

We like to emphasize creating turnovers. We did a tremendous job of running drills that promoted turnover production during the pre-season practices. However, as the season went along, we found we were doing less scoop-and-score, tomahawk, and ball-stripping drills. If you get away from the things you are supposed to emphasizing, the less effective you will be at that skill. You can find that out from your drill checklist.

When I was with the Cowboys, we finished number one in total defense twice. We went back and did a study of those two years. I would be willing to bet you, if they did the same type of study of the 2008 season, the results would be the same. The longest runs in the national football league always came in the second half of the season. Teams started off doing well through the first four or five games. We considered runs over 15 yards to be long runs. In that year, 60 percent of the runs over 15 yards occurred in the second half of the season.

The reason for that happening is very simple. During pre-season training camp, that was the emphasis. Everyone tackled and got off blocks every day of training camp. As the season wore on, those things were not the emphasis of the drill work. With the use of the checklist, you are constantly aware of what you are teaching your players.

In our pass-rush drills, the first drill listed is a run curve drill (Figure 6-1). I started doing this drill back in the late 1980s. There is nothing outstanding about this drill except it teaches your defensive linemen to get off the ball. In doing this drill, we time the defensive linemen and try to plant the seed in his mind of speed. We set up a cone for the takeoff point of the defender. There is no movement key in this part of the drill. The defender takes off when he is ready. We set a stand-up bag at the depth of seven yards. That is the depth of the front foot of the quarterback in a five-step drop.

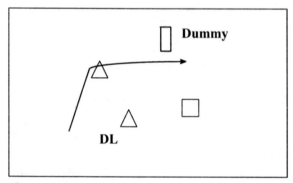

Figure 6-1. Run curve

We set a cone at a point which represents the set point of the offensive tackle's outside foot. The defensive lineman has to get off the ball, curve around the cone, and cross the face of the dummy. The whole thing we are trying to teach is how fast the defender can do it.

If it takes the defender 1.2 seconds to perform that move, he has 1.8 seconds to make the tackle. We assume the ball will be thrown in three seconds.

The next part of the drill is run curve with the ball. Reacting to the movement of the ball took 1.7 seconds. They lost five-tenths of a second in their reaction time. That lets them know what they have to do to get to the quarterback.

Right now we have 60 film clips of defensive linemen from the NFL. We have films of Julius Peppers, Dwight Freeney, and many others. Our players come in and watch those clips to help them become better players. It helps our players develop their own pass-rush moves.

We do the gauntlet drill to help players understand there is generally more than one blocker to defeat (Figure 6-2). If the tackle defeats the guard, he may have to take on the center or running back to get to the quarterback. The gauntlet is a series of stand-up dummies, staggered so as the player weaves through them he has to use both hands to attack each dummy. On the first dummy, he may use a right-handed club move and a left-handed move on the second dummy. In those drills, they run the club, rip, and dip moves. We have a dummy at the finish with a ball attached so the defender can strip the ball.

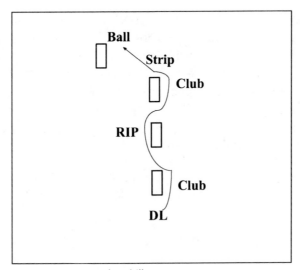

Figure 6-2. Gauntlet drill

We use all kinds of variations of drills with the hoops. You can make the hoops very inexpensively, and they will pay great benefits in the pass-rush game (Figure 6-3). The more competitive you can make the drill, the more you will gain from it. We play chase and tag on them. If the first player can catch and touch the second player, the second player has to go again. Make the drills as much fun and as competitive as you can. You have to use your own imagination and creativity to come up with different ways to incorporate the skills.

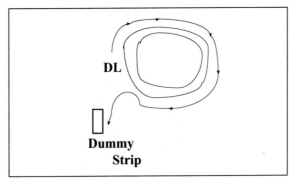

Figure 6-3. Hoops

The thing you want to watch is how tight the players stay to the hoop. The tighter they can stay to the hoop, the more flexible they are in their hips. The players that run the tightest to the hoop are probably going to be your best pass rushers. If you put a dummy holder in the middle of the hoop, it helps them to be more physical as they run. Have them perform rips on the dummy as they go around the hoop. We do the drill with the linebackers and defensive backs that we plan on using in a pressure scheme. When you watch your game films, you can see the skills from the practice field taken to the game field.

I have great respect for the fact that you coaches are here today. I got into coaching 35 years ago. I taught high school biology and coached boys and girls track in addition to coaching football. I rode on many school buses just like all of you in this room. However, the main reason I became a coach was to make a difference in the lives of the kids I was involved with. There is no greater calling today. The future of our country relies on the coaches in this country. You are the ones that can truly make a difference in the lives of the kids. You can help kids. You can help them stay out of trouble, and you can become a role model for them.

I believe that 95 percent of you in this room are a father figure for some player in your program. Those kids do not have the father figure in their lives that they so desperately need.

It was a pleasure to be with you today. Come see us in Chapel Hill, and thank you very much.

7

Defensive Concepts Emphasizing the Defensive Line

Mike Fanoga
Western Kentucky University
2003

I want to give you a quick summary of our defense. In my first year at Western we had a big thick playbook. I wasn't very happy with it because there were some things in there that we didn't use. I believe less is better. The more reps your players can do the better they become. This year we decided to condense our playbook and make it a thin copy. All our players have a copy of it and bring it to all team meetings. I wanted to make them responsible for the playbook. If our players don't bring their playbook and a note pad to meetings, they get fined. Our fine is running after practice. I want the defensive line to have the section of the playbook that relates to them. They don't need the secondary section of the book.

You always need a defensive philosophy. In our playbook we have our philosophies for the offensive team, defensive team, and the special teams. When you form your philosophy make sure it is sound, basic, and easy for your players to understand. Our defensive philosophy is: *attack-confuse-attack*. I'll talk more about that later.

We have team goals we emphasize with our defense. We develop weekly goals for our defense. They are very simple but necessary in getting our players to focus on some specifics for each game.

The first goal is to win the game. We all want to win and that is the place to begin to build. We feel if we can *hold our opponents to 13 points or less*, we have a chance to win the game. We want to *create three or more turnovers*. That is probably the biggest goal we have. This past season we had 15 fumble recoveries and 20 interceptions. During the course of the game, we want to *force the offense into a critical mistake.* To get your defense off the field you have to be proficient on third-down plays. We want to stop the opponent on 30 percent of their *third-down plays.* We want to prevent the offense from getting big plays on the defense. We want *nothing over 12 yards in the running game and nothing over 18 yards in the passing game*. When our offense turns the ball over on a fumble or interception, we want our defense to come in and stop the other team's offense. We call that sudden change. *We want a 100-percent stop in the sudden change category.*

We post our weekly goals in our locker room and fill in the ones that we complete. We want our players to see what they accomplished and where they fall short. They can see from the goal sheet what it takes to win a game.

The next section is important, but I am going to go through it quickly. These are principles that are important in playing great defense. It is extremely important to be able to communicate with your players. You have to talk to your players. Let them know that you love and care about them. If there are problems they want to talk about, make sure they know you are available to counsel them or simply be someone who will listen to them. Let them know you care about their welfare and not just about their football ability.

To play in the defensive line, a player has to improve and master the techniques it takes to play the game. The player has to become a *technician*. I feel this is my biggest asset as a coach. I want to think I do a very good job working on individual techniques for each player.

If a defensive football player wants to be successful, he must have tremendous effort. I want my players to understand it is important to give a 110-percent effort when they step on the field. All I ask from my players during a game is an honest effort. Running to the football is nothing more than effort. The game of football has gotten very sophisticated. We are requiring more out of our players in making adjustments and reading offenses. Players have to be smart to play the game today. The intelligence part of the game is important. They don't have to be brilliant to play the game, but they must have a good football IQ. I guess that is what we call *functional intelligence*. They have to play the game smart and think on the field.

The game of football requires players to have *emotional stability*. That keeps them from overreacting to situations that arise in the heat of battle. That keeps a player from getting the killer, dumb penalty when you can least afford it. He has to be able to handle the winning as well as the losing. Every game is filled with small individual battles between players. A player has to play with a calm demeanor and at the same time be aggressive. He has to play the game with *harnessed aggression*.

You have to coach good practice habits and stress to the players to always finish the play. It is not enough to simply do your job; you have to complete every play. Running to the ball and getting in on the play is a finish to the technique the defender played to get off a block. We have a slogan at Western that deals with pursuit. We took it from a movie, but it reflects what we want them to do. When we talk about running to the ball we tell our players to *get in the gun line*. We want everyone on the defense to be within five yards of the ball when the whistle blows. If our players are not in the gun line, they get shot and have to run after practice. It really showed in our team this year. We had people swarming to the football. We want people breaking up passes, turning and running to the ball, playing violent, and becoming a ballistic missile out on the field.

We post signs in our locker room to get our players to focus on what is important. One of the signs we hang in our locker room is: *Think like a Winner*. They see the sign coming into and going out of the building. We talk about it in our drills and emphasize it during practice. The biggest thing we work on in coaching defense is pursuit. Getting in the gun line has become our faith and motto. That phrase has become synonymous with pursuit at Western Kentucky.

We have a practice-and-players policy sheet we go over with our players. That gives our players a guide to what they should expect from our practices. The player policy lets them know what is expected of them at practice and all other activities they may be involved in. That is a part of our ongoing attempt to communicate with our players.

The biggest defensive skill a defender has to master is *tackling*. The defensive team that can't tackle won't win many games. You have to define what you expect from your players. Give them the objectives you hope to accomplish in your team tackling. You have to teach them the techniques that go with tackling. If you watched our championship game, I think you would have been impressed by the way we tackled. We did not miss a tackle in the championship game. We work on tackling every day. Each position coach has tackling drills every day we practice. The progression we teach in tackling is the *approach*, *contact*, and the *finish*.

When your offense turns the ball over to the opposing team it creates a sudden-change situation in the game. The attitude we try to get over to our kids is a happy occasion. We want the challenge of trying to go out and stop the offense. We have a word we use in this situation. The word is *mana*. It is a Hawaiian word that means *power within a person*. Before the defense goes on the field, they gather around the coach and have a mini-pep rally.

We break the field into zones to describe the type of effort we want from our defense. The first zone is called the gut zone. We describe the *gut zone* as the area between the opponent's goal line and the opponent's 25-yard line. When the opponent has the ball in the gut zone, we want to hold them in that zone and not let them out. We want the opponent to kick from a backed up position.

The second zone is called the *normal zone*. That zone extends from the 26-yard line to the opposite 26-yard line. In that zone we want to attack on first down. In the third-down situation we will blitz on occasion if it is long yardage.

The *red zone* is the area between our 25-yard line and the five-yard line. In that zone the defense wants to be in attack mode and mix in some man coverage.

The last zone is the *goal line zone*. That zone stretches from the four-yard line to the goal line. In that zone we are in goal line defense most of the time.

The offense has a two-minute offense for the last two minutes of the game or a half. We have to do the same thing on defense. We must have a plan to defend during the last minutes of a half because most teams are going to be in a no-huddle offense. We have to be prepared to play without a huddle and get into a proper alignment.

Each of our coaches has a sign posted on their door, which relates to the playing habits of playing the game. It states that every day and *every play there are things to be done*. There is a list of items on each sign. They are broken into pre-snap and post-snap responsibilities. In the pre-snap situation the players have to consider alignment, stance, field position, and responsibility. In the post-snap situation there is read, react, execute, delivery a blow, get off the block, and tackle. These are things that they have to do as they line up and get ready to play.

We have *three nevers* that we teach all the time. They are to *never* get knocked down, *never* get knocked off the ball, and *never* run around a block. These *nevers* are also posted on our doors in our coach's office. These are situations we want to constantly reinforce to our players.

Next is our *scouting report*. Each coach has a responsibility to make up his part of the playbook and the scouting report. Our graduate assistant has responsibility for the front cover of the scouting report. He has to come up with a thought for the week to go on the front of that report. For our scouting report on McNeese State in the championship game he came up with: *Those Who Stay Will Become National Champions!*

As you walk into our facility, our head coach has that slogan posted on his door. It is ironic to think about that now. I never thought we would get that far. We just played our butts off in those final games and came away with the championship.

The next page of the scouting report is a breakdown of personnel, formations, top runs, and top passes. Our defensive coordinator puts this part of the report together. The first thing you see on this sheet is *overall record*. Since we were playing McNeese State in the last game, the first thing they saw was the 13-1 record. The next thing is the name of the team, their national ranking, and the games that were used to scout them. In this case we used the last five games. We list the opponents and the final score of each game.

We are a very personnel-oriented team. We like to know who the top personnel are and what they do in the game. That helps us make our calls. We list the top personnel by numbers and the percentage of time they run or throw the ball. For instance, McNeese State's top personnel's grouping was what we refer to as 21. That means they have two wide receivers and one tight end in the game. From that set they ran the ball 70 percent of the time and passed it 30 percent of the time. We list their top formation, top runs, and top passes. We list their top formation with their top personnel (Figure 7-1).

McNeese State's top formations from their 21 personnel package were pro and slot. In each formation we list the percentage of times they ran the ball as opposed to the times they threw it (Figure 7-2).

Top Personnel	
21 – 70/30	20 – 30/70
11 – 65/42	22 – 100/0
32 – 100/0	

Figure 7-1. Top personnel chart

Top Formations		Top Passes	
Flex	Pro	2 Spot	QK – 2332/2322
Slot	Slot hip	Flex – BJ get open	Shallow crossers
Top Runs		Curl/flat	I slot – P43 058B3
Belly	Toss		
Iso	Power		
Draw	Jet sweep		

Figure 7-2. Top formations and plays chart

The defensive linemen love the next sheet on the report. That is where we get our tendencies and techniques. We test our team on the scouting report. Most of the material comes from that sheet. The first year I was at Western we had a huge scouting report for each game. We have taken all the verbiage out of the report and condensed it to a four- or five-page report. We get all the scouting report to the team on Tuesday afternoon. Each of our defensive coaches is in charge of one section of the scouting report. The outside linebacker coach is in charge of the section called *field zone run/pass percentage*. That section of the report lists the field broken down into zones (Figure 7-3). This chart breaks the field down and gives us the percentage of times they run the ball or throw it in each zone.

Field Zone Run/Pass Percentage 60/40	
-1 to +10	100/0
-11 to −39	53/47
−40 to +40	54/46
+39 to +26	63/37
+25 to +5	77/23
+4 to +1	68/32

Figure 7-3. Field zone run/pass percentage chart

I am in charge of the short-yardage section of the report. As you can see, this tells us what they like to run in the short-yardage situations in the game (Figure 7-4).

Short Yardage
I pro – 52/53 belly
I slot – 43 lead
I flex – 52/53 belly-fake pitch

Figure 7-4. Short-yardage chart

McNeese State's favorite sets in the short-yardage situation were I-pro, I-slot, and I-flex. From the pro set they like to run what we call 52/53 belly. From the slot set they ran the 43-lead play. From the flex set they ran the 52/53 belly fake pitch.

In the goal line situation, I don't have to tell the defensive line what they run. It is the same series they use in short yardage. The difference is the formation in which they are aligned. Most of their formations are tight formations with two or more tight ends (Figure 7-5).

Goal Line
1 tight – 53 belly
PQA/M to tight – 45 blast
11 run to slot hip – 53 belly F/P

Figure 7-5. Goal line situation chart

Each coach has a responsibility to break down the red zone situations. I'll show you an example of our red zone breakdown (Figure 7-6).

Red Zone – 70 x – 80/20
21 – 79/21 = 1 pros/slot – 52 B/53 B/44 L/48 G – 2 reverses, 1 trick
20 – 58/42 = 1 flex = run – belly/43 LO/AGS Detroit hip = pass
22 – 9 runs – 1 tight – 44 L/49 G/53 B/48 G
11 – 4 runs
32 – 1 run

Figure 7-6. Red zone situation chart

Our scouting report showed us that McNeese was in the red zone 70 times in those five games that we scouted. They ran the ball 80 percent of the time and threw it 20 percent of the time. From their 21-personnel grouping they ran the I-pro/slot. From those formations they ran 52/53 belly, 44 lead, 48 G-sweep, two reverses, and one trick play. We break each personnel grouping down in similar manner.

I am also in charge of doing the section that deals with the backs set. I list each back set and show the number times the ball is run or passed from that set (Figure 7-7). From the ace set, McNeese State ran the ball 58 percent of the time and threw it 42 percent of the time.

Back Set	Run/Pass
I	75/25
Ace	58/42
SG	16/84
QN	36/64
AGS	15/85
KG	0/100

Figure 7-7. Backs set chart

We played McNeese during the regular season at their place. They beat us in that game. They were a very good team. It was a nasty and hostile atmosphere and a difficult environment in which to play a game. After the first game one of my defensive linemen was really down about the defeat. I told him we had just gotten our tails kicked but we would meet those guys again down the road. In the championship game we played them in Chattanooga. We were ready for McNeese in the Division I-AA Championship Game.

The final section on this page is the run/pass tendencies. We list them by percentages. McNeese ran the ball 60 percent of the time and threw it 40 percent of the time. We list the tendencies by down-and-distance situations. We break our down-and-distances into 12 categories (Figure 7-8).

Run/Pass Tendencies (60/40)	
1st +10	73/27
2nd +L	50/50
2nd +LL	54/46
2nd +M	74/26
2nd +S	82/18
3rd +L	18/85
3rd +LL	28/72
3rd +M	18/82
3rd +S	100/0
3rd +3	50/50
4th 1-2	7 runs
4th and 3+	1 pass

Figure 7-8. Run/pass tendencies

We have first-and-ten, fourth-and-one to two yards, and fourth-and-three yards plus. In the second- and third-down situations we use long, medium, and short yardage to classify what they are doing.

The next sheet of the scouting report is a two-deep listing of personnel. That lets us know who is playing in the game. We list the players by name with their height and weight. Next we list several sheets with the plays they run. We draw each play they like to run from their personnel groups and show how they block the plays. I am in charge of the pass-protection sheet. We show how they are protecting in each formation. We show the formations they like to throw from and the protection that goes with each formation.

We also give our defensive players a tip sheet. The first section on this sheet is *alignment*. We give them tips about stance whether it is heavy or light. We watch the splits of the linemen and what they like to do from a tight or wide split. We give them the opponent's snap count and what they use for their hard count.

Each coach is responsible for giving his position group a quiz on the scouting report. It is a 10-question quiz about the information in the scouting report (Figure 7-9). My sheet starts out with some goals listed at the top of the sheet. For McNeese State I listed: *play with mana, play with power,* and *play with quickness.* I followed that with a statement to challenge them. For McNeese it was: *Those who play and pour out their hearts will become champions tonight.* After that comes the quiz.

I conclude the sheet with a mission statement. It stated: Magnify Your Stewardship and Finish! I told my players the day we played McNeese State that everyone would be watching them on TV. I told them they needed to play hard and show everyone what our program was all about. I told them this game could open some doors for

Hilltopper Linemen Quiz Versus McNeese

1) I-back means? _____

2) What type of alignment will they show us? _____

3) How will they block us up front? _____

4) Anytime we're in a 3 technique we must be ready for what? _____

5) We must get or come off line of scrimmage and also need to be the _____

6) What is their favorite outside run play? _____

7) What do they like to do in the red zone? _____

8) What is their passing formation in the red zone? _____

9) What kind of offense is McNeese State? _____

10) What do we need to accomplish this week? _____

Figure 7-9. Scouting report quiz

those who had dreams about the next level. If they played well people would follow them. These guys played their butts off that day and we became champions.

After each game the coaches grade the film. We grade our players on production. Each production has a point value assigned to it (Figure 7-10).

If a person makes a tackle he receives two points. If he gets an assist he gets one point. You can see the point value and how we rate the players. In addition to the positive scores there are negative scores. If you fail to *get in the gun line*, that is a minus one. A missed assignment is minus three, and a missed tackle is minus two points.

We total the plays each player is involved in, add up his total points, and compute the player's ratio. We divide the number of plays into his number of points. That gives us a ratio for the number of plays that a player was productive. If the players ratio figures out to 1.2 to 1.5 score, that is good. That means he is making a productive play almost every play.

We do the production chart on Sunday night and have it posted on the production board in the locker room on Monday. That is the first place the players go. They want to see how they did. We also give them a percentage score on their play in the game. The rating sheet is divided into five columns with the headings of play, player, (+ or -), production, and assignment/technique comment (Figure 7-11).

Hilltopper Production Chart		
ITEMS	PTS.	GAMES>>>>
Tackle	2	
Assists	1	
Tackle for loss	3	
Kickoff tackle (-20)	5	
QB harass	3	
Sack	5	
Big Hit	3	
Exceptional play	3	
Caused fumble	5	
Recovered fumble	5	
Onside kick recovery	7	
Pass breakup	4	
Interception	7	
Blocked kick	6	
Score on defense	8	
Gun line	-1	
Missed assignment	-3	
Missed tackles	-2	
Special Comments		
PLAYS		
TOTAL PLAYS		
TOTAL POINTS		
RATIO		

Figure 7-10. Production chart

Hilltopper Grade Sheet				
PLAY	PL. #	+ OR -	PROD.	COMMENTS
#1	LDE			
	RDE			
	NT			
#2				

Figure 7-11. Grade sheet

Coming down the page there are three line divisions for each play. This means for each play run the three defensive linemen are graded. Each player gets a percentage grade from the number of pluses he has, divided by the number of plays he played. What you don't want to see are players with high- percentage grades and low-production ratios. That means his assignment and technique is good but he is not making any plays.

As a coach at Western Kentucky, you have to be involved with some kind of special team. My area is the extra point and field goal block team. When we start practice we start with five minutes of field goal blocking. We blocked four field goals this year and one of them was in the championship game. The first block is called MC Hammer (Figure 7-12), which stands for middle block. We don't change any personnel on our block team. Whoever is in the game stays in the game and aligns on the block team. The left and right corners play their side. The Mike linebacker goes to the left side and the Will linebacker goes to the right. We have a nickel and a linebacker in the game and they deploy with the nickel to the left C gap and the in the right B gap. The defensive ends are in the left B gap and the right A gap. The nose tackle is in the left A gap. In the middle of the formation we have what we call our leapers. Those are the players that are going to jump and block low kicks. These are safety positions, but we want our highest jumpers in those positions.

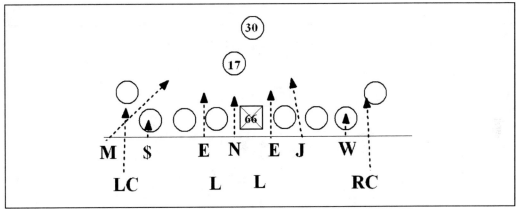

Figure 7-12. MC Hammer (middle block)

If the ball is on the left hash mark, we call hammer right (Figure 7-13). Nothing changes for anyone on their alignments. The only assignments that have changed are the right end and joker. They become the blockers. The Mike linebacker has to make sure the kick is off. If the ball is blocked, he may have a chance to scoop it and score. If there is a bad snap and the kicking team makes a fire call, he has the kicker. Everyone else has a man on the play. The joker and left defensive end are blocking the left offensive guard off the line of scrimmage. We are trying to get the leaper through or at least get him deeper in the backfield.

If the ball is on the right hash mark we call hammer left (Figure 7-14). The alignments are the same. The nose tackle and defensive left end are the blockers. The linemen are in a power charge. They lead with their helmet hard and low. The linemen should extend the hands into the offensive lineman like an incline press. They need to get their pads under the pads of the offensive lineman and work upward. They should bench press the lineman and keep coming hard with their legs moving and their arms extended.

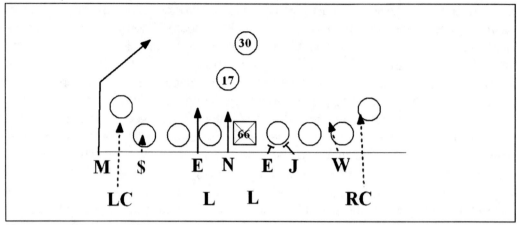

Figure 7-13. Hammer right

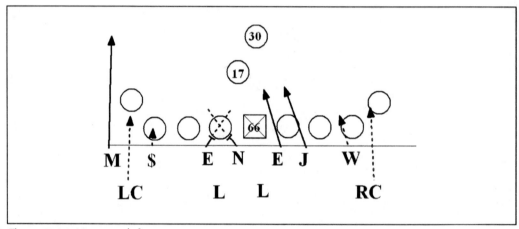

Figure 7-14. Hammer left.

They need to get vertical as well as horizontal push. The left leaper has to adjust his path and everything else is the same as the hammer right.

If we want to try and block the ball coming off the edge, I call that an H&R block (Figure 7-15). We give a Liz or Ricky call to tell us which side is coming. The best kick blocker on the team should be put to the side the block is coming from. We cover man-to-man on the receivers with the Mike and Will linebackers having the tight ends. The free and strong safeties have the wingbacks. If we are coming from the left, our best blocker is coming from outside the wing. We align him in a cocked position to the inside. We want his outside foot back. He aligns wide enough to get a good close angle to the spot four-and-a-half yards in front of the ball. On his first step he takes his outside foot across the line of scrimmage. On the second step he steps with his inside foot. The third step is a drive step to the inside to adjust his course. On the fourth step he takes off and lays out with his arms extended. We want his eyes open so he can move his hands to the ball. The next rusher is coming inside the wing to draw his block. That gives the blocker a chance to get on the right angle to the ball. If we make a Ricky call, the block comes from the right side. Everything remains the same as far as responsibility, except the blockers go to the right side.

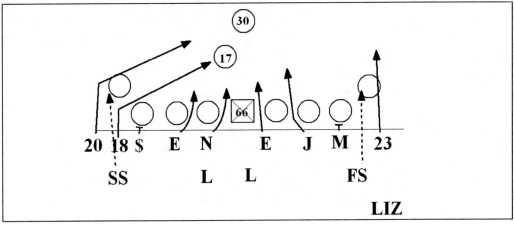

Figure 7-15. H&R block

Let's talk about defense real quick before I run out of time. We are a 3-4 defense. We coach our players to attack what is attacking them. We want to attack the offensive linemen. We want to penetrate, not read. I spent some time with the Philadelphia Eagles last year doing an internship in a fellowship program. They really emphasized a wide base with good knee bend for their defensive lineman. They spend a tremendous amount of time working on get off.

When I talk about the target area, you need to know about *vision point*. The defensive linemen have to see and read the hips of the offensive lineman as they slant. The defensive lineman in his stance comes off with a 45-degree step. He is looking at the hip of the offensive guard. If the hip goes down on a down block, the defensive lineman comes inside off his hip. If the hip comes toward him, his hands shoot out and he makes his move off the block. Another vision point we use is the V of the neck. On the snap of the ball we get great takeoff and attack the V of the neck.

To play defense, the lineman has to play with his eyes. He has to see what is happening. We attack off the line and read on the run. We have to see which way the offensive linemen are going. If we have a fill call we attack the V of the neck. The course of the lineman is changed. He wants to come flatter to the scrimmage. If his vision point is the hip, his charge is more upfield with penetration and vertical push. I want them to see the blockers and cross face every chance they get. If the defender is getting a reach or a zone block on a fill call, he is going flat down the line and has to redirect when he reads the reach. On a pass protection or fan-out block the defensive lineman has to cross face.

When the defensive lineman takes on a block, there are three elements he has to consider. They are *my body*, *his body*, and *eyes*. I got this from the Philadelphia Eagles. You attack with your body, use the offensive blocker's body as a shield, and play with your eyes. In the 3-4 defense, the defensive end is playing in a 4 technique. On some of our defensive calls he has to use a loop step. He is going to loop outside on the tight end and play the C gap. He has to see the alignment of the tight end. If the split of the tight end is tight, he takes a small step to get to the inside shoulder of the tight end or 7 technique. If the tight end has a wide split, he has to take a larger step to get into position. He is taking a lateral step and controlling the C gap. If the tackle is trying to reach him, he gets his hands on the tackle and stays inside the C gap.

The alignment of our nose tackle is head-up on the center. He is getting as close to the ball as he can. Our defensive ends are in 4 techniques head-up on the tackles. They are backed off the ball 18 inches. We want them to have a little clearance off the ball. We are a slanting defense about 70 percent of the time. The other 30 percent, we are an eagle, over, or under front. When we are playing what we call a 70 front, our defensive ends are using a jam technique on the offensive tackle (Figure 7-16). That is another term for a bull rush on the tackles working their way upfield. The nose tackle is aligned on the center and doing the same thing. The Mike and Will linebackers have A gap responsibility. The joker linebacker is dropping into coverage and the nickel linebacker is rushing. We are playing cover 2 in the secondary.

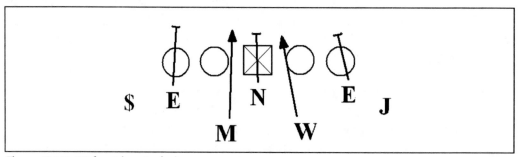

Figure 7-16. 70 front jam technique

When we call 72 (Figure 7-17), it tells our players the defensive line is slanting to the right. The right defensive end has a loop technique if he has a tight end to his side. If he is to the openside of the set, he has a jam technique and contains outside. The nose tackle doesn't worry about the block of the center. He is slanting at the offensive guard and reading his hip. If the hip goes outside, he attacks the hip because the play is going outside. The nose tackle is the core of the defense. He is the heart and soul of the defense. He cannot get blocked by the center. He has to tilt his hip and get on the guard. The left defensive end is slanting inside and reading the hip of the offensive guard. If the guard is down blocking, zone blocking, or pulling, the defensive end attacks his hip. If the defensive end has a fill technique, he is coming flat to the line of scrimmage. If the center tries to block back on him, he wants to go cross face as quickly as he can. The nickel linebacker knows he has containment, but he is slanting too. The Mike and Will linebacker are scraping over the top on flow. The joker is dropping and has the curl zone to the flat area.

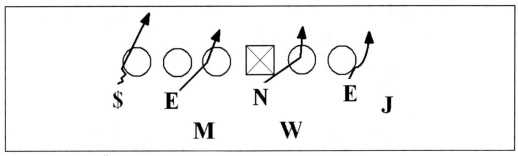

Figure 7-17. 72 call

The 73 call is the opposite slant. The defensive front is slanting left. The left defensive end has to read the split of the tight end. If he has a tight split, he takes the small loop step into the C gap. If the tight end's split is wider, he has to take a longer loop step. Everyone else is playing the defense the same. If the defensive call is 74I, that tells the nose tackle to shade the center.

If we make a *reduction call* that means we are going to reduce away from the call. We are going to reduce away from the tight end or the split end. The reduction call moves our defensive line to shade techniques away from the call. If the call is to the defensive right side, the right defensive end moves from a 4 technique to a 3 technique, and the left defensive end moves from a 4 technique to a 5 technique away from the call.

The nose tackle moves to a shade on the guard away from the call. If we make a *bonzai* call, that changes the direction of our slant from one side to the other side. If we have a split-fill call (Figure 7-18), the front is going away from the split end. If the tight end comes out to the left and the split end is right, our angle charge would be toward the tight end. However, if the tight end shifted to the other side before the ball was snapped, that would reverse our call. The Mike linebacker would call *bonzai* and change the angle from left to right. The defensive front is slanting using a fill technique as their charge course. That means their angles are flatter to the line of scrimmage. They are redirecting on blocks at them and cross facing on blocks going the other way.

If we run a tight fill, it is the opposite of the split fill. The front is slanting away from the tight end. If the tight end changes sides, we get the bonzai call, which changes our direction on our slant. Behind both of these fill defenses we are playing cover 3. This is very simple for our kids to learn.

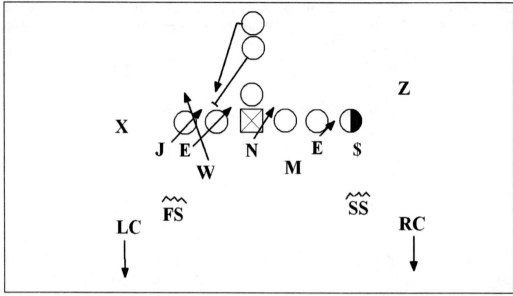

Figure 7-18. Split-fill call

We also have a double fill (Figure 7-19). Any time the defensive line hears *double* they know they are coming inside. This is a pinching defense. Both sides of the defense are coming inside. The nose tackle is playing a jam technique on the center. The defensive ends are slanting hard inside keying the offensive guards. The joker and nickel linebackers are slanting inside also. We use this defense in our goal line defense. Ninety percent of our short-yardage defense is our base defense. The Mike and Will linebackers are keying the backs. If it is a run, they are shooting their gaps. The Mike linebacker on flow toward him is scraping outside. On flow away he is scrapping inside. The Will linebacker is doing the same thing. On pass the linebackers have the backs coming their way.

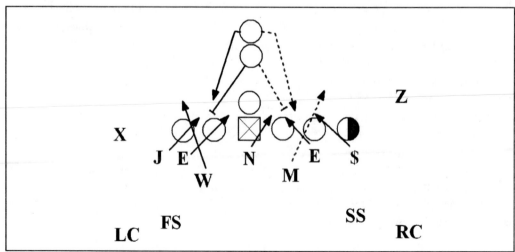

Figure 7-19. Double-fill call

In our Okie fronts we have four defenses we run. We run what we call *south, west, southwest,* and *freeze.* I'll talk about them in a minute. We play four basic coverages. We have *black coverage,* which is a cover 1. The *blue coverage* is our cover 2. Our *green coverage* is cover 3 and the *silver* is our cover 6, which is our quarter-quarter-half coverage. Our blitz and move calls are southwest twist, wham, magic, and 33. We can also blitz with the nickel package. That is called *snack-nickel.* If we want a blitz coming from the secondary, we call *snake-safety.*

The first Okie front I want to show you is our *west* (Figure 7-20). In this defense the angle is coming from the weakside. The joker has an inside slant and is coming outside. If a back releases toward him he takes him in coverage. The defensive end is slanting inside, attacking the guard, and getting across the face of the offensive guard. The nose tackle is slanting at the V of the offensive guard's neck and getting upfield, looking for penetration. The Will linebacker is taking a tight path off the defensive end tail and blitzing the B gap. The defensive end to the strongside has containment responsibility. The nickel linebacker is dropping into coverage. The Mike linebacker has the middle-hook zone on pass.

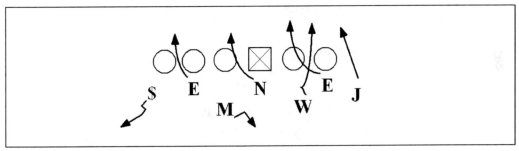

Figure 7-20. West defense

The second Okie front is called *south* (Figure 7-21). It is the mirror opposite of the west defense. The only difference in this stunt is the blitz is coming from the strongside with the Mike linebacker doing the blitzing.

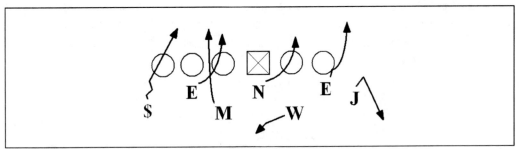

Figure 7-21. South defense

The next Okie front is called *southwest* (Figure 7-22). This is a combination stunt. We have everyone coming. Both sides are pinching to the inside. The Will linebacker is blitzing the B gap behind the slant of the defensive end. The Mike linebacker is blitzing the strongside A gap. The nose tackle is jamming the center instead of slanting to the strong side.

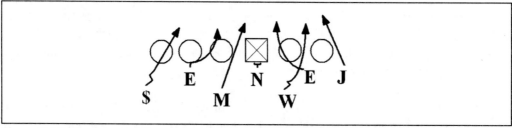

Figure 7-22. Southwest defense

This next stunt is one I really like because it is a good run and pass stunt. The stunt is called *southwest twist* (Figure 7-23). The nickel and joker linebackers have outside containment on this defense. We want to bring this stunt from the boundary into the field side. Our defensive ends stem into 3 techniques on the command of the Mike linebacker. On the snap of the ball, the nose tackle slants toward the weakside guard. The strongside defensive end is slanting into the strong A gap. The weakside defensive end is twisting into the strongside B gap.

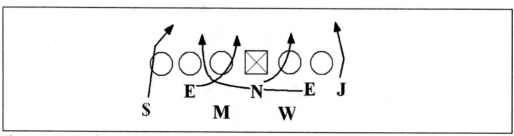

Figure 7-23. Southwest twist

The other stunt I like is called *33 wham* (Figure 7-24). We stem into the front so it looks the same as the southwest twist. On this stunt the nose tackle is slanted into the weakside A gap. The strongside end is blowing the B gap to his side. The Will linebacker is blitzing the strongside A gap. The weakside defensive end has to take a wide charge outside because he has to contain the pass to that side. The joker is dropping into coverage and the nickel linebacker is rushing. Behind all these stunts we generally play a cover 3.

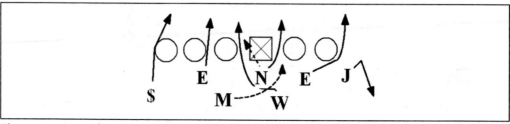

Figure 7-24. 33 wham

If we want to bring the Mike linebacker instead of the Will linebacker, we call *33 magic*. That puts the nose tackle into the strongside A gap and the Mike linebacker blitzes the weakside A gap. The responsibilities for the defensive ends and outside linebackers are reversed from the wham call.

8

Defensive Line Techniques and Drills

Jim Heacock
The Ohio State University
2003

The first thing I want to do is talk about the *philosophy of defensive line play* and then get into some of our drill work and techniques. If I have time at the end I'll show you some of the things we are trying to do with the spread offense. In our first six games this year we only saw 10 plays by teams in a two-back offense. The Wisconsin game was the first team that ran a two-back offense. The spread offense is the trend in college football offense today.

There are two areas where Coach Tressel did an unbelievable job with our football team. The first area was vision and the second area was focus. When he talked about vision, he put a picture of the Fiesta Bowl on the wall. I guess he knew back then that we were destined for something big. That is when the team got the vision of the goal and started working in that direction.

The second area I believe he talked about today was the topic *focus on the moment*. It was unbelievable the focus of this football team. I think we had a good defensive line this year. I think we played *lights out* against Miami, but that is the way we played all year long. There were a couple of reasons they were able to do that. We emphasized a couple of things to them. The first thing we stressed was *team*. We decided that everybody was going to be a positive member of this football team. The team is more important than the individual. That is a hard concept to get over to your team. Everyone seems to want to know who the next Lombardi winner is going to be. They all want to know who the Heisman Trophy winner is going to be. Everyone is talking about individuality. We got our defensive line together and told them from the start we were going to be a team. It is amazing what you can accomplish when they believe that.

The second thing we stressed is *attack*. We wanted to be an attacking front. We wanted to have a relentless mentality for 60 minutes. We wanted to get off on the ball and make something happen and be consistent with it.

We wanted to stress *activity*. I had some great defensive fronts when I coached at Washington. We had a bunch of first-round draft choices in the NFL and some great players. But I have never coached a defensive front that was as active as this group. We as a coaching staff were expecting this group to make plays. The day of just keeping the linebacker free to make all the plays is over. The defensive line has to make plays for us to win games. We moved our defensive ends into inside positions. They had never played in there before. What we were trying to do was create mismatches and move more speed onto the field. The defensive end we moved inside made two sacks in the Fiesta Bowl. We took inside linebackers and moved them to defensive end positions. The reason we did this was to make plays in the defensive line.

We told our players they had to *improve* as the year went along. Their last football game should be their best game of the year. That is the coach's responsibility. If your kids are not improving as the season goes along, the coaches are not doing a good job of coaching. Your kids have to get better daily. When I think back to my early coaching jobs, when my players weren't playing well it was because I was trying to do too much scheme work. If we played a bad game I changed defenses.

Good coaches use repetition to improve their players. They decide what they are going to do and use *repetition* to perfect it. The repetition of techniques is the best learning process we have. Repetition eliminates mistakes in a football game. If you have players making mistakes, it is generally because you have not had enough repetitions at that technique. Remember what you see on film is a reflection of what you are teaching. If your players are making mistakes, it is your fault.

I think this year our coaching staff did a good job of *adjusting* at halftime. Our second-half statistics were outstanding. Our fourth- quarter statistics were tremendous. In the second half of our games this year, we had only three second-half rushing touchdowns against us. Our players did a good job of adjusting their play in the second half.

Your assignments have to be flawless. If we cannot do it by Thursday, we have to get rid of it. Never go into a game with some flawed piece of a game plan. If the defense doesn't know what they are doing, the only thing that can happen is bad.

If things don't go the way you like, that is called *adversity*. As a team we got focused and turned the intensity up a notch. Against Purdue, we had a fourth-and-one from their 31-yard line and threw a touchdown pass to win the game. There were games this year when adversity kept setting in, but our team kept fighting and stayed in the game.

We have a team *policy*. We don't have many rules for our players to follow. We have some team rules, but we don't have time for distractions. We don't have time to have team meetings about rules and policies. We tell them the team policies and if they don't do them they are not going to play. That is the end of that conversation. We expect them to take care of business on and off the field. If they are going to create problems, they are not going to play.

The last thing in our philosophy is to *expect to win*. If we expect excellence we have to push our players some times to get them to perform. The reason we are getting after them is to make them better players. If they can't understand that, then we have a problem. If the players want to be the best they can be, then they are on the same page as the coaching staff.

I give our defensive linemen a checklist. These are things I believe are important. The first and most important thing is to *defeat the blocker*. I say that at least a hundred times a practice session. If I am a defensive lineman, someone on the offensive line is going to block me every play. If the offensive lineman blocks the defensive lineman, the defensive lineman is not going to be a factor in the play and the offensive lineman wins. If the offensive lineman can't block the defensive lineman, the defensive lineman will be a factor in the play and the defense wins. When the play starts, the defensive lineman is not thinking about anything except defeating the blocker. All he is thinking about is knocking the face off the offensive lineman.

Defeating the block is just like boxing. If I am boxing a fighter, but I am looking at the corner man, I'm going to get my head knocked off. You can't look at the quarterback when you start rushing him. The defensive lineman must give 100 percent of his concentration on defeating the blocker before he can think about sacking the quarterback. Before the defensive lineman can make a play, he has to defeat the blocker. I still believe football is a tough game played by tough people. I think mental and physical toughness is something you have to have in the defensive line. We are going to hit, be physical, and be tough.

Attitude and effort affect performance more than anything. You have to have great attitude to play in the defensive line.

I'm spending too much time talking about these things. I'll put them up for you to see and we'll move along. We have already talked about repetition. Defensive linemen must rise to the occasion and make plays. The last thing is *defensive line pride*. We were able to control the tempo of the game and we created great pressure from our front four.

We coached pre-snap preparation this year. I taught more this year at Ohio State then I ever had before. At Ohio State we do a lot of moving and zone pressures. That requires us to have a stance that allows us to accomplish what we are trying to do. We are more balanced in our stance then we have been in the past. I am pretty old school when it comes to stance. You won't see us in the sprinter stances you see in the NFL. We are still pretty much in a heel-to-toe relationship in our stance. We went to a zone-pressure scheme because we ran out of all-American cornerbacks. We went to Oklahoma to fine-tune our defense. Oklahoma had gone through the same situation as we had. That is where we installed our zone-pressure package. That allowed us to rush five guys and still play three under and three deep, or four under and two-deep zones in the secondary.

Alignment and assignment are still important pre-snap preparations. The ultimate key to victory is the team that executes their assignments. We really stressed that this year. If you look at the big plays that were against you, it was probably because someone made a mental mistake. You have to eliminate mental mistakes if you are going to be successful.

This next part is the part that I tried to emphasize this year. I had never done that in my coaching career. I gave a lot of lip service to it but never really emphasized it. These are the variables in the football game that the defensive linemen had to deal with.

Defensive linemen have to know what is *going on* in the game. They have to have *awareness* on the field. They need to know the down-and-distance, special plays, personnel, sets, field position, score, time on the clock, and the weather. We really worked on that in practice this year. We talked about it and made them aware of all the things that are going on in the game.

We are a *gap-assignment team* (Figure 8-1). Someone is responsible for every gap on the line of scrimmage. We assign letters to each gap on either side of the ball. Our gaps run from A to E on each side of the ball. In our defensive scheme the defensive linemen have to be aware of the gaps they play and the ones they are responsible for.

Figure 8-1. Gap assignments

The trend in college football today is the *spread offense*. We have to make sure we understand our theory on rush lanes to play against this offense. Most everyone is in some kind of spread with the quarterback in the shotgun set. I don't think containment is a big a factor as it used to be. The way to get great pressure on the quarterback is to come underneath the offensive tackles. The key to stopping the success of the shotgun is getting in the face of the quarterback. I'll talk about that a little more in a minute.

Let me get into some of the drills we do. We break our drills down into segments from the time the ball is snapped until the tackle is made. The first things we work on are *stance, alignment,* and *assignment*. When we talk about defending the run, the first thing we have to do is perfect our get off. That is probably the most important thing we do. A defensive lineman has to react to the football. Every drill we do is started with the movement of the football.

The second thing we drill is *delivering a blow*. When we strike a blow, we want our thumbs under the arm pits of the offensive lineman with our elbows in tight to our body. We are a standard old school in this type of teaching. We want our eyes to see the V of the neck. We tell our players that the low man will always win. We want our pads under their pads.

The next thing we drill is *separation*. Holding by the offensive line is bad in college, but I know it is getting bad in high school, too. That is why these drills are tremendously important. We teach locking out on the offensive lineman with our hands and arms. From separation drills we go to *disengage, pursuit,* and *tackling drills*.

That is the way we step up our drills. Each day we do one drill that includes one of those skills. That is what I mean by breaking our drills down into segments of teaching. We go through the progression from start to finish.

We do the same thing when practicing the pass rush. The first type of drill we teach relating to the pass rush is the *get- off drill*. From there we go to what I call *set-up drill*. I listen to offensive line coaches talk about their techniques. The one thing they all talk about is staying balanced. In our set-up drill, we work on getting the offensive linemen off balance. We stutter step and fake to make the offensive linemen move. We reach with our left hand and make the move right. If we can make them lean left, we have a chance to get by them on the right side. If we get them to lean any direction, we have a chance to get by them.

We work on our *pass-rush technique* in drill work. If you do the same thing every time the offensive lineman will block you. In our pass-rush technique, for every move we use we have to have a *counter move*. In addition to teaching the techniques of pass rushing, we teach counters off each move in drill work. The last type of drills we work on is the actual *sack* of the quarterback.

I'll put this drill film on and run through it really quick. But there is one statement I want to make before I do that. One of the best things I do is done during our agility period. It is probably the most fun too. When I look back on my career there are so many things in my coaching career that I screwed up on. But my agility period has become a series of drills to make sure I cover every type of skill we could possibly use during the course of the year.

We work a *low-block drill* every day in our agility period. When I was at Washington we played Southern California. Rodney Peete was their quarterback at the time. Southern Cal really liked to chop the defensive linemen when they ran their plays. I spent the entire week of practice before the S.C. game working against the low block. In the game on Saturday they cut us down like a bunch of trees. I told Coach James that I had spent the week working on that block. He told me I needed to spend the whole year working on them. Work on all the skills you could possibly need before you need them. Don't wait until the game before to teach your players a skill they need. Teach it year round and all you will need to do is refresh the skill on which you have already been working.

One drill we work on daily is throwing the far arm at the quarterback on the pass rush. If I am a defensive end rushing the quarterback from the left side, as I beat the blocker and get to the quarterback, I throw my outside arm toward the quarterback. If I reach with my inside arm, I go right on by the quarterback as he steps up into the pocket. If I throw my outside arm, it turns my butt toward the sideline and steers me into the quarterback, not by him. We drill that every day for that simple reason. In the bowl game we had a 3 technique that beat his block, threw his far arm, and caused a fumble by the quarterback.

In the first drill we are teaching two or three things. I am teaching foot movement, agility, and playing a low block (Figure 8-2). We are stepping over a gauntlet of three dummies to work on our foot movement and agility. At the end of the dummies, I have two managers rolling big balls at the players. The players chop step over three dummies, and low-play the two balls that are rolled at them. They punch down on the ball and keep their feet moving. They punch the ball away from them.

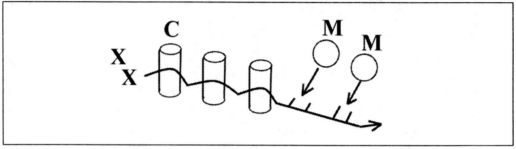

Figure 8-2. Dummy/ball drill

If you want to add something to the drill, have someone throw a ball on the ground as they come off the low blocks. We do this drill every day. If you don't have those big balls, use hand dummies to throw at them. Make them be an athlete and not a clumsy lineman.

We put them in a chute and make them bend their knees (Figure 8-3). We turn them sideways and make them shuffle down the chute. As they come out of the chute we roll more balls or throw dummies at their feet.

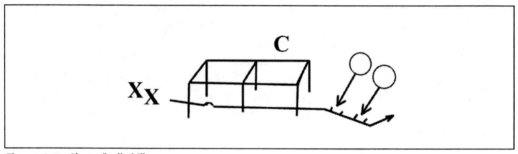

Figure 8-3. Chute/ball drill

We do another similar drill, but instead of rolling balls at them we work on throwing the far arm (Figure 8-4). We place a stand-up dummy at the end of the chute and a stand-up dummy that represents the quarterback in his pass set. The lineman shuffles through the chute, clubs the dummy at the end, rips through and attacks the quarterback with his far arm.

When we do these drills we want the defensive linemen going full speed. We want them to go as quick as they can. I like to show our linemen why we do certain drills. When I show them a drill tape, I always tack on some game footage that shows the skills we drill in practice.

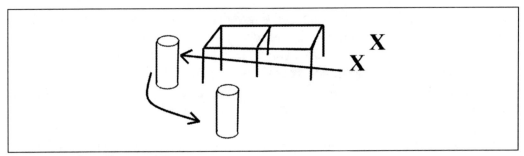

Figure 8-4. Chute/far-arm drill

Another dummy drill we use is a *pass-rush gauntlet drill* (Figure 8-5). We space three stand-up dummies in a line. We put another dummy in the drill to represent the quarterback. A defensive lineman starts at the first dummy. He has to use a set-up move and a pass-rush move on that dummy. He does the same thing on the second dummy, except he uses a counter move. He does the same thing to the third dummy. He starts with an outside move, followed by an inside move and another outside move. As he comes around the last dummy, he turns inside and rushes the quarterback dummy, attacking it with his far arm.

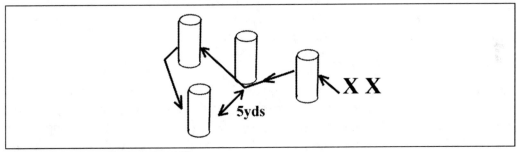

Figure 8-5. Pass-rush gauntlet drill

We use a simple *get-off drill* to teach that same skill. I line up two linemen facing the coach. He is moving a ball and watching the initial step of the linemen. The coach has the ball on a stick. The ball on a stick is nothing more than a football attached to a broom stick. It allows the coach the freedom to stand and watch his players and move a ball to trigger their start. When we teach get off, we want the players to take a short six-inch step. I don't want them to take a long stride. I feel when they overstride it makes their pads come up. I want them low and driving out, not high. We are working on a good balanced base with our feet nice and wide. We work the get-off drill into the chute also.

The next drill we work on in our progression is *delivering a blow*. We start teaching that on the sled. We start in a six-point stance. A six-point stance is a kneeling position in front of the sled pad. The idea is to punch the dummy with the hands. We move the ball and watch the technique of the lineman. We are watching the punch and hand placement. We watch for the hips sinking and the thrust forward. We want to see the eyes go into the V of the neck.

From the six-point stance we go to the three-point stance and do the same thing. It is a progression of teaching that breaks down each move. If you watch these two guys on the tape, I'll show you when you know they are into the drill. They strike the sled, lock out with their hands, and get off the sled. After they complete the drill they go to the end of the line and head butt each other. When they get that excited about a drill, you know you are on the right track.

After we get off the sled, we go into a *1-on-1 drill*. We are in close quarters and go half speed so no one gets hurt. It teaches the technique of get off, strike, and lock out. We watch the same techniques we saw on the sled. The punch, hand position, short first step, eyes in the V of the neck, sinking of the hips, and locking-out techniques are all displayed in this drill. The last thing we look at is to make sure their feet are continuously moving. We don't want our players to stop their feet. We want them to chop them all the way through the drill.

This next drill we do involves a move we call the *dog technique*. We got this from the Tampa Bay Buccaneers. This is the way they play defense. They move on movement and attack the outside tip of the offensive blocker. We are reacting on the run to the blocking scheme. If we are playing a spread offense, we like to use this technique. We want to get off the ball and upfield for the pass rush.

We work all kinds of 1-on-1 drills to teach *separation and disengagement*. In one drill we tell the offensive lineman to throw his hips to the outside and try to get them around the defensive lineman. We teach the defensive guy to bench press the offensive lineman and lock out. We are looking for a good back and body angle, with a good wide base. After they lock out the block, they rip through with their inside arm and make a play on a ballcarrier. The players have to be violent with their arms and hands to play in the defensive line. The defensive lineman wants to use the offensive lineman like a door. He doesn't want to go around him; he wants to go through him. As he locks out he cannot loose ground. He locks out, twists his hips outside, pulls hard with his outside hand, and rips his inside arm past the offensive lineman.

We do this drill on the *Crowther sled*. We do it on this sled because it will spin in a circle if the drill is not done right. As the player comes off the ball and engages the sled pad with his hands, if his base is too narrow the sled will start to work in a circle. This teaches a good base and strong hands.

Before I quit I want to talk about the spread offense again. When we started out we were talking about stopping the spread offense. In the second phase we talked about slowing down the spread offense. Now we are talking about dealing with the spread offense. In our first game last year we played Texas Tech, which was one of the better teams in the country with the spread offense. We played Washington State, who did a great job with the spread offense. We played six teams last year that ran the spread offense.

We studied the heck out of the spread offense in the off-season because prior to this year we did not play it very well. The first thing we decided to do was to use different fronts against the spread offense. We used at least two different fronts. We went with a four-man front and a three- man front. Two years ago when we played South Carolina in the Outback Bowl, we stumbled upon the three-man front. We had gotten behind and didn't know what to do. We went to the 30 front as a stop-gap defense. We decided to make that our second front. The good thing about that was we didn't have to change personnel. We used our rush and drop ends as part of the 30 package. By doing that we were able to stem at the line of scrimmage.

On the quarterback's pre-snap, we tried to disguise what the defense was doing. The quarterback in the spread offense was waiting for the coach on the sideline to call the play from what the coach in the press box saw on the field. We disguised the front by not changing personnel and stemming on the line of scrimmage. The whole idea was to confuse the quarterback so he wasn't quite sure what defense he was going to get.

The next thing we came upon was critical to our game play. We had to *stop the run*. We found out that people who ran the spread offense were successful if they could run the ball. The play we needed to stop was the *quarterback-follow play*. We wanted to make sure we got movement in the box and got after the run.

We wanted to get pressure on the quarterback and hit him. We had 158 hits on quarterbacks this year. That is in addition to all the sacks we got. I feel strongly our success in the fourth quarter came from the fact we were hitting the quarterback so much. By the fourth quarter the quarterback was throwing the ball early to get rid of it. We wanted to make the quarterback start running in the passing game.

The more I studied the spread offense, the more I felt we had to get someone into the inside throwing lanes. We talked to Coach Tressel about that idea and he told us to go ahead with our plan. We were going to get someone in the face of the quarterback at the risk of losing containment. We were not going to let the quarterback stand in the pocket and pick us apart. We were going to make him run for his life. We called this stunt *cover me* (Figure 8-6). We felt the best way to pressure the quarterback was to give the defensive end a two-way-go on the offensive tackle. We gave the defensive end a power rush inside the offensive tackle to get to inside the throwing lane. The tackle was going to power rush but he was working outside and was responsible for containment. If the quarterback broke containment, we chased him. We had good success against the teams we played.

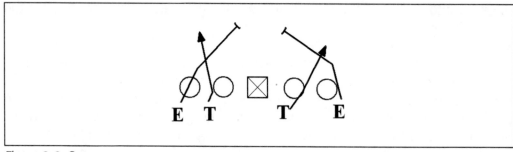

Figure 8-6. Cover me

We can also do it the way Tampa Bay does. They make the *cover-me-tackle* call (Figure 8-7) and the 3 technique charges at the inside shoulder of the offensive tackle and power rushes upfield. The defensive end jammed the tackle and came under the charge of the 3 technique. That got quick pressure in the face of the quarterback. I know the quarterback from Washington State had a really low completion ratio when we had him on the run. When he was in the pocket, he was unbelievable.

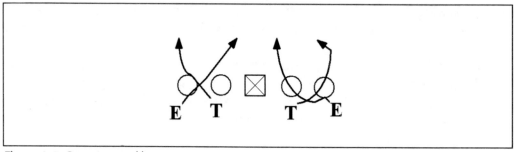

Figure 8-7. Cover me tackle

You have to be physical with these types of teams. We turned up the heat in the fourth quarter. We rotated six defensive linemen into the game. I used a sophomore and freshmen in the rotation this year. They got game experience the whole year and are coming back next year. If anyone got hurt, you weren't replacing him with someone who had not played. It kept all six of the guys into the game plan. The night before a game, they were not playing around because they knew they were going to play the next day. We were great in the fourth quarter because we were fresh. The last four or five years we have not had a drop off in our defensive line's performance because we are rotating these underclassmen during the season and giving them experience.

We use a pattern in the rotation. We start off by rotating every three plays. We have a six-play max for the defensive linemen. As the year goes on, the better players played more plays. I'm not stupid enough to leave my best player on the bench too long. The thing we tried to do was stay fresh for the fourth quarter. In the bowl game against Miami we played first and second down with a strong run player and on third down we brought in a strong pass rusher.

Our goal against the spread offense was to not allow any big plays. We wanted to make them go the long field to score if they could. We had to play with great poise. There are great multitudes of things that go on during a football game. The offense is constantly changing personnel. They have a no-huddle scheme. It seems the pace of the game has increased and there is tension all over the field. You have to remain poised and calm to play against that type of offense.

The last thing we have to do to deal with in the spread offense is to *run to the ball*. That is one thing the defensive line did really well this year. We demand that they sprint all out from the start of the play until the whistle blows. If they are tired and didn't run to the ball, they knew they were coming out of the game. We preached that all the time. We went back and looked at one of our games this season and found five defensive plays that won the game for us. I told them they may pursue 50 times in a game and nothing happens, but the next game they may run to the ball once and cause a fumble. Every time they run to the ball it makes a difference.

9

Motivating Defensive Linemen

Steve Jacoby
De La Salle High School (California)
2009

Thank you. I am excited to be here. It is an honor to be here in Atlantic City. We played Don Bosco Prep last year in California, and we play them in New Jersey next year. One of our two losses last year was to Don Bosco.

I want to talk about De La Salle High School and how we achieved the success we have had. I want to share with you how similar our program is to your programs. All the public schools say we do not know what it is like to have to run a program in their situation. They think we can recruit and get anyone we want, which is not true.

I am guessing that most of you in this room have much better facilities than we do. We do not have our own field. We do have a coaching office for the entire department that would fit in the corner of this room. I am not talking about football offices. I am talking about the entire athletic department.

We do not have the technology that most of the schools we play have. We do not have an indoor camera for any of our teams. Our weight room is outdated, old, and dilapidated. However, we work as hard as anyone in his weight room does. We have not had a new sled in 17 years. We live on the sled. It is just about worn out. There are a lot more similarities between your program and ours than you care to think about or even realize.

We have a 100-yard field that we share with junior varsity and freshman programs. We also have to share the field with the soccer program. We very seldom get to work on a regulation field. When we practice, we work on half a field.

Our facilities and stadium are not very good. They are old. However, we have first-class players and a great coaching staff. With all the disadvantages we have with the physical facilities, we are blessed with the kind of program we run and the success we have enjoyed. We have overlooked all those things and gone on to be very successful in California.

This situation challenges you as a coach. What I want to expand on is what we do and how we do it. I do not profess to be the greatest line coach in the world. I will share with you what we do. You will find it is not any different from what most of you do already. I want to talk about how we get our players to perform and get better as the year goes on.

When Don Bosco Prep came to our place and beat us, that was the turning point in our season. We were not a good football team then. We won our first two games by a few points. Those two games were not typical as to how we prepare. In the Don Bosco game, we were up 21-7 at halftime and lost the game 23-21. We totally dominated the game in the first half, and did not score a point in the second half. It completely changed what we did as coaches and the attitude of our players.

I am prouder of what these kids did this year than last year, when we won the state championship. This year, we were not a good football team, and we did not have a lot of talent up front. Those players toughened up from the Don Bosco game till the end of the season, and they worked their butts off.

They developed a foxhole mentality. We challenged our players to be the best that they could be. People use words like *brotherhood*, *love*, *drive*, and *commitment*, but they are only words unless you teach the team what they mean. Those things are a very important part of our program.

If you are considered to be part of the brotherhood, you are a Spartan. That is what every player in our program strives to be. That is the ultimate goal of players in our program. They want to be a part of the brotherhood of Spartans.

We do not talk about individuals in our program. We tell our players the most important player on the field is the player next to him. When our players start out as freshmen, we want to teach them about our offense and defense. However, we also want to teach them what it takes to achieve what they want.

It is traditional at De La Salle for the freshman to move the sleds. They actually have to pick up the sleds and move them onto the field. The sophomores carry the sled pads, and the juniors carry the bags to the field. This is a process of building team unity through performing difficult tasks together.

When we lost the state title this year, our weight program started eight days later. That was a tense and difficult time for our players. They came into the weight program with mixed emotions. The season ended on a sour note, and we were back in the weight room starting to prepare for next year. The players have rededicated themselves for next season.

I want to give you a quick overview of our defensive line. We run a four-man front. We play with a 1 technique and a 3 technique for the inside tackles. We shade the inside shoulder of the backside guard and outside shoulder of the callside guard. The defensive ends play in a 6 technique to the tight end, and a 7 technique to the openside or the weakside of the formation. We vary our alignment to the ball, depending on the scouting report.

In some situations, we crowd the line of scrimmage, and in others we play off the ball. The first game we played this season was against a team with a crazy offense. It was more like the wing-T than anything else. In that game, our defensive line backed off the ball by one yard. That gave us time to react to what they were doing.

We are a big blitzing team. When we lost to Don Bosco in the third game of the season, we had problems. Our players were not doing what they were supposed to do. Coach Ladouceur told the defense, we were not going to run anything but the base defense for the next five minutes. He understood we were not doing things right. He wanted to go back to the basics and tried to let our players play with confidence.

As a defensive line coach, we do certain things on a daily basis. However, if there is anything you get out of this lecture, remember this point: You cannot lower your expectations for your players. I found myself starting to accept mediocrity in the play of my defensive linemen. It was so bad that I began to accept poor play and bad technique in the defensive line. It does not matter at what level you coach. It could be youth leagues, little league, or college; do not accept that kind of effort.

The good thing about this season was the leadership displayed by our seniors. As coaches, we began to notice during practice that the seniors were taking on the role of player-coaches. They assisted the younger players and helped them with their techniques and skills. We talk about having ownership in the program. The seniors took on the responsibility of mentoring the younger players though tough times. We talk about that when we line up every day for practice. We get the defensive line together, and I tell them they are the most unorganized staff in America.

As the defensive line coach, I believe we have simple things to do. They have to step right and fly to the ball. We have this sled routine where we teach steps and movement on the ball. The defensive linemen have to get off the ball, play their responsibility, and fly to the ball. When we watch film, I want all the defensive linemen in the picture at the end of the play.

When we go live in practice, I stand behind the defensive line between the linebackers and coach the defensive line. I coach them every play. After we finish our individual defensive line drills, we work 1-on-1. When we work against the offensive linemen, we find out where we are in our development as a defensive line. We work a 2-on-1 drill with two offensive linemen on one defensive lineman. They work the down block and combination blocks on the defensive lineman. He plays and reacts to what type of blocking scheme he sees.

We do that every day. Our defensive line bangs for 60 to 80 plays a day. We do not have problems with anything physical. We go every day with our ones against our ones. We want to see the competition every day because we need to see where we are in our development.

We put them in two lines. I give the signal of where to go, and everyone watches the completion. When you go best against the best, you find out if you can play. In those drills, we find out who can do what you ask them to do and who cannot. After those drills, we have a live drill against the scout team. As I said, our kids bang for 60 to 80 plays a day.

I made a commitment to get our players to play better this year. I told them we were not very good, and I did not know how to make them improve on their effort. My best assessment that I learned, is never tell the kids "You are just crappy." I never tell a player that he is not worth a dime. I say, "You are not doing what we need to do, and I cannot trust you." We use the word trust all the time to express our feeling for them. Trust, responsibility, and accountability are huge pieces of everything we do.

I want to cover these things quickly. I will try to get to specific line techniques. We line up all of our kids in a four-point stance. We have the foot to the side of the shade as the balance foot. It is back in the stagger. Most people do align with the inside hand down and the inside foot back. I love to get movement in the front but still be able to play the zone play. We are very fast, so we developed our slant game. If we slant right, our right foot is back. It can change your alignment a slightly.

When you work against your scout team, it is imperative they give you a good picture and maximum effort. Anytime we work against our scout team, they must have trust and be accountable for their effort. If I ask my defensive linemen what the scout team is running and what they like to do, they should be able to answer me. Knowing our scout team is a huge part of our accountability.

When we go through our progression every day, we start out with sled work. When I got to De La Salle, we had terrible defensive linemen. All our kids were offensive linemen, and they were amazing offensive linemen. Everywhere I went, all they wanted to talk about was the offensive line. The only thing I wanted to know was "How do you get sled work?" If the offensive line uses the sled every day, how can I work my linemen on it? We had to develop a sled routine to get the defensive line on the sled. Our sled was 17 years old. We did not have a sled that really worked.

When we got on the sled, we put everything together. We worked the routine until they knew it perfectly. I broke it down to stance, start, and get-off. I talked it, got them to jog it, and then ran it. Every day, when I put my defensive linemen into drills, they should be able to do the drills without me being there. That way, if I am late, when I get out there, the kids are already going though the drills. They don't have to wait for a coach.

I know there are some things that we coach and teach that are not acceptable. However, if you don't hold them to the highest degree of accountability for their effort and performance, who will? Nobody has ever pitched a perfect game, which is what I love about football. There are no perfect games. There's never been a perfect game played. Nevertheless, there can be a perfect outcome, and that is what our kids control. We believe in the perfect outcome. That is when you tell your kids, "This is not good enough." When they stay after practice to work on timing and striking, you are getting the kind of effort you want. I'm not going to teach you guys any drill work you do not already know. What you need to focus on is effort. Defensive line coaching is a dirty job. What I like about coaching the defensive line is the dirt.

I want to talk about how we motivate and how we get performance out of our players. After I came to De La Salle High School, there was a viewpoint that became apparent to me. For our opponents, we were the biggest game of the year for them. We became a nationally known team and had our players playing in California, Hawaii, and Louisiana in national all-star games.

We have to do what we do every week, knowing we are preparing the team for the best shot our opponent can possibly deliver. We never focus on that fact, and our players never approach a game that way. Where we derive our work ethics comes from a very simple premise: We want our players to excel to what they think they can be. As coaches, we have to get our players to believe they have to give more to achieve what they want.

We want our players to become Spartans. We want all of our players to be a positive part of our program, regardless of the differences in their backgrounds. We never talk with our players about being a football star. We do not talk about winning. We talk about being the best you can be and giving the maximum effort. Winning is a byproduct of that attitude.

When we talk about brotherhood, it is not a word to be thrown around lightly. When we talk about being a Spartan, it has meaning for our players. It develops character, and it is truly a brotherhood among our team members.

To get your players to play at their highest level, you have to commit yourself to being a coach. That is harder to do than it sounds. I have two daughters at home. I have to make sure they observe my best effort. On the football field, if I am not prepared and do not work hard, how can I ever expect my players to work hard and give their best effort?

We cannot lower the bar to win and achieve. We have to raise the bar, and the wins will take care of themselves. When I looked at the Don Bosco film, I told myself, "I can live with the loss." What I cannot stand, and what came out of the game, was the effort our team played with in the second half. All the things that we did in the first half and all the things we had talked about simply went away. We dominated the game in the first half and became a failure in the second half.

The things we talked about, such as tradition and oneness, went down the tubes. If you have a great program, you do not want to finish 7-3. You want to be 10-0. We lost two games this year after going undefeated the year before. However, being everyone's biggest game was not the reason we lost two games. That cannot be the focus for your team. The focus of the team has to be on making each individual on that team rise to the maximum that they can be.

I have a family, and you have to be committed to your family, which I am, but you have a commitment to your players, also. I am a coach for the Spartans, and I care about those players deeply. I hope everyone in this room made the commitment to coach high school football to help the players on that team. I am going to coach the players on my team as hard as I possibly can. In the drills, I coach them every play. That toughness with which you coach them allows you to get more from them.

De La Salle High School began to set goals for the team a long time ago. How many of you coaches are into goal-setting? The goal-setting at De La Salle became an awakening for our young people. We wanted them to develop goals, but we wanted them to share their goals with their teammates. When they shared those goals, they are held accountable for them.

We had our young men developing goals. The coaches guided them in selecting goals that were measurable, attainable, and meaningful to them. We have a meeting where the players share their goals with the group. We give each player a 3x5 printed card called a goal card. We give the players a schedule of the goal meeting and tell them their cards are due that night.

On the goal card, we have three areas of goals. We have practice goals, weight room and conditioning goals, and game goals. Those are the three areas that are extremely important to any football program. Every player in your program has a goal card, and everyone know the goals he has chosen.

We run gassers as part of our conditioning. One of the goals a player might put down is to run all the gassers in the time allotted. He might put down that he will increase his bench press by 25 pounds. An example of a game goal is to be the best supportive player on the scout team.

On Thursday night, we have our meeting. The player stands up in front of the entire group and shares the goals he has written down. After he read the goals, he picks a player in the room. He walks over to the player and hands him his goal card. They embrace and share the brotherhood. The player who received the card is now accountable for that player's performance.

These players have written down their goals, shared them, and committed to their goals with one another. Everyone gets motivated and accepts the responsibility for the behavior and conduct of the players on the team. This has to come from somewhere. It is no longer a group of individuals or a football team. It is a whole family. They are walking around, representing their family, and their actions reflect on the family.

We also have something we call "chapel service." It is nondenominational, and we talk about ownership in our program by our players. Coach Ladouceur helps mold the character and values of our players. They choose a song with lyrics that mean something to them. They have to play the song, and pick a passage from the Bible and talk about it.

This service is a takeoff on the 300 Spartans and the courage and togetherness they shared in their brotherhood. When we gather in our meeting room, it is a very informal setting. The coaches and players sit down and take off their shoes. We discuss the meanings of the songs, and Bible verses, and what those things mean to them. We are seeking inspiration from the group and some soul-searching into their lives.

I love to see young men getting to the point where they are performing up to the level they should be. The players start to believe in the goals they have set from themselves, and their goal card become very important to them. They bring the card to you and want you to see the things they have achieved. They have a purpose of value and believe they can succeed in their goals.

Football is a game that is difficult to play. Everyone gets knocked down at some point during a game. It is not getting knocked down that builds the character in the players; it is what they do from that point forward. They have to get up and continue to struggle and play on. It is not getting knocked down that has value, it is getting up and continuing to fight and play that builds the type of character we are looking for in our players.

There is always going to be another day and another play. As coaches, we must get the players to see the best within themselves and get the best out of themselves.

We played our last game on December 20 and our players were in the weight room on January 2. We do not stop that program until the last game of the season. Not every coach works in the school where he coaches. They arrive at school at 6:30 in the morning to prepare for the day. We are not like some of the elite programs in our state where the head coach does not teach. We all teach in addition to coaching. These coaches go the extra mile to teach and coach. They do it so they can help these players. We have to take an active role in recruiting. These players come from bad neighborhoods, and they have every excuse not to play football. What we do is offer a way out of those neighborhoods.

The players come from all different neighborhoods and have to ride a public transportation to get to school. Some of them spend a lot of time on the bus just to play in this program. You have to care about the players. You have to commit your best effort to the players. I love being at De La Salle, and I love coaching the players I have. We are all a part of a big family. Your expectations you have for your players are a big part of the motivation that goes into the program. We use the goal cards, we use the chapel service, and we practice hard and are committed to the oneness of the Spartans.

We won 151 games in a row, playing all the top competition the country had to offer. NFL Films came out and did a piece on De La Salle High School. No one outside the program has ever been allowed into the chapel. We allowed NFL Films to come into the chapel to see what went on. I can talk about what goes on within those walls, but until you experience it, you have no idea the good that comes from it. The chapel changed our whole outlook and the environment within our team.

Last year, we won two games and lost the third game to Don Bosco at home. We were a terrible team. After that game, some of the players who we did not think could help us rose up and worked as hard as they have ever worked. They bought into what we were selling. That carried us to the game against Centennial High School in the finals of the state championship. We lost that game 21-16, but our players walked away from that game knowing they had done their best. They knew they were responsible for the success of one of their teammates through the obligation of the goal card.

I just wanted to share my experience and the love for the kids and our school with you coaches today. We show the NFL film to our players as a motivational tool. The film features a lot of well-known and respected coaches and players. It has Bill Walsh and John Madden, just to mention two.

Gentlemen, I appreciate your attention. I tried to give you some idea of the way we try to motivate our players to perform at their highest level. Thank you very much. It has been a pleasure.

10

Defensive Line Techniques and Stunts

Jeff Jamrog
University of Nebraska
2002

It is great for me to represent Coach Frank Solich and our defensive staff at this clinic. Everything we do at Nebraska comes back to a simple philosophy. We want to stop the run. We want the offense to throw the ball and throw it in a hurry. Everything we do in our drills, whether it is with linebackers, defensive line, or defensive backs, is predicated on that philosophy. I emphasize stopping the run in all my drills.

The thing we never want to happen to us is to have someone run the ball. It is the worst thing that can happen to you. I know because it happened to us this year. All eleven of our players came to the sideline feeling bad. If you get beat in the passing game, it is not as bad.

I hope I can give you some tips about drill work that will help you. I have gone to other colleges and pro teams to get ideas that I can use. We are not a unique program, and we don't have a lot of original ideas, but we adapt what we have learned. We have studied other schemes and made them fit what we are doing at Nebraska. What works for us may not fit what you are doing. We have a lot of people come to our campus to see what we are doing.

As far as drills go, as a coach you need to explain to your players why you are doing a particular drill. We do all our explanations in meetings and not on the field. We never want to waste time on the football field.

We always use movement to initiate any drill. Use a football or your foot to make players react to movement. Never run a defensive drill on cadence.

It is very important to expect and demand effort from your offensive linemen in individual drill work. I have coached the front seven, and it never seems like you have enough individual time. Coaching the defensive line at Nebraska, I have the most individual time of anyone. However, that seems like it is never enough. The thing I stress to our offensive players is to give our defense a good look. It is important for pad levels in drills to carry over to team drills and ultimately to the game.

It is important to get as many reps as possible. We are fortunate at Nebraska to have a large squad. We have 155 players on our team. When we go to team drills, it is a big advantage for us. We are able to get reps for our first, second, and third team players.

We believe in coaching on the run. The practice field is not the place for a walk-through. Do it before practice or after practice. Don't waste time in practice. Don't stop a drill to correct a mistake. You should keep the drill going while you are coaching an individual.

Have your drills set up and ready to go. Know what you want to do in the drill and what you want to get out of the drill. Get your managers or injured players to help set up the drills. I don't want people standing around while I set up the drill.

Go full speed in the drills, so you get a good look at what is supposed to happen. You don't want to get people hurt because someone is going full speed and the other guy is not.

Always grade the film and show it to your players. We stole this idea from Florida State. They film and grade all their winter conditioning drills. It is important to have a plan year round for your players. When our new players report to Nebraska, we have about three days before the varsity comes in. We take time to expose all our players to the drills we are going to be using. We walk through the drills and go through them slowly. When the upper classman report and we start practice, everyone knows what is expected of them.

We use a green football in our drills. I got this idea from the Tampa Bay defensive line coach. The whole idea is stimulus-response. The clearer a stimulus a player has, the quicker response you will get. The green football blends into the green grass or

Astroturf. On Friday night when the brown football is used, it looks crystal clear. Your players will have a clear stimulus and a clear response. That response translates to getting off the ball. That is one thing we want to have as a defensive lineman.

It is important to not trick your defensive players early. Start out slowly telling them what blocks they are going to see and how to play them. We teach them the base, reach, cut off, and trap blocks. We teach them the pass set up and what it looks like. After that we work on each phase of those blocks before we get into the combination blocks, double teams, and down-G schemes.

Always start your defensive linemen on a line. We want to crowd the ball as much as we can. We start our young players off the ball a bit until they get some experience. The better they get with their footwork and get-off, the closer they can get up on the ball.

I like to incorporate two or more skills into a drill. For instance in their shuffle over the bags drill, I'll put a pop-up bag at the end of the shuffle. They shuffle over the bags, club or rip the pop-up bag, and sprint past the quarterback. You could do the same shuffle drill and finish with an angle tackle.

Another example would be the cut-block drill. In this drill, the defensive end learns how to play cut blocks. We have three tube dummies lying on the ground. The defensive end comes down the front of those bags and punches down on them as if he were playing a series of cut blocks. As he comes off the last dummy, we could throw a ball on the ground and have him work on fumble recovery or scoop and score skill.

We want our defensive linemen to have great peripheral vision. We send them over the bag and make them look for number cards the coach holds up. That keeps them from looking at their feet and lets them feel the bags.

You can't take for granted that players have speed and quickness. You need to work on body coordination and foot quickness all the time. You need a daily plan and checklist for things you want to get done. I have some advice I would like to pass along to you. Every drill that you do should be written up with a checklist for that drill. After you list all the drills you do, I would put a column on the left of the drills as to when you are going to do them. That way you don't forget to do a drill or de-emphasize a drill that doesn't need to be done often.

I firmly believe you get from your players what you emphasize. If your players do your drills well, you will see a correlation on game day.

I never want to teach blocking schemes until I completely cover defeating the 1-on-1 block. There are four blocks a defensive lineman has to play. He has to play the base, reach, cut-off, and high-hat blocks. Before we go any further, we are going to be able to whip our man 1-on-1. We flip-flop our defensive linemen so they have to learn a right-handed stance as well as a left-handed stance. When we start in the 1-on-1 drill, we do it from both stances.

I think it is important to praise your players when they do a good job. Keep encouraging them to work hard, and praise them when they do. Too many times, the only thing a coach does is to point out the negative things a player does. You need to praise your players when they do things right and try to motivate them in a positive way.

It is important for the defensive linemen to be prepared for things they are going to see on game day. We were trapped once last year. I feel the reason for that is the way we work in practice. We work on trap block at sometime in our drill each day. Even if the trap is not in the game plan, we work on it during that week. If a team does not trap in the scouting films, it does not mean they won't put something in for us if they feel we have a weakness for that type of scheme. We want to be prepared to play trap every week, even though it may not occur.

In your game planning, make sure you work on the schemes you are going to see in the game on Saturday. We have a list of skills we are going to ask our players to do. We will have different drills to teach those things. Our defensive linemen are no different than yours. All linemen must have great get-off ability. They must have great agility and be able to change direction. All defensive linemen have to take on blockers. All defensive linemen must have great hands. That is one of the prerequisites for all great defensive linemen. We do a lot of drills starting out in a six-point stance on a sled. We learn how to shoot the hands on ball movement. From the six-point stance, we go to a three-point stance, shooting the hands, but not taking a step. After we have done that, we get in the three-point stance, shoot the hands and take the first step.

You need drills that teach the stunting game. The more stunts a defense runs, the more they need to practice them.

You need pass-rush drills. You have to teach pass-rush moves and counter moves. We try to get all our defensive lineman to learn and become good at one pass-rush move and one counter off that move.

We have zone blitzes as part of our defensive schemes. We don't do it very often, but it has to be taught. You need drills to teach that skill. We have a drill for dropping our defensive linemen into coverage. We don't rep that drill a lot because we don't use that scheme a lot in the game situation.

We have second-effort drills we work on, as well as pursuit drills. Pursuit is nothing more than effort and desire. A person chases the ball because he wants to make every tackle.

Tackling is the last thing in our drill work. Some defensive-line coaches don't work on this skill as much as the linebackers and defensive back coaches. But, tackling is an important skill in the defensive game plan. It is hard to get backs in a defensive-line tackling drill. We end up tackling each other, but that is not too realistic because of the size of the defensive linemen, although there are some huge fullbacks in our league.

It is important to do drills. This drill is called the line drill. It is a drill where the player does not know what you are going to do, and his reactions become tremendously important. Reaction is what football is all about. One of the drills that is done in any pro combine practice is a line drill. The player starts out and sprints five yards in one direction, touches a line, sprints 10 yards in the other direction, touches that line, and sprints back to the original point. It is a reaction drill that is timed. We have some players playing at Nebraska who have fabulous times in that drill, but on a football field, they have poor agility.

There are players at Nebraska who test out great in that drill who will not see the football field. We also have had players that don't test out at all that become great football players because they know how to react.

I want to show you a *get-off drill*. I am four yards from two defensive linemen. I tell them the down and distance, because it affects the stance they will get into. If it is a run situation, they will be in a more balanced stance. If it is a pass situation, they will be in an elongated stance with a narrower base.

They get in their stance, and I drop my hand. They are getting off as fast as they can and come straight ahead. There are a number of things I can do. If I move my hand right or left, they plant, turn flat, and sprint down the line of scrimmage.

The next thing I do is drop my hands and start backpedaling. They should think pass rush and make a quick pass-rush move. If I continue to drop, they sprint by me in a good vertical pass rush.

If I start backpedaling for a couple of steps and come forward, that is the draw. They get off, plant, and retrace their steps to the original position.

I can drop my hands and point flat to the line. That means the flanker or jailbreak screen. They sprint back in an angle to get to the screen play. If I point at an angle, they assume quick pass downfield and pursue downfield. I got this quote from an NFL coach that I really like: *"It is the tedious repetitions of the simplest movement that produces the greatest results."* Players sometimes get bored with the drills we do. I show them drill films from pro camps and combines. They find the same drills there that we do, and it leaves an impression that the drill may be important.

The next thing I want to cover is our base front and alignments. After that I will talk about some inline stunts and movements. We have one-, two-, three-, and four-man games, which could be adaptable to your scheme. I have them on film that I will show you later. Some of these stunts have been good to us at Nebraska.

The front that we have considered our base front is called *even-strong*. We flip-flop our nose and tackle. The nose will go to the running strength of the formation. He lines up in a 2-technique, which is head up the offensive guard. The tackle will also be in a 2-technique on the guard to the weakside. The rush end to the strongside is in a loose 9-technique, and the rush end to the weakside is in a loose 5-technique.

We are playing with a three-linebacker scheme. The Sam linebacker is off the line in a 60-technique. The Mike linebacker is head up on the center in a 0-technique off the ball, and the Will linebacker is in a 40-technique head up on the weak offensive tackle.

In our coverage, we roll down one of our safeties to be in our eight-man scheme. The corners are usually manned up on the wide receivers, with the free safety in the middle. The Sam linebacker has the tight end. The Mike and Will linebackers have the tailback— whichever way he comes.

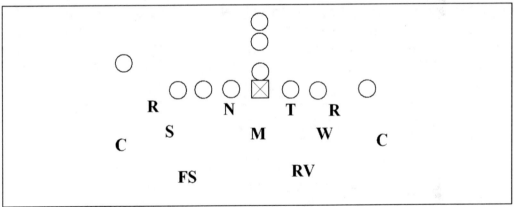

Figure 10-1. Even strong

We are a gap-responsibility team. The nose is stepping with his outside foot into the B-gap strong. He is in a right-handed stance, with his inside hand down and his inside foot back. The tackle would be in a left-handed stance, with his inside hand down and his inside foot back playing the A-gap weak.

In this front, our Mike linebacker overlaps a lot. If we get a wide-reach block by the guard on the nose, the Mike linebacker runs backdoor on a lot of plays from his head-up alignment. We get fast flow by or Mike and Will linebacker, with the rover coming down to the cut-back side.

The next front is called *even*. All that basically does is move the strong rush end into a 67 alignment on the tight end. That technique is head up on the tight end. The nose and tackle are still in their 2-technique alignments, and the weakside rush end is still in a 5-technique.

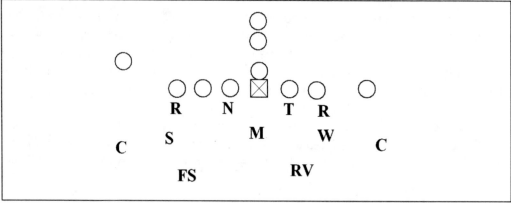

Figure 10-2. Even

The next front is called *over*. The tackle moves to the 3-technique to the strongside. We secure him in the B-gap to the strongside. His right foot is splitting the crouch of the offensive guard. The more experience he has at that technique, the tighter he can align. Obviously on passing downs, he will get in a wider alignment. We play his technique a little differently than most people because we step with our outside foot with a short power step on our first step. The nose is playing a shade to the weakside of the center. He has the A-gap weak. He is stepping with his inside foot aiming for the neck of the center.

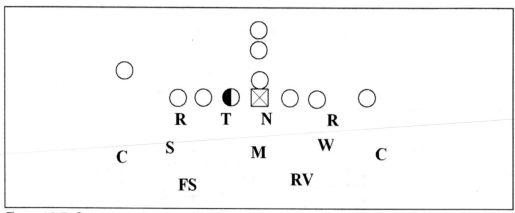

Figure 10-3. Over

If we call *over strong*, it is the same defense except the strong rush end is kicked out into a wide 9-technique alignment. The word "strong" indicates that point to the defense end.

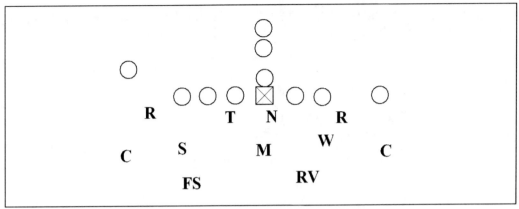

Figure 10-4. Over strong

This next front has been a very popular front. It is a form of the double-eagle defense. We took this idea from Arizona back in the 90's when they had their "Desert Storm defense." We adapted it and played it a little bit different than they did. There are a number of ways you can get into this front. One way we do it is called *bubble over*. It is an over defense for the nose and tackle.

The Mike linebacker is lined up in the weakside B-gap at the heels of the defensive linemen. He is a B-gap player versus the run. If the guard pulls in front of him, he flows over the top. The tackle in the 3-technique plays a loose 3, and a lot of times we will slide-tilt him inside. He steps with his inside foot to protect against the zone-blocking scheme. We push hard on the guard and get in the crack in the B-gap.

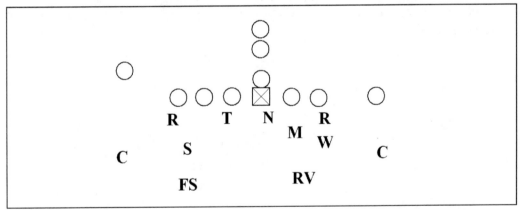

Figure 10-5. Bubble over

We can call *bubble under* and change the defense. We bring down the free safety. We play cover 0, which tells the free safety he has the tight end. The Sam, Mike, and Will linebackers are on the two backs in the backfield. If both backs went toward the Sam and Mike linebackers, the Will linebacker would be a short-hole defender in the middle of the field. The rover will be in the deep middle, and the corners are locked up on the wideouts. The nose is in a strongside shade of the center. The tackle is in a weakside, loose 3-technique with a slight tilt inside. The Mike linebacker is playing the B-gap to the strongside at the heels of the defensive linemen.

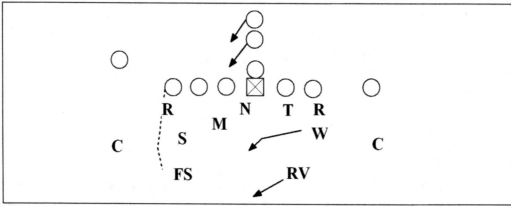

Figure 10-6. Bubble under

If we call *bubble over Mike,* we are blitzing. That tells the Sam and Will linebackers they have the two backs, the free safety has the tight end, and the rover is in the middle of the field. If we call *"bubble under Mike,"* it is also a stunting defense. I'll show you the stunts in a minute.

The last front I'm going to talk about is what we call *single front.* We walk the Mike linebacker up over the center. The coverage for the Sam and Will linebackers and the defensive backs stays the same. We can play a three-man game with our nose, tackle, and Mike linebacker. In one game this year, we replaced the Mike linebacker with another down lineman.

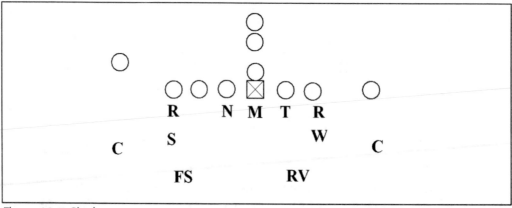

Figure 10-7. Single

A lot of people want to know why we run defensive-line stunts. Stunts are very good versus inside zone plays because they free up the defender and get penetration. They are good against teams that like to pull linemen. If you mix up your stunts, it confuses the offensive linemen. It is hard for the offensive linemen to make great body contact on a stunting defensive lineman.

Stunts are effective when people try to down block on defenders. It frees up the defensive line, and keeps them from having to go 1-on-1 all day. It causes indecision in the offensive line. Anytime you can get an offensive lineman to redirect his original charge, we think we have the advantage. It breaks up their aiming points and breaks down their footwork. I tell our players they are better than the offensive linemen they are playing against. I tell them if they get too big or out of shape, their next stop is the offensive line. I tell them they are the best athletes on the football field.

By being a multiple-packaged defense, we feel like the opponents have to spend additional practice preparing for us. They have to limit the amount of things they may do, so they can be more prepared for what we do. At Nebraska, we have enough players that we can get four teams working at the same time. That increases the number of reps you get.

Stunting can muddy up rush lanes and lets you play the draw better. As much man coverage as we play, it scares me when the quarterback takes off and runs the ball from a pass drop. We feel like stunting helps us free up on the pass rush.

There are some pass protection schemes that stunts work well against. I'll show you some of those.

Obviously, there are some disadvantages, but we feel like the advantages out-weigh the disadvantages. Stunts are not particularly good against the outside zone play. If you guess wrong on a stunt, it could hurt you. When you stunt, you create gaps for linebackers and secondary players to fill.

The first stunt is an individual stunt called a go stunt. We line up head up, but we want to penetrate our gap responsibility. The nose is a B-gap player on the right side. He wants to step with his left foot on a 45-degree angle and rip with the right arm. He tries to skim the guard as he rips with the right arm.

The tackle is an A-gap player. He steps with his left foot and rips with his right arm into his gap. We want vertical penetration and change the line of scrimmage. We react to blocking schemes on the run. The nose is skimming the guard, but is keying the guard and tackle. They will give him his reads.

The tackle skims the guard, but is keying the center. We always skim the man on which we are aligned, but we also key the man on the other side of our gap. We like the go stunt. These are one-man stunts. It is hard to rip up field from a 2-technique, but we like this stunt.

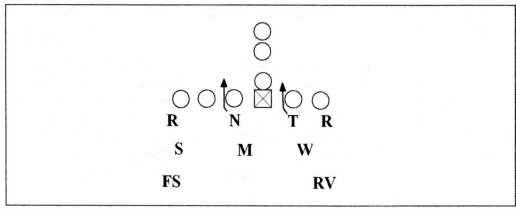

Figure 10-8. Go

The down side to this stunt is it allows offensive linemen to get up on linebackers too easily. Our guys like the go stunt as a change up.

Another one-man stunt we run is called *nun*. This is for the shade nose. I think to be effective playing a shade technique on the center, you must allow your nose to play across the center's face. It can give you a big play sometimes. Usually we blitz the Mike linebacker in the B-gap. If you don't, it makes you a little soft in the B-gap.

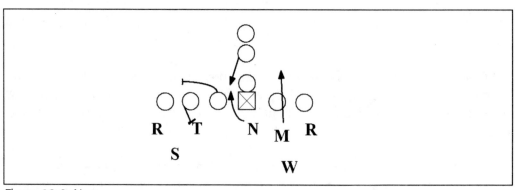

Figure 10-9. Nun

On the next stunt, we run out of a shade front at times. The stunt is call *whip*. This is a two-man game for the defensive line. We are going to fast flow our linebackers weak. The free safety rolls down to the strongside. The nose goes to the A-gap, and the tackle goes to the B-gap. That gives you weakside movement in your front.

On the whip stunt, we have taken a shade nose and given him B-gap responsibility. What we have done is aligned him as a shade on the center, run him under the block of the guard, and gotten him into the B-gap. It works great if it is a zone play that way. The nose is running away from the center who is supposed to block him.

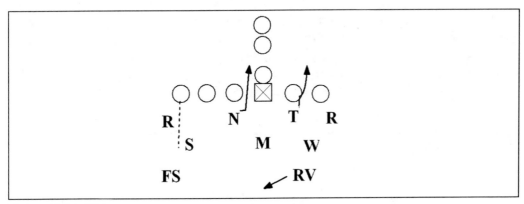

Figure 10-10. Whip

The next stunt is good against the run and the pass. This is a two-man stunt. The first lineman's movement is critical. The man who goes first must gain penetration into the B-gap. If he doesn't get the gap, the stunt won't work. These stunts are TE and ET stunts. The first man has to penetrate to the back of the blocker. The second man has to sell vertical rush upfield first. If he just slants, the stunt will break down. The guy who goes second is the "loop" man on this stunt. This is a delay stunt. We want to come around tight on the defensive tackle and be ready to make a move on another blocker.

We don't grab and pick people as we go through the stunt. We want the mindset that the nose thinks he is going to make the tackle or sack, and the end does too. We don't want one of these guys to think that he is giving himself up so his buddy can be the hero. We want the mentality that both players are thinking sack.

This stunt is called the *jet stunt*. The tackle is the first guy to go. He is the man that penetrates, and the rush end is the man that loops. We want to run this stunt when the center is turning away to the other side in protection. If the penetrating tackle can get the gap, we are going to be successful. The key is the rush end not changing his alignment or cheating in any way. He has to sell his vertical pass rush so the offensive tackle kicks out on his pass-blocking scheme. We don't tell the end to take any particular amount of steps. It is a feel type of thing. When he feels the tackle has gotten the B-gap, he breaks off his upfield rush and comes inside as tight to the tackle as he can.

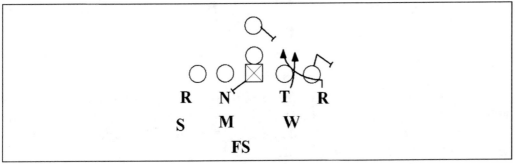

Figure 10-11. Jet stunt

We like this stunt because it can be used on running downs as well as passing downs. The only thing that is different is the end. He is going to read the offensive tackle as he starts up field. If it is a reach block by the tackle, he doesn't complete the stunt. He plays the reach block and gets into his C-gap contain responsibility. The tackle on the penetration becomes the containment on a pass play.

If we call *twist*, that becomes a four-man game. The stunt is basically a double jet run to both sides.

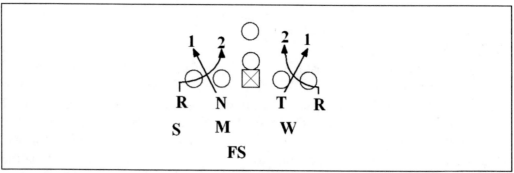

Figure 10-12. Twist

The next stunt we run is called *stab*. This is an ET stunt. That means the end goes first and is the man that penetrates, and the tackle comes second as the man that loops. This stunt has all the techniques of the jet stunt, but reversed. The end is the man that *penetrates* and must get the B-gap for the stunt to work. The tackle has to sell his inside rush and feel the rush end getting the gap. He comes off the hip of the rush end and outside rushes. This is an excellent stunt if the center turns toward the tackle. It is also good on run downs.

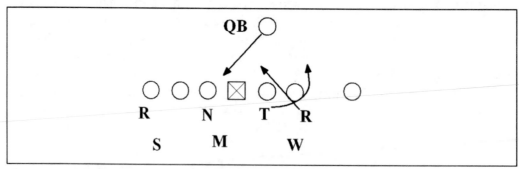

Figure 10-13. Stab

This stunt is really good against teams such as Northwestern, and teams who are in the shotgun offset-back look. They run their zone play, but tell the quarterback if the end is closing hard, to pull the ball and run a bootleg out the backside. This play works well against that type of running game.

This stunt is a great stunt out of the bubble over front. We call it *bubble over Mike stab*. We rush the nose hard in the A-gap and run the stab stunt with the Mike linebacker and rush end. The rush end goes first and is the penetrating end. The Mike linebacker comes second off the end's butt and is the loop man. This is a great stunt. We have the end chasing and making plays on the running back, and the Mike linebacker coming around for the bootleg by the quarterback.

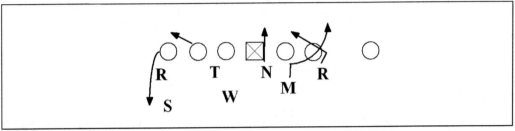

Figure 10-14. Mike stab

The next stunt we put in to change up our rush ends. This stunt is called Detroit. It is a four-man game. The rush ends start upfield on their vertical pass-rush lanes. This is not a stab stunt. The rush ends are four or five steps up the field before they comes inside. We want him to collapse the pocket, so the quarterback can't step up to throw. They plant and do a late counter inside.

For the second part of the stunt, we game plan which man is to go first. If it is a right-handed quarterback, we tell the tackle to go first, and he is contain to that side. The nose goes second the opposite way and is contain on that side. We like this stunt because the coverage has everyone manned up. When the quarterback sees the ends go inside, he thinks he can escape outside. We have had some slow tackles come on the delayed rush and make the tackle out there. This has been an excellent stunt for us.

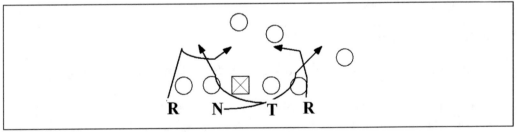

Figure 10-15. Detroit four-man game

If we get in the under front, we have a four-man game we like to run. It is called *Mike switch*. We run the Mike switch with the jet call. The Mike linebacker attacks the center, and the nose loops off his butt and behind through the B-gap. To the open side, the tackle and end run a jet stunt. The downside to this stunt is there is no short hole-player in the middle.

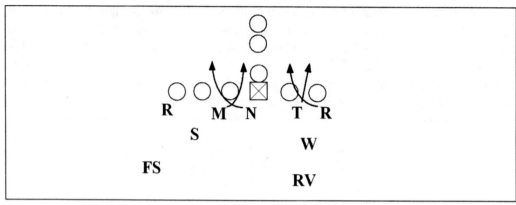

Figure 10-16. Mike switch jet

If we got into a single front and called *single switch*, it would be like the Mike-switch call. The only difference would be that Mike would read before he ran the stunt. If it were pass or run flow to the nose, the Mike linebacker blitzed the B-gap. If it were a run flow away from the nose, the Mike linebacker flowed and played run to the weakside.

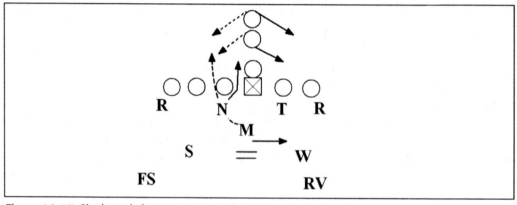

Figure 10-17. Single switch

Those are some stunts that we have run at Nebraska that have been good for us.

There are some blocking schemes that we always go over to prepare for a game. There are only so many things that an offensive lineman can do to you. We give handouts every week as part of our scouting report that tells them the blocks they are going to see. We rep those blocks in practice and study their cut-ups of blocking scheme from film.

The first things I talk to them about are the basic "1-on-1" blocks. They are the base, reach, and cut-off blocks. Some people are really into cut blocks as a cut-off block. They don't cut you too much on the playside, but they could on some reach blocks.

From there, we go into the 2-on-1 blocking schemes. We work on double teams, power scrape, and scoop blocks. We get a lot of down-G blocks. We have a base rule of thumb for the down-G block. If the blocker's head is in front of us, we are going to wipe across the blocker's face. If the blocker's head goes behind the defender, we are going to flip our hips, backdoor the block, and get flat down the line. Most offensive line coaches don't want the cross face escape.

The veer release trap is the most common one you will see. That is when the man the defender is aligned on will block down inside. The good guards will head fake outside before they go inside. When we play the trapper, we spill everything outside. We take our outside shoulder and rip through the trapper's inside shoulder and try to make a play.

The toughest ones to read are the pass influence and pull influences. That goes back to reading the player inside and outside your gap of responsibility. If the guard pass-blocks, and the tackle is run blocking, it is an influence trap.

The last thing I'm going to talk about before I show the film is pre-snap reads. The first one is down and distance. The second thing to consider is time and score. A lot of coaches in their game planning break down an opponent's films. They plan their defensive scheme by down and distance, personnel grouping, and things like that. At Nebraska, we do the same thing, but we do it with the opponents whether they are ahead or behind in the game. If you are using a computer to give you offensive tendencies, remember this point: When you put your numbers into the computer on the opponent, if they were ahead, the results will be totally different than when you put in the number when they were behind. When we evaluate this situation, we look at 0-0 or a tie score as being behind.

The next thing we look at is the stance of the offensive linemen. We look for heavy or light stances. We look at the pressure on the hand, the level of the back, and the distance from the elbow to the knee. All of those things will tell you if the lineman is going to pull, pass block, or fire straight ahead. If he has pressure on his hand and his tail is high, he is going to roar off the ball. If the distance between the elbow and knee is great, he has weight forward; if the distance is really small, that means he is going to pull or pass block.

We call our light and heavy stances on our defensive line. If both the guard and tackle are in light stances on one side and the guard and tackle on the other are in a heavy stance, we know the counter trey is coming.

We watch the split of the offensive lineman and the depth they are off the ball. Offensive linemen like to split wider if they are trying to open a hole inside the defender. They like to get off the ball to get a better angle inside or outside.

Offensive linemen have to know whom they are going to block. They have to use their eyes to find him. Watch the eyes of the offensive linemen. They peek and glance around; watch what they are looking at. The personnel grouping, formation, and backfield set, are all keys for the offensive tendencies.

11

Defensive Linemen Run and Pass-Rush Techniques

Larry Johnson
Penn State University
2009

I am glad to be here. Let me set the pace for you. I am going to give you information that will help you as an offensive line coach. This is not just a drill segment. I am very basic. I am a fundamental football coach. Everything I do is based on finding ways to improve my players

That is my philosophy. For the rest of this lecture, you are going to have to bear with me. I am going to make you defensive line coaches by the end of this session. I am a teacher, and this is the new way of getting it done. By believing in something, it will help us get the job done. I am going to tell you some things about football before we get out of here. I am going to trick you. I am going to feed your soul.

I am going to show you my drill tape. It consists of things we have used to make our players better. Some of the drills you may not have seen before. I am going to show you some of our bag drills.

I want you to have this quote to help you understand what we are all about. "Visions without action equals hallucinations." Let me repeat that quotation: "Vision without proper action equals hallucinations." What that simply means is that you have a vision. If you do not do anything to improve that vision, you are just hallucinating. Football coaches get great ideas and decide they are going to do certain things in their program. After some time, they let the ideas go and the ideas fall through. I tell our players all of the time, "If you have a vision, you must follow through. If you do not follow through, you are just hallucinating."

I am going to set a pace. I am looking for a new brand of coaches to join me and the way I coach. Let me tell you a few things. You can tell by my voice that I do not need a microphone. I love what I do. I love coaching the defensive line. I think I have the best job in the country. I am working for the best coach in the country. I have a great job. I get to do what I love, and that is to coach football. I do not take my job for granted. Every day I walk on the field, I am prepared.

Here are three things I think every coach must do. I do not care how good you are, or how long you have been coaching, you must follow these three principles:
• Make sure you are a good teacher.
• Relate to your players.
• Be organized.

I am lucky in that I came from the classroom as a high school coach. I am very fortunate to be at Penn State. I have just changed chairs from one classroom to another. I feel no different than most of you, and I know what you are going through.

You must be able to relate to your players. If you can relate to your players, you are going to get great things from them.

You must be organized to coach. I have never walked on the field in my drill segment without being prepared to teach. I do not walk out on the field and say, "Let me see, what can we do today?" Kids today will pick up on that. They know if you are just making up drills as you go through practice.

If my drills do not show up in a game video session, I am doing the wrong drills. I will caution you now: if you are doing drills to be doing drills and they do not show up in a game film, you are wasting your time.

We are going to teach our players to play fast in our drills. We are going to teach them how to play full speed. Full speed must be acquired. It is a skill. When we get the young players, they do not know how to play fast. If you want your players to run to the ball, you must teach that skill. You cannot just assume that is going to happen. You must practice as if it is a game. If you practice as if it is a game, when you get to the game, it is not a surprise to you and your players.

If you come to see us practice, you are going to see we practice fast. We are going to be efficient, but we are going to practice fast. I have two great managers. I could not do without them. They are like assistant coaches to me. I pick all of the drills we are going to use in practice that day and I give it to them along with everything we are going to do in practice that day. I make sure everyone knows what we are going to do.

If you have to set up the drills, you are wasting time. We have drills for 12 minutes, and they are set up ready to go when we are ready for them. If you have to set up the drills, you should find a manager or someone on the staff who is not a coach to set up the drills.

I am going to go over some basic things for defense that I think you need to know. I am not a big stat guy, but I am a big run guy. If you cannot stop the run, you cannot play football. I tell my linemen stopping the run gives you the honor to rush the passer.

Everything we do is predicated on stopping the run. I am talking about stopping the run in our base defense. If you cannot stop the run in your base defense, and you have to blitz all of the time to stop the run, then you will not be able to fix the defense. You will not be able to fix it when you need to fix it because you will not know which gap they are going to run into. We play one-gap football. This allows us to play faster because we are only playing in one gap.

I love playing one-gap football because I can fix it fast. The big point that is important to me is the rush defense. Sacks are important, depending on what part of the season we are in. Nevertheless, the rush defense means a great deal to us. We are going to be in the top 10 in the country in rush defense. You look at the last four years, and you will see we were in the top 10 all four years. We have been seventh in rush defense the last four years. We only had one back to gain over 100 yards against our defense this past year. That was in 13 games.

My first goal going into a game is to stop the run and make the offense one-dimensional. Stopping the run gives the defense the honor to rush the passer. That is something we believe in for everything we do. We are going to stop the run first.

I want to give you the things we do in developing defensive line drills.

DEVELOPING DEFENSIVE LINE DRILLS

As you prepare your defensive line drills, you must keep a certain mentality in mind while conducting the drills. Defensive linemen have one of the most important assignments in football. Their job is predicated on their ability to rush the passer or get to the ballcarrier. The main ingredient for a good defensive lineman is the need for quickness and determination. There are certain areas of consideration when conducting your drills.

Most high school coaches have a tough job because some of you have to coach both the offensive and defensive lines. You must make sure you transition from an offensive line coach to a defensive line coach. You cannot teach the same techniques on offense and defense. It is tough to transition from offense to defense. You cannot assume because they are offensive players, they can pick up the defensive techniques.

Speed is important. I am not a 40-yard-dash coach, but I do look at the 10-yard times. A defensive player must have excellent foot speed. He must always keep his feet alive and moving. If they can run for 10 yards and go from sideline to sideline, they can play for me. I have never had a player who could run a 4.9, or a 4.9 player to play for me. That is not important to me. Can he run, can he hustle, and can he play at full speed? That is important to me.

A defensive lineman must be able to accelerate. Initial quickness must always be emphasized. The desire to accelerate on the movement of the football is the principal athletic trait a defensive lineman needs. Areas of concentration will be to accelerate, react quickly, and develop good physical coordination. If a blocker is quick enough to get his hands inside the framework of the defensive lineman's numbers and get his elbows locked on him, forget it. The defender will not get to the passer.

A defensive lineman must be able to coordinate the action of his hands, feet, and body as he rushes the passer. When rushing the passer or playing the run, a defensive lineman must keep his feet moving. Remember that point with your drills.

A defensive lineman must be competitive. An attitude is one of the most important football qualities defensive linemen should have. He must never give up. He needs to have a mean streak, in wanting to get after people. For that reason, we make our drills demanding and tough. He must want to be a good defensive player.

A defensive lineman must be tough, and he must not be denied. How will he react when playing against a bigger and stronger opponent? He must possess inside power. He must be able to control the line of scrimmage.

Let me move on to the five essentials of a defensive lineman.

THE FIVE ESSENTIALS

- *Stance:* You must not overemphasize the stance parameters of the defensive lineman. What is important is the stance that allows the lineman to take a neutral position. He should be able to move in either direction with an explosive power step.
- *Attack:* We do not teach the big-first-step coaching point that a lot of coaches use in their desire to gain penetration. We feel the big first step puts the defensive lineman at a disadvantage against every type of block, save one. The only blocking scheme a big-first-step technique is effective against is the high-hat read (pass protection). Against all other blocks, the big first step puts the defensive lineman on an edge or in a position where he is unbalanced against a blocker using short power strides. In order for a player to contact the blocker in a fundamentally sound body position, it is extremely important for the player to utilize short, powerful steps while maintaining a good base.

- *Neutralize:* The effective defensive lineman must neutralize the blocker's impact and stabilize the line of scrimmage. Neutralizing a blocker or a combination-blocking scheme involves several reactions: getting an upfield push on a pass protector, spilling a trap blocker, disrupting a combo block, and so forth. In order to consistently neutralize a blocker or blocking scheme, the productive defensive lineman must be able to move quickly and efficiently in eight different directions.
- *Escape:* This is where the kinship of the defensive line play and wrestling is the strongest. A primary characteristic of an effective defensive player is his ability to quickly and violently shed a blocker. Against the run, escaping predominantly entails lateral movement ability. Against the pass, the defender may have to throw his blocker aside with a club move in order to clear the pass-rushing lane. Good technique and leverage is simply not enough. The escape factor is a critical component to defensive line play, and it should be practiced on a daily basis with specific drills that hone the players' technique in escaping from contact with the blocker.
- *Pursuit:* An effective escape puts the defensive lineman into position to effectively pursue the ballcarrier. No one can outhustle our defense. In addition to outhustling our opponent, our players (through the use of the proper escape technique) will pursue the ballcarrier according to the proper angle and leverage. Hustle and angles are the two components of effective individual pursuit.

We do not overemphasize the base stance, but we do get into the stance. I do believe in the base stance. I do not overcoach it, but I want to make sure it is balanced. I teach stance and start the first day of practice. That is the most important thing we do.

The defensive lineman must neutralize the block before he can get off the block. He may use the swim technique and get by with it one time, but he needs to neutralize the block, because the swim technique will not work all of the time. We talked about escaping the blocks. It is part of coming off the block.

The last point is pursuit. This is something you must teach every day. You must finish every drill. When we show the video in a few minutes, you need to watch us finish every drill. Finishing teaches pursuit. If you do poor drills and do not finish, you can forget about pursuit.

If you do not teach finish when you run the bag drills, you are not teaching pursuit. You are just teaching a bag drill. I want to teach pursuit on every drill.

I want to bring up another point not related to the X's and O's of football. I can do all of the coaching aspects of the game without using profanity. I have been coaching over 30 years, and I have never cursed on the field. I have never cursed in the course of a game. I will tell you why I have never cursed when coaching. My high school coach was a great coach. His name was Herman Boone. Have you see the movie Remember the Titans. That was my high school coach, when he was coaching in North Carolina. He was a great coach, but every third word was a curse word. He did it thinking he was motivating players. He used profanity every other word.

While I was playing for Coach Boone, I would tell myself if I ever became a coach, I would never use that technique. I will tell you why I never wanted to curse in coaching football. When you curse in front of those young athletes, you train another society. They will be using those curse words later in their life. We are supposed to be growing young men, not teaching them bad habits. We do not want to tear down young athletes; we need to build them up.

I assure you that you can coach and not use profanity. I have coached for 30 years, and I know it will work.

I am asking for one coach to join me in changing the society on this matter. One of you needs to come over and join me in this endeavor. Join me and say, "We can do this in the right way." I will guarantee you will get more out of the players if you have passion for them, and you do the right things. I just need one coach to join me. We will create a new society of coaches.

Let me show you these coaching points on the techniques. We want air under the heels on the stance. The free hand is near the line of scrimmage. We want the hips higher than the hat. We want the inside hand down, and the inside foot back.

On attack, I do not want to step on someone's toes here. When we watch high school films, we see a lot of players that do not know how to get off blocks. They will attack, and then they pursue the ballcarrier. They drop their hands and start running to the ball. When they drop the hands, they get blocked downfield, and they do not know why they get blocked downfield. They have not been coached to get off blocks. Getting off blocks is a part of tackling.

On the starts, we use a six-point start. We teach this on day one on how to take off. The reason I teach this is because I am interested in the pad level. I am a "pad-level coach." We want to see if they can come forward out of the six-point stance. I want to know how fast we can get their pads going forward. We run the drill every day.

We want them to get off the ground and get the pads forward. We are going to run through the blocker and attack the line of scrimmage.

Next, we go to a one-leg balance drill. I got this drill from a track sprinter. All of you have seen the sprinters starting blocks in track. Everyone thinks they push off the back foot. Their stance is tight. They are not really pushing off the back foot. They are really pushing off their front foot. They gain ground with the second foot. When we take off, we want to go across the line of scrimmage. We do not want to take off and just get to the line of scrimmage.

We teach the lineman to balance in their stance, and we push off the front foot. By doing this, I can gain ground. I have to balance, and then push. We still are taking a six-inch power step, but we are gaining ground as we cross the line of scrimmage. We are attacking the line of scrimmage.

There are two keys in that drill. It is great take-off practice. We are gaining ground, and we are going across the line of scrimmage.

The next step is to take the drill to the mat and work on hip explosion. We are not swimming, we are not diving, but we are snapping the hips on the get-off.

We do a redirect drill. The reason we do the drill is to make sure we are running to the football. This eliminates seams.

After we teach the steps on the drills, then we go to the chute and work on them. You can build a chute without going out and buying an expensive one. We do all of the moves coming out of the chute.

I want to cover some drills. The first drill is the hop drill (Figure 11-1). We do these drills in pre-season and early on. In addition, we do them in our winter workouts. What we are looking for is knee bounce, and high knees, and watching them finish on the drill. We always teach finish. We are developing bounce, foot movement, and finish.

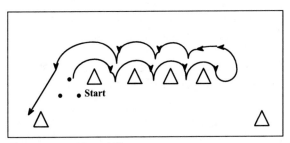

Figure 11-1. Hop drill

Next is our lateral balance step drill (Figure 11-2). I love this drill. We are working on balance and finish.

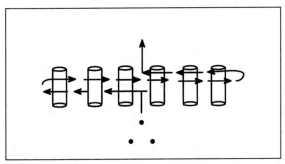

Figure 11-2. Lateral balance step drill

We do a ton of bag drills. The first one is the inner drill. We do not use high bags with the defensive line. Get rid of those high bags with the defensive linemen. We want to run over the bags we use. The bags we use are half-moon bags. They are flat on the bottom and round on the top. We do not have to worry about the players getting their knees up high. We want to know if they have the ability to change directions at full speed.

We start in a three-point stance. We go over the bags and move up to the next level (Figure 11-3). Then, he goes back down the bags.

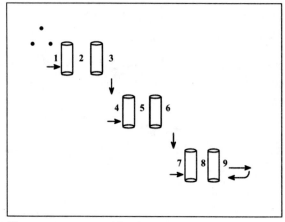

Figure 11-3. Up and back

We add the next phase of the drill and have the lineman finish the drill (Figure 11-4). He goes up the bags, turns, and finishes the drill.

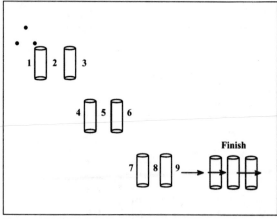

Figure 11-4. Up and finish

Here is another lateral step drill that we like. We have the bags set up at different angles (Figure 11-5). We always have the finish aspect of the drills.

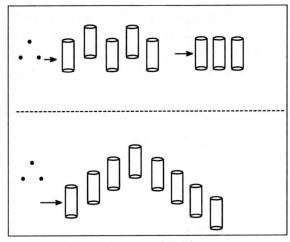

Figure 11-5. Lateral step and finish

Every drill that we have done over the bags, we can do in the chute. If they bump their head, it is on them. You can use all of these drills.

Here is a four-bag drill that I use (Figure 11-6). The drill gives them four sets of bags to go over. It is a great conditioning drill during the pre-season.

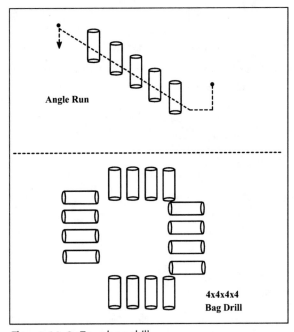

Figure 11-6. Four-bag drill

I do not like to use pursuit drills with players down on the ground. I do not want to put a player in a position that he should not be in. We keep them up in a two-point stance, or a four-point stance. I point to a cone and have them run to the cone. Once they get to the cone, they have to come back to the middle and go again. I am trying to simulate a game. It is a start-and-go drill. It is how we play in a game. We make them backpedal, turn, and run. We want to give them moves they will be using in a game. We give them several moves, and then we give them a finish to the drill. We usually go three men in the box to get the drill done in a small amount of time.

We run another drill where they must get back to the middle. They do not care about their shoulder pads; we are teaching them how to run. We make them finish as we do on all drills. We make them think they are doing a drill, but we are really teaching them how to run.

We talked about pursuit. What it takes to pursue is worth mentioning:
• Pursuit is first a mental process.
• Visualize pursuing and making great plays.
• Physical conditioning is necessary so you can have great pursuit on every play.
• Speed: react fast and quickly. You can improve your speed and quickness.

The question comes up how to pursue. This is what we do in terms of pursuit:
• Play technique and gap responsibility first.
• Concentrate on lateral movement when the ball comes your way.
• Take correct course (pursuit angle) to the ball so you are in good position for the cutback.
• You have to want to be the first to the ball.
• Whoever is responsible for contain must turn the ballcarrier inside to the pursuit. Everyone else works inside-out to the ball.

What should you do once you arrive at the ball? This is what we want:
• Come to balance (come under control).
• Good bent-knee striking position.
• Step to and through the ballcarrier (take one extra step).
• Club and wrap-up driving your numbers through their numbers.

What does pursuit do for you?
• Eliminates the long touchdown.
• Discourages opponents.
  ✓ During the course of a game.
  ✓ Strikes fear and intimidates future opponents.
• Promotes consistent team performance.
• Creates turnovers all over the field.

Let me talk about tackling. The definition of tackling for us is simple. A tackle is a desired collision between the defensive man and the ballcarrier. *The defensive man must win!*

The objective of tackling is this. It is to stop the ballcarrier in his tracks for little or no gain, and to gang tackle. Tackling is 50 percent determination and 50 percent technique. It takes both aggressiveness and good technique to be a great tackler.

This is what we want on the techniques and fundamentals:
- Meet the ballcarrier in a good hitting position.
- Eyes should be focused on the ballcarrier's numbers.
- Don't give the ballcarrier a two-way cut.
- Keep the butt low; keep the head up. First contact should be made with the chest or numbers. As the chest or numbers make contact, roll the hips.
- Do not leave your feet. Keep a wide base, and take short choppy steps. Drive through the ballcarrier, and take him backward.
- On contact, work the arms from low to high, wrap viciously, and pull the ballcarrier toward you. Squeeze and grab cloth.
- If you get caught in a poor hitting position, somehow make the tackle. Grab arms, legs, or anything you can get hold of, except the facemask.

On open-field tackling, this is what we stress:
- Gather yourself, and come under control three to four yards from the ballcarrier, with feet chopping, and move toward the ballcarrier.
- Keep your eyes on the belt buckle, and get into a good hitting position. Make the tackle.
- Give the ballcarrier only one way to go, and then take that direction away from him.
- Leave your feet only as a last resort.
- Use the sideline whenever possible.
- Force the ballcarrier back into pursuit when possible.

Let me cover a couple of tackling drills. This is the first one we use. It is "Joe Pa" all the way. It is the mat tackle. We are not going to hit the ballcarrier in the center of his chest with our helmet, but we are going to slide it off toward the ball. For drill sake, we are putting the helmet down the middle. We put our arms on his buttocks, and set our hips down. We do not lift! We hit, dip the hips, and come up through the ballcarrier. The reason we use the mat is because we do not want them to hit the ground. What we want to do is to "run the feet," and then make the tackle.

We teach the angle tackle the same way. I do not want to angle tackle and drive the man sideways. We want to get the helmet in front of the man and drive him backward, not sideways. We want to drive the helmet through the man and drive him back. The key is to turn the hips and head and drive the man back.

Here are our pass-rush rules:
- Have a plan.
- Pre-snap read.

- Maintain a consistent stance.
- Pass rush from a shade alignment; be on the edge, same arm, same foot. Trust your hips.
- Create momentum and take it away.
- Use your hands.
- Know the quarterback.
- Run through the sack.

I am not a big spin guy. I do not like my linemen spinning on the pass rush. If they spin and they miss, and the quarterback throws a touchdown pass, they are in trouble with me.

If the quarterback throws a touchdown, I do not want our defensive linemen blaming it on the deep defenders. I tell them they did a lousy job and did not rush the passer fast enough to prevent the touchdown. I want them accountable. I do not want to give them an excuse for not getting to the quarterback. The entire team has a job to do, and we cannot blame one group for a touchdown that everyone on the field was responsible for the score. That is what I believe, and that is what I work on.

We study the quarterback. We want to know the type of passer he is. If he is going to step up in the pocket, we are going to come after him. If he is a quarterback who scrambles, we are going to consider that in our pass-rush game plan.

We do not want to jump and run through a sack. We do not want to leave our feet before the pass is out. We want to run through the sack.

Pass-rush drills include the following. We attack the elbow and then club and rip. We finish with a rip move. Let me give you these drills on the tapes so you can see what I have covered.

TAN STUNT: TACKLE AND NOSEMAN

Tackle: Take a 45-degree step, aiming for the back hip of the center. Pin the hip, and then work out to the quarterback.
Nose: Collision the guard. Once the tackle makes contact with the center, come around to cover.

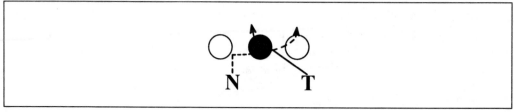

Figure 11-7. Tan stunt: tackle and noseman

NUT STUNT: NOSE AND TACKLE

Nose: Move to a 2i alignment. Take a 45-degree step, aiming for the back hip of the center. Pin the hip, and then work out to the quarterback.

Tackle: Collision the guard. Once the nose makes contact with the center, come around to cover.

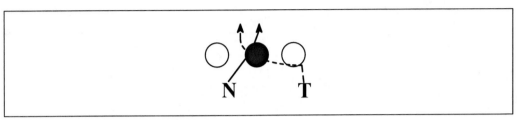

Figure 11-8. Nut stunt: nose and tackle

TEX STUNT: NOSE AND END

End: One step upfield. Plant off the foot, turn and drive to pin the hip of the guard. After collision, work to the quarterback.

Nose: Align in a 2i technique. Two steps inside and "flash hands" to hold the guard. When you see the end cross your face, come around tight to contain.

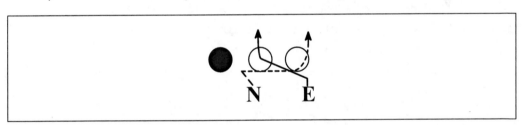

Figure 11-9. Tex stunt: nose and end

EXIT STUNT: TACKLE AND WILL LINEBACKER

Tackle: Drive hard upfield, aiming for the inside half of the tackle, and then work for containment.

Will: Two steps upfield and "flash hands." Plant on second step, and aim for inside shoulder of the guard.

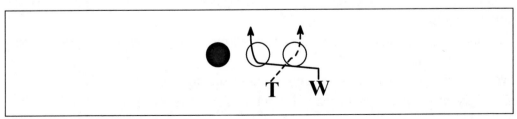

Figure 11-10. Exit stunt: tackle and Will

WET STUNT: TACKLE AND WILL LINEBACKER

Tackle: Drive hard upfield, aiming for the inside half of the tight end, and then work for containment.

Will: One step upfield and "flash hands." Plant on first step, and aim for the inside shoulder of the tackle.

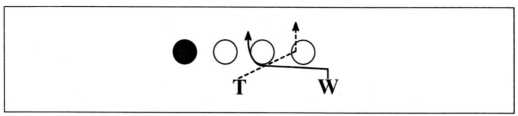

Figure 11- 11. Wet stunt: tackle and Will

DOUBLE COVER STUNT: TACKLE, WILLAND NOSE, AND END

Tackle: Align in a 3 technique. Hit the guard. Flash hands, and come around tight to contain.

Will: Take two hard steps upfield. Take a reckless inside rush.

Nose: Hit the guard. Flash hands, and come around tight to contain.

End: Take two steps upfield. Fake a reckless inside rush.

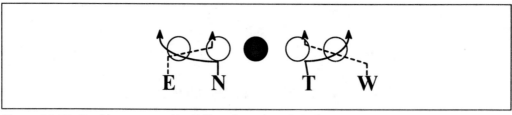

Figure 11-12. Double cover: tackle, Will and nose, and end

RAMBO STUNT: TACKLE, WILL AND NOSE, AND END

Tackle: Align in a wide 3 technique. Drive hard upfield, pick the back hip of the tackle, and then work to contain.

Will: Take two hard steps upfield. Step hard for the guard, and pick the guard. Aiming point is the rib cage.

Nose: Hit the guard. Flash hands, and come around tight to contain.

End: Take three steps upfield. Plant the outside foot, and come underneath.

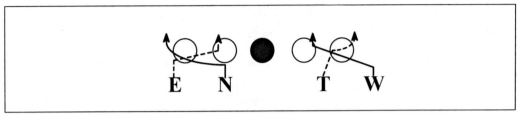

Figure 11-13. Rambo stunt: tackle, Will and nose, and end

CONAN STUNT: TACKLE, WILL AND NOSE, AND END

Tackle: Drive for the inside hip of the tackle. Pick the tackle, and work for containment
.Nose: Tex stunt
End: Tex stunt
Will: One step and long stick to the A gap.

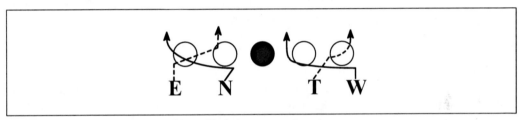

Figure 11-14. Conan Stunt: Tackle, Will and nose, and end

ROCKY STUNT: TACKLE, WILL AND NOSE, END

Tackle: Align in a wide 3 technique. Drive hard upfield, and pick the back hip of the tackle.
Will: Long stick. Read the center. If he turns to you, cross his face. If he turns away, come inside of him.
Nose: Hit into the guard to hold him, then come around tight, working for containment.
End: Contain the rush, and do not take an inside move.
Coaching Point: Versus a tight end, check to Rocky II.

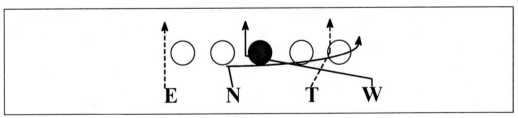

Figure 11-15. Rocky stunt: tackle, Will and nose, and end

The NCAA will not let me give you my drill tape, but I have started a youth ministry program at my church. I can sell you the tapes for 10 dollars. I do not make anything from this, as I give it all to the youth program at my church at Penn State. Let me know if you want one. All of the drills are on the tape.

Let me close with this. I have three minutes, and I will be done. I hope I have showed you something in the time I have spent with you that will make you a better defensive line coach, a better man, and that will help you make it a better world.

I want each of you to ask yourself this question: What have been the 10 best years of your life? If you tell me it was when you got married, or when I did this last year, or I did this 10 years ago. I am going to stop you at that point. I am going to tell you the way it must be. The best 10 years better start tonight! It starts this hour, this minute, and this second. You have promised yourself that you are going to make yourself a better football coach.

It is not what you did last year; it is what you are going to do right now. Every morning when I rise, I say this scripture. It is from the Bible, Philippians 4:13. "I can do everything through Christ who strengthens me."

Then I make this comment to myself: "I have to make this a great day." I know we all only have so many years left in this life. If you want to make the next 10 years the best 10 years of your life, if you make up your mind to start now, it will happen. You will be a better football coach. Don't live on yesterday. You cannot live on the last state championship. Live on what you do this moment. If you will live that way, every morning when you get up, you will become a great coach. You will be fired up in everything that you do.

This is natural for me. The enthusiasm I have here today is no fake for me. This is natural. I am like this all of the time.

The only time I calm down is when I walk into my house. I am one of those coaches who has to wear many hats. When I walk into my house, I am a husband, a father, as well as a coach. You have to do that. Do not let your kids not see their father.

I have one story to illustrate this point. My wife and I are the parents of twins, Tony and Teresa. When they were in the early years of school, they played a game at school. It was a game similar to show-and-tell. The teacher asked Tony if he could tell the class his mother's name. He replied, "Christine Johnson." Very good, Tony! Can you tell us your father's name? Tony replied, "Coach Johnson." He did not know my first name, but he knew I was "Coach." That was a reality for me. He said that because that is all he ever heard. He did not know my name was Larry. What is the moral of the story? The kids must know who you are. From that point on, I changed my life. Don't lose sight of that point.

I need one of you to brand yourself with me so we can create a new generation of football coaches. That is all I want. God bless you!

12

Defensive Line Techniques and Stunts

Greg Mattison
University of Notre Dame
2004

My topic is coaching the defensive line. The defensive line is critical in playing defense. If you have a good defensive team, it is because you have a good defensive line. If you have great linebackers and great defensive backs, but only an average defensive line, your defense is average.

The defensive line coach has to be a great teacher. I take pride in my defensive linemen being intelligent. Do not pigeonhole your linemen by saying they only need to know a few things to do the job. If you do not teach your players the entire aspect of every stunt and defense, you will have problems with their performance.

I know we have a lot more time than high school coaches, but I give my linemen a mini-playbook every day. They have a tip sheet for everything we do in practice that day. I think you have to do a great job in the little things in teaching.

The defensive line coach has to be a great motivator. The best way to motivate your players is to make them accountable to you. The only way I know to make them accountable is to give them a grading system. I grade players with a plus and minus on techniques. If the only grades you have are plus and minus, you run the risk of having a robot who is a good technician but never makes a play. We grade all of our players on a production chart. In addition to positive points within the grade system, there are negative points.

The first thing our players want to see after a game is the production chart. I think a combination of plus and minus grades and a production chart is a good way to motivate your players.

I think defensive linemen are special people. To coach those people, you have to have a great passion and enthusiasm for the game. Your players will feed off the defensive line coach. If the coach is having a bad day on the practice field, the players in his group will have a bad day.

When you coach the defensive line, you have to be demanding, but also consistent. From the beginning of practices, the players must know only one way exists to do things. They have to do things your way, or it is not acceptable. When someone does something wrong, he hears about it. There is no one in the program who is protected from correction.

For a defense to be successful, they have to stop the run. My teaching motto is SATKR. That is an acronym for stance, alignment, technique, key, and responsibility. All those traits have to be present for a player to be a great defensive lineman. If one of the traits is missing, he will not be as good as he can be.

When our players come to camp at the beginning of the year, I treat them as if they know nothing. The stance we put them in is not the only stance in America, but it is the one in which we believe.

When we teach our stance, we talk in terms of a three and a half- point stance. The best stance to be in is a four-point stance, but it is impractical. You cannot pass rush and stem as easily from the four-point stance. I want to make one point, which I will make again and again tonight. What you see on film is what you are coaching. We want our defensive line at Notre Dame to be the best technique line in the country.

The first element in the stance is the width of the stance. We want the stance to be shoulder-width apart. That equates to how the player walks. That is how wide the feet should be apart. If the stance is too wide, the defensive lineman has lost time in getting to the man he is facing.

A defensive lineman wants his toes and heels in a straight line. That is critical to a good stance. The most important thing about coming out of a stance is how fast the defender can get to player he is against.

I want the defensive lineman to have the weight on the inside of his feet. In linemen's stance, they should be knock-kneed. If you make them grab grass with their big toe, that will put pressure on the inside of the foot.

We want a toe-to-instep relationship in the stagger of the feet. When the defender comes off the ball, he is always gaining distance toward the man he is against.

The inside foot of the player's alignment is back. To get in the three and a half-point stance, we start in the four-point stance. Once we get in the four-point stance, we lift the inside hand off the ground.

The player's hands are loose as he gets into his stance. We do not want him to form a fist with his hand. That keeps the player tense. When you get in a stance, the shoulders are square and straight. That is the stance from which we want to play the run.

I am not going to spend too much time talking about alignment. Everyone in America is playing gap control defenses. That is what we tell our players. They will align as to their ability to control their gaps.

If the defender has a B gap responsibility, he has to align on the offensive blocker in an alignment that allows him to get into and control the B gap. If that means his inside foot is down the crotch of the offensive blocker, that is his alignment. If he cannot control the B gap from that alignment, he has to get wider. The problem, obviously, is the further the defender gets away from his technique, the more susceptible he is to other blocks.

When we talk about technique, I never mention footwork to our players. We want to explode our face and hands toward the target, and the feet will follow. A key point about contact is to explode with the heels of the hands through the man, and not to the man. If you do not talk about punching through the man, you end up playing patty-cake.

We want to punch to grab. We do not want the hands to fly off the target after the defender hits the man. When we talk about hand placement, we want our hands above our eyes. That allows the defender to play with his chest over his knees, which puts the defensive lineman in a good hitting position.

We never talk about rolling our hips in our explosion drills. The only time we roll the hips is during the tackle. If the defensive lineman rolls his hips, he is belly to belly with an offensive lineman who outweighs him and is going to hold him. We want the natural separation that comes from playing with the hands out.

When we key a blocker, we look right at the face mask. I try to convince players there is no one on the practice field or the game field except the man on which he is aligned. If you can get that point over to your players, you will win more battles than you lose. The defenders who get in trouble are the ones that are looking all over the place for the ball.

The only thing I tell my players about responsibility is for them to get their hips in the heat. We are a shade team, and most of the blocks we play are reach blocks. I do not want to hit and steer the blocker. I want the hit and to get my hips to where the force is coming from. In most cases the force is coming from up the field.

If the offensive blocker knows where the defensive lineman is going, he will win more than he loses. He knows the snap count and is probably bigger than the defender. If the defender plays a perfect technique, we still will lose. The defender must have the ability to go three ways. The offensive lineman has to wonder where the defender is going. The offensive blocker has no greater fear than missing the defender completely. We angle, loop, and stem to give us movement from a shade technique against an offensive blocker.

When you teach your linemen to stem, make them take pride in the movement, and do not let them get sloppy. We want them to move quickly. If you are a stem team, make sure you work on angling. If the offense snaps the ball while we are stemming, that charge becomes an angle charge. We continue the movement off the stem into an angle charge to our responsibility.

You can cue your lineman to stem in three ways. You can let the linebacker make the call, or the noseguard make the call. If you know the opponents cadence, we can stem off their cadence.

The last thing I want to cover before we get into the angle movement is the criteria for loafers. We did not do a good job of this last year. That is my fault, not the players'. I put the product on the field. If I do not teach them well enough, that is my problem. You can never justify a player loafing on the field. To grade a loaf, you have to define what it is.

We base our loaf grades on the following criteria: changes speed running to the ball, teammates passing him in pursuit, caught lying on the ground, and not laying out on the pile before the whistle blows. The last criterion is critical to being a great defense. We were an average defense last year because of that. Two years ago we had a great defense because we kept coming until the whistle blew.

There are some techniques involved with the three-way-go scheme. When you play a shade defense, offensive line coaches tell me the most difficult thing they have to deal with is the defender angling across the blocker's face. There are some critical points to these kinds of movements. Never cheat the alignment to run an angle stunt.

If we are angling inside, we only have to play two blocks. We have to play the drive and reach blocks. If the block is a cut-off block, by angling we have played the perfect squeeze technique.

The defender is aligned on the outside shade of the blocker. On a drive block, the offensive blocker is angling outside to get to his block. That makes it easier for the defender to angle across his face. The reach block is better because the aiming point on the defender is wider than the drive block.

When the defender angles from a shade alignment, he always reads the man he is over, not the man to his inside. As he angles, he wants to narrow his stance. The most important thing in the angle technique is to gain distance with the first step. The angle is not a forty-five degree angle. We never step forward on the first step. It is a flat step to the line of scrimmage. If you step forward from a shade technique, the defender runs into the blocker every time.

By taking the flat step down the line, the defender, on his first step, is over the blocker's head gear. If the blocker tries to reach the defender, his helmet goes outside on the defender. When the defender reads that, he does not try to come back across the face. He plants his inside foot, comes off the blocker's butt, and runs flat down the line of scrimmage to the outside.

If the blocker tries to drive block the defender, on the first step the defender's head is inside the drive blocker, and he wins the battle. If the blocker goes inside, the defender squeezes inside and comes off the offensive blocker's butt. This technique applies to every position we play in the defensive line.

The defensive end playing over the offensive tackle has a tough time if the offensive tackle knows he has containment responsibility. The tackle thinks he can come off hard every time, and the end will never come inside. When we give the tackle the inside angle, that slows him down immediately. If our end has containment, we tell him to come late on the containment, when he has an inside angle.

We frequently call two stunts in our run defense. The first stunt is called a spear stunt (see Figure 12-1). The aiming point for the defensive end is the offensive tackle's hip. If the tackle did not move, our defensive end hits him right in the hip with his face mask. He is coming flat to the line of scrimmage. We tell the end he can never be wrong. The only way he is ever wrong is to get too high. If the tackle blocks out or pass blocks on the defensive end, the end should be under the block.

We do not tell him to get under the block. He is on a railroad track coming flat down the line of scrimmage. He is taking on anything he meets on that track. The

Figure 12-1. Spear stunt

3 technique defensive tackle cheats three inches back in his alignment. That allows the defensive end room. On the snap of the ball, the tackle takes two shuffle steps to the inside. The thing that destroys this stunt is the defensive tackle getting in too big a hurry to run the stunt.

The defensive tackle has to give the defensive end time to get down inside. If the offensive tackle is coming down on the defensive tackle, the end crushes his charge and knocks him down. The defensive tackle never has to worry about getting blocked. If the tackle gets too fast, he ends up forcing the defensive end wide, and that becomes an awful stunt. The tackle wants to come off the end's butt and become the defensive end. The defensive end becomes the 3 technique.

The defensive tackle cannot run up the field. This is a run stunt, not a pass stunt. If the tackle runs up the field, a huge gap is left on the line of scrimmage. He is able to tell whether it is a run or pass by the offensive tackle's block. If the blocker disappears down the line, the defensive tackle needs to stay on the line of scrimmage. If the blocker has set up in a pass blocking set, he rushes the passer.

The linebacker playing behind the stunt does nothing. He plays as if there were no stunt. His technique has not been affected. The linebacker is not involved with the stunt. If there is a tight end to that side, the stunt is off. We only run this stunt to the open side of the formation. This is a good stunt to run with the under front.

When we play the over defense, we use this stunt. This stunt is similar to the spear stunt, but different. We run a whip stunt. (see Figure 12-2). Before the snap of the ball, the Will linebacker walks up on the line of scrimmage and does the same thing the defensive end did on the spear stunt. We want the defensive end to tighten down on his 5 technique, cheat inside, and back off the line of scrimmage. That gives the Will linebacker room to get inside. If the end is wide, the Will linebacker bows his charge. The defensive end has a rule that controls the way he plays. If the tackle blocks on him or inside, the end comes around late. If the tackle blocks out on the Will linebacker or uses a pass set, the defensive end goes inside. These are two good stunts we run to the open side of the formation, against the run.

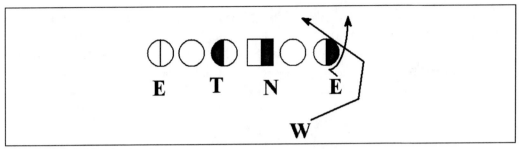

Figure 12-2. Whip stunt

The jet alignment is a technique we use for our defensive end (see Figure 12-3). The end is in a cocked 5 technique stance on the offensive tackle. We want his inside hand exactly two feet from the outside foot of the offensive tackle. That is critical in this technique. The end has his inside foot back in his stance. On the snap of the ball, we go two steps as hard as we can, extending and thrusting our upper body and hands at the hip of the offensive tackle. Our aiming point is his hip, not his headgear.

This technique is where we talk a great deal about closing the air between the blocker and the defender. That is the catchphrase we use to describe the space between the defender and the blocker. Whenever the tackle's hip goes away, the end has to close the air with his feet. The end runs a straight track down inside at the hip.

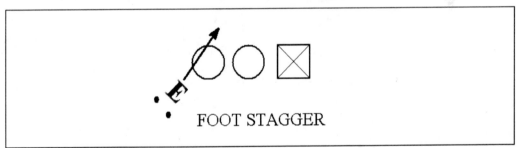

Figure 12-3. Jet alignment

As the end attacks the hip of the tackle, everything happens. The first rule the defensive end follows is to have no air between the end and tackle. We know on nine out of ten blocks, the hip is going away from the end. If the hip goes away, the end continues to close until there is no space between him and the tackle. At that point, the end squares his shoulders and shuffles down looking for the cut-back run or bootleg.

There are a number of blocks the defensive end has to play from the jet alignment. The first block is the base block. If the offensive tackle tries to base block the defensive end, he completely blows up the offensive tackle. He runs his track inside with such speed that the offensive tackle cannot turn him out. This allows you to play this position with an undersized end that has speed.

On the reach block, the tackle is closing the air with the block (see Figure 12-4). When the defender sees the helmet come outside, he squares his shoulders, gets his hips to the heat, and rips upfield. "Getting the hips to the heat" means he turns his hips upfield against the blocker and upper cuts or rips upfield with the inside arm.

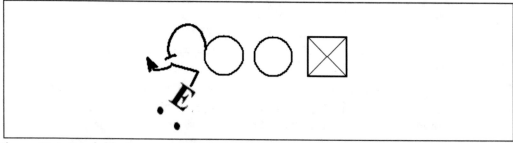

Figure 12-4. Reach block

If the tackle goes inside and flattens out but does not cross the line of scrimmage, the defensive end knows it is probably the bootleg (see Figure 12-5). If the tackle goes away inside and fans up across the line of scrimmage, the defensive end know it is a reverse. If the offensive guard is pulling to protect the bootleg, the end attacks the guard and gets his hips to the heat.

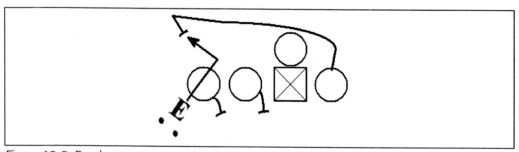

Figure 12-5. Bootleg

We do not tell our defensive end to look for the blockers (see Figure 12-6). If the defensive end closes all the air between him and the tackle, the offensive blockers will find the defender. The defensive end spills the blocks coming from the fullback on the kick-out or the pulling guard on the counter. However, I want him to take the block on with his head inside, but I want his hips working upfield. He spills the ball, but he tries to get out of the block to help with the tackle.

If the defensive end did nothing but close the air on the down block and get as close to the tackle as he could, that is a great technique. He does not have to find the blockers because they have to find him. If the defensive end does not close, he is in trouble.

We have a saying at Notre Dame. The saying is, "If you cannot play a 6 technique, you cannot play at Notre Dame." That is a true statement. We take unbelievable pride

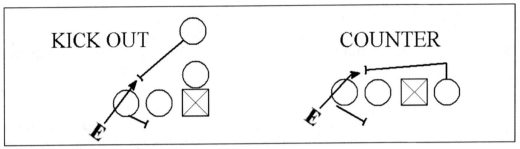

Figure 12-6. Kick out and counter

in how we play the 6 technique. A 6 technique at Notre Dame is nose to nose and toes to toes on the tight end.

There are three types of blocks the 6 technique has to play. He has to play the power scoop, the cut-off, and the influence block. We play our 6 technique with the defender's outside foot back in his stance. We are firm believers that you cannot attack one man and key another man. The combo block of the tackle and tight end on the 6 technique gives me nightmares. No worse feeling exists than what you feel watching a tackle and tight end zone block the 6 technique with the linebacker trying to scrape to the ball.

The reason we play with the outside foot back is to be able to maul the tight end (see Figure 12-7). If the tight end tries to power scoop the defensive end, the 6 technique puts him in the backfield. If you have an average defensive end, have him run off the football as hard as he can. Have him put his face through the tight end and drive him back. As soon as the 6 technique gets his feet to the line of scrimmage, it is time for him to get his eyes inside. Knocking the tight end back off the ball eliminates the power scoop.

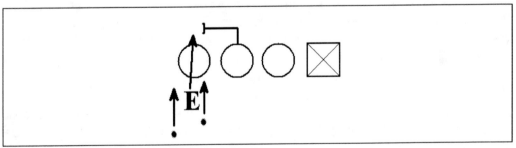

Figure 12-7. Power scoop

There are some negatives to playing that type of technique. If the tight end releases outside on a pass, the 6 –technique's momentum runs him away from the quarterback. The second thing is the cutoff block. We have never worried about the cutoff block because we are bigger and more physical than the tight end. We stuff the tight end back into the hole and make the tackle with his butt.

The 6 technique end is a C gap player. Any time a lineman pulls across the face of the 6 –technique, he can void his C gap as long as he stays inside the football. If the ball cuts inside the 6 technique, he is wrong. The linebacker is pursing outside the defensive end.

What teams try to do to our 6 techniques is influence them (see Figure 12-8). They know the tight end cannot block him so they fake the outside reach block. They hope he widens and becomes an easy target for the fullback to kick out. Anytime we see the helmet go outside, the 6-technique closes as quickly as he can on the offensive tackle.

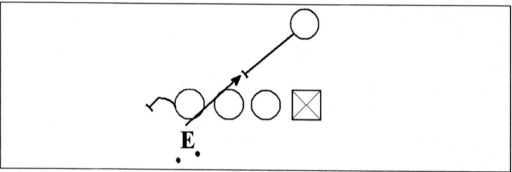

Figure 12-8. Influence

We have one coaching point for playing a block. Too many times the defensive lineman becomes an offensive lineman when he plays the block. They do all the technical things correctly except they do not look for the ball. When they attack the blocker and get their hips to the heat, they have to get their eyes back inside. The ball is going to be on the inside most of the time.

To be a successful pass rusher the player must believe that no one can block him. When the offense wants to throw the ball, generally there are five blockers and four rushers. We challenge them on a pass play by telling them that three of the four pass rushers will be in a one-on-one situation with the pass protector. As hard as it is to pass block, if the rushers cannot get to the quarterback, they need to go to the offense.

Do not teach a lot of pass rush techniques. Pass rushing is like wrestling because we shoot the move and make the lineman cheat to stop it. After we shoot the move, we have a counter move that gets us clear. We have five moves we teach. I do not expect all the defenders to use all five of the moves. They find what they do well, and use it. We teach the bull rush, speed club, slap club, counter club, and spin.

In the bull rush, the defender explodes with his hands. He attacks half of the offensive lineman. We make three-point contact with the offensive lineman. We contact the chest with our hands, and the chin with the face mask. We want to accelerate the feet and push with the hands to get to the quarterback.

In the speed club, we club with the arm and leg together. If the arm and leg are not together, we are beat. We club the middle of the offensive linemen's back, grab jersey, and rip through the outside arm. The hands and feet have to keep moving to be a good pass rusher.

The slap club is a slapping movement on the offensive blocker's hand by the opposite hand of the defender. That allows the defender to get the speed club into the middle of the offensive lineman's back.

On the counter club, the defender has to sell the outside move with alignment and foot movement. On the first step, we sell the outside move. On the second step, we plant and come inside and club using the club leg together with the arm.

In the spin moves, we sell the speed club on the first step. We plant the shoulder into the numbers, swing with the arm all the way around, and slap the back of the offensive lineman. Make sure you accelerate the feet coming out of all moves to the quarterback.

Before I quit, I want to show you some games we use in our pass rush. The first game is between the 3 technique and the 1 technique. It does not matter who is in those positions. We call this a twist (see Figure 12-9). The "t" in "twist" tells us the tackle goes first. The tackle comes first and gets his helmet to the hip of the center. If the tackle gets his helmet into the crease, we win. If the guard comes off the tackle to block the nose, the tackle makes the sack. The center cannot block him with his helmet on his hip. The nose guard attacks the center on his shade side. He delays and comes off the tackle's tail into the gap of the offensive guard.

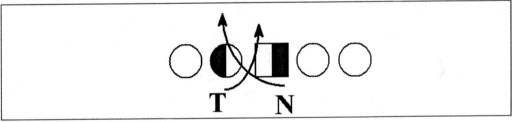

Figure 12-9. Twist

We use the thumbs game on the outside (see Figure 12-10). The tackle goes first, and the end comes second. This involves the 3 technique and a 5 technique or 6 technique end. The end is the key to the game. He has to get off the ball fast to make the offensive tackle open his hip to him. The 3 technique is speed clubbing on the guard and working for containment. The end plants and comes underneath the offensive tackle. Nine out of ten times, the center is waiting for the end. The end is running full speed and should beat the center's block.

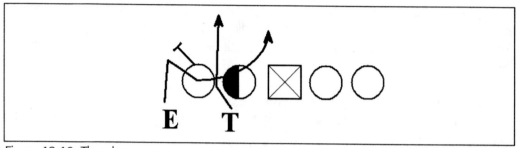

Figure 12-10. Thumbs

If we want to bring the end first on a game we call "ears" (see Figure 12-11). The "e" in "ears" means the end comes first in the stunt. On the end's first and second steps, it looks like the thumbs game. On the second step, he comes under the offensive tackle using a spin or counter club. The tackle takes two shuffle steps inside to freeze the offensive guard. He plants and goes outside for containment. If the end gets his headgear in the crease of the guard, the defensive tackle makes the sack.

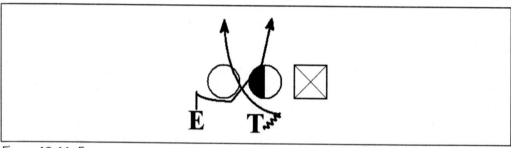

Figure 12-11. Ears

When the defense runs a stunt, they cannot be selfish. If they cannot get the sack, they must make sure their buddy does. We run the Ed game with the 1 technique and 5 technique (see Figure 12-12). That would occur on the bubble side of the under-defense or the weakside of the over-defense. The nose guard has to occupy the center and the offensive guard. He cannot smother the center and let the guard come off on the end coming underneath. The end sells the upfield move and comes under the tackle. The noseguard occupies the center and guard, and comes outside for containment.

Do not run games just for the sake of doing something on the defensive line. Have a purpose for running each game you run. If you think the offense is going to run the draw, the twist is a good move. It screws up the offensive scheme and protects your linebackers. Any time the offense is protecting by using turn back protection, the ears game is an excellent call. If a team runs a lot of sprint draws against us, we run the Ed game.

If we do not know what to run, we run a four-man game. That means no matter what the offense is doing, they will be in the wrong protection. This game is called Tex

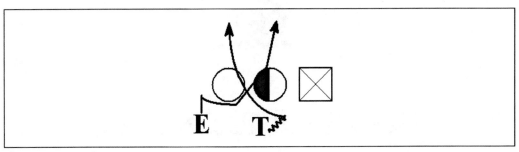

Figure 12-12. Ed

(see Figure 12-13). Everything is planned, and we are not grab-bagging just to be running something. On this stunt we run a thumbs to the 3 technique and 5 technique players, and an Ed to the 1 technique and 5 technique players.

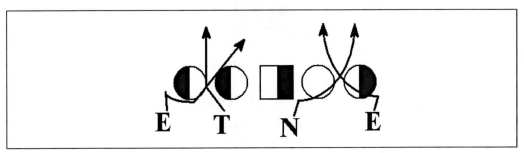

Figure 12-13. Tex

We run games because we know what the protection is going to be. Against a shotgun set with a back sitting next to the quarterback, that tells you the center generally blocks away from the set back's position. We give a "green" call, which means we come off the center shade and run two 3 techniques (see Figure 12-14). We know the center is turning away from the back. We run no stunt inside toward that direction. We void the center gap and run the stunts to the outside and the center's backside. We can run double thumbs and double ears and bring pressure without running into the center.

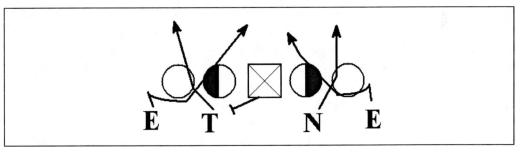

Figure 12-14. Green double thumbs

Thank you for your time and attention, and thank you for having me.

13

Pass-Rush Techniques

Jim Muehling
Indiana University
1993

I am going to talk about defensive line play with regards to rushing the passer. I will talk about the elements that we use as far as the pass rush, the pass-rush moves, the drills we use, and some of the power moves we teach.

First, I want to talk about our philosophy of rushing the passer. This is dictated by the defense we are playing. We play a couple of different fronts. We play a 4-3 front that is more of an attacking front. We lay our ears back and move on the snap of the ball. It is a ball-key defense. We have an area that we are attacking on the snap of the football. On our nickel front, which is a four front, it is a little less aggressive at the snap of the football for the inside people because we are short one linebacker. We have two linebackers instead of three in our nickel front. We slide the fronts some, particularly with a two-back set. We will give them more of a 50 look with a nose man. It is less aggressive than our 4-3 package.

We use two types of pass-rush moves. We use the speed rush and the read-and-react rush. Once you get into the moves, there is no difference in the moves. You start executing the move, and the principle of the moves does not change. The philosophy of your defense will dictate the kinds of moves you want to teach on the pass rush. If you are an attacking-type defense where you want to lay your ears back and come hard, you do not have a lot of reads for the front people. You are going to teach a lot more speeds and rip and slip moves, such as the butt and olé moves, which I will cover later.

In our philosophy, we talk about the desire to get to the quarterback. A lot of players are a little tentative at this. If you are going to chew out a kid because of the draw play, you need to make sure you have the right person who is responsible for the draw. It all depends on who you assign the draw to. It is like hitting a golf ball. Do you want me to take a wood and hit it as hard as I can, or do you want me to take an iron and hit it straight down the fairway? It depends on what you want. You have to let the kids know what you want.

You must make time to get better. We spend three periods a day in practice trying to get better on the pass rush. The time will vary on each period, but we do have three periods to teach the pass rush. I think you can do the same with the pass rush in high school. You have to make time to get better. I know that some of you have players that go both ways. Some of you have defensive specialists, and you can get a lot of things down on the pass rush.

We spend 5 to 10 minutes per day on pass-rush technique. We work on takeoff, ball key moves, and breaking the corner down. We spend a minimum of 10 minutes on group work every day, defense against the offense. We use a drill we call machine gun, where we set up cones and have them rush the passer. The tackle goes with a guard; however, the guard is only for alignment. He steps out of the way once the ball is snapped.

We go 1-on-1 on the pass rush. We go bang, bang, bang! We are just like a machine gun. We go one after another. The coach on offense blows the whistle. We get a lot of three- and four-step pass rushes. We set a ball on top of a dummy at a depth of five or seven yards deep to simulate a quarterback setting up to throw the pass. That is where the tackle is working toward.

We do not like to do a lot of full-line work. We do a lot of half-line work. We do team work later in the practice session. We go ones versus ones and twos versus twos at the end of practice. While the group work is going on, the skeleton drill is going on at the other end of the field for our linebackers. We incorporate some offensive backs for protection in our drills. Also, we will bring up some linebackers. However, during that drill, it is the front linemen going against each other.

Next, we have team pass period for 10 minutes. We may go 15 minutes, depending on what we have done in the other 15-minute drills. Early in the year, we may not do any team work during practice. Later in the year, we may do more team work and less group work.

Let me get into the principle of the pass rush. We have 10 principles that we cover in our pass-rush package.

Principles of Pass Rush

• Speed for speed! We spend a lot of time, since we are in the 4-3 front, looking at the football. As soon as the center flinches his hands, we move. Also, we work under the chutes, and we move from a painted line. We make sure that the ball is in the middle of the defense. A coach checks their stance and moves the ball. We make sure that they are getting off on the ball. We work on the takeoff drill every day. It may be for only one minute or for only 30 seconds per day. We come out of our stance and get ready to attack, speed for speed! We want to get the offensive lineman in a disadvantaged position with our speed. We want to take the bend out of his knees where he has to kick out of his alignment. With our speed, we are going to get his weight moving off the center of gravity as much as possible. This puts him at a disadvantage by forcing him to go backwards. This is what we mean by speed for speed. We have to teach him to come out of his stance.

• Speed off the read! Many of you in high school may play a read defense. Once you do read pass, speed off the read to rush the passer. We will put them into a position where they are locked up and go from there. We are always using our hands on the rush. We will cover these moves later. We are trying to reach through and get that cloth behind his shoulder pad. We want to pull him forward so we can get by his hip. If you use your hands on the pass rush, you always use the foot on the same side as the hand you use. Do not cross the hands and feet. We stress this coaching point: step through; step through. Close the distance between the blocker and the quarterback.

• Constant up-the-field movement, no lateral moves. We constantly tell them to get their butts up the field. We want to close the distance between the quarterback and blocker as quickly as possible.

• Force blocker's shoulders to turn; work to the corner. The offense is trying to keep their shoulders square to the line of scrimmage. They are trying to keep their hips square so they can react to the pass rush. They will take away one side or the other. Most of the time, they will try to force us to take the long way outside. On defense, we want to force shoulder turns by applying pressure to one side and pulling the inside shoulder or by getting the outside shoulder turned. That is what we are trying to get. We are trying to get a shoulder turned. We are going to push it, or we are going to pull it. Let me talk about the hand moves. We are trying to throw speed moves. We do not get both hands on the man, usually. When we do get the hands on the man, we go for the shoulder pads. We shoot our hands for the wide corners of the shoulder pads.

- Take the bend out of his knees; force the grab. I am trying to get to the blocker as soon as possible. I always keep leverage on the blocker. I want my pads below his shoulder pads. I want to be able to force up and into the blocker, or I can get the force where I can pull down through him to get the bend out of his knees. I used a big coach to demonstrate this move with me at one clinic, and he got mad at me because I pulled him down with too much force. Today, I have my son with me to demonstrate.

If I get the bend out of the blocker's knees, he cannot move. As soon as his knees get straight, he can't move. This is true on defense as well as on offense. We want to take the bend out of the blocker's knees as quickly as possible. We want to force the grab. We want him to grab for us to save his own rear end from getting beat. We want to force the hold so he will get a flag on the play. We feel that the holding penalty is not called enough, but the offense feels it is called too much. If we can force the hold, the officials will call it every once in a while.

- Maintain body lean; lead with the hard stuff! Give the blocker as little soft stuff as possible. We want to lead with the shoulders out over the knees. I want to pass rush with my shoulders out in front of my knees. I do not want to rush straight up. I do not want two chickens fighting. We rush with body lean. They give us this big helmet, face mask, and shoulder pads, so we lead with the hard stuff. Don't give them much of the soft stuff, which is your body. If the blocker is trying to grab you, make him grab the hard stuff and not the soft stuff. This is the reason that we tell them they are too high. They must have body lean.

- Maintain power position. Keep your shoulders lower than the blocker (kick off if necessary). What is a power position? You are getting ready to clean the blocker. You are going to power clean the blocker.

- Force the retreat; don't let the quarterback set his feet. We know that you are not always going to get to the quarterback. We would like to change his rhythm and the tempo of the throw. That is one of the things that we keep track of on our production points. We give awards for our sacks. We can't just pat them on the back. We award them for tips, forced bad passes, and other good plays.

- No recoil off blocks! Keep pressure hard, fast, and constant. We are going north and south on our pass rush. Keep the pressure up the field and not lateral.

- Work to get on the same yard line as blocker. If you do, he's beat (pressure back into quarterback). We want to get on the same yard line as the blocker. If we can do that, we have him beat. If we can look him in the ear hole, he is beaten. We try to get to the point—to the tip of his shoulder or the tip of his hip.

• Stay on ground until throwing motion starts, skywalk, hands high (tip drill). How many times have you see the rusher leap up in the air to block a pass, and then the quarterback ducks under him and makes a big play? We run a drill to work on this technique. We want to keep the feet on the ground and keep up the field until the throwing motion starts. When the throwing elbow goes up, that is when we will stop and get our hands up in the air. On the release of the ball, we are jumping and tipping. In the drill, we have them call out, "Pass," when the quarterback makes his drop. When the off arm comes off the ball, we call, "Ball." This is to let the defensive back know that the ball is ready to be released. The scout-team quarterback throws a volleyball-type pass so the rushers can practice tipping the ball. They can knock it down or reject it. If they catch the batted ball, they can run with it. They have a lot of fun with the drill.

Pass-Rush Lanes

On our field, we use the dome-shaped pass-rush lanes; we have a five-step and a seven-step lane. We have the lanes drawn on our grass field, and we use them in our machine-gun drill.
  • Simple points of aim (near number, near shoulder)
  • Lines on practice field for dropback
  • Drill work with a rabbit for one-half roll and sprint
  • Give the rusher some freedom to do it.
  • Understand how blitz affects lanes T's in A/E's contain (or E's/under).

Types of Pass-Rush and Rush Moves

Read Rush

Let's say you are in a 50 defense. You have a 5 technique, a 4 technique, a 6 technique end, and a nose man. You have an end coming off the backside. You have a four-man rush coming off the read. You are reacting off that read to execute the pass-rush move.
  • Define—First, I play run, and then I read pass. Now, I have to execute my pass-rush move. That is a read pass rush.
  • Principles—On the read rush, we use the following points.
    ✓ Three-point explosion—Arm extension, take the bend out of his knees, and I can get his shoulders raised. The hands are two points; the face looking in is the third point.
    ✓ Power position—You must have power position on the blocker when you use a read rush. You must be able to get him up in the air, and you must be able to get your shoulders underneath him. We work off the push and the pull.
    ✓ Take away knee bend.

- Lift and rip, jerk and slip—These are the basic two moves that we use. We call it the slip because Coach Mallory does not want to call it a swim move. It rhymes with rip, and we are not going to swim at Indiana. Coach Mallory hates the term swim.

Speed Rush

Define—We are a ball-key team. When the ball moves, we attack. That is a speed rush. If it is a run, I must adjust as I attack the line of scrimmage. If it is a pass, I must execute a pass-rush move on the run. That is a speed rush.

- Principles
  - ✓ Elongated step
  - ✓ Cloth grab
  - ✓ Breakdown
  - ✓ Move execution
- Get to the corner!

Pass-Rush Moves (Read and Speed)

(Both) indicates that you can use on read and speed rush.

- Rip (both)—At this time of the year, this is what we do in the weight room. We take weights or plates, because we do not have enough dumbbells. We use a drill we call 10 o'clock–2 o'clock. We take the weights in our palms and try to get the arms extended to 2 and 10 o'clock on the face of a clock. We want to get the arm under the man and drive it up through the man. They do three sets of eight reps. That is the way we work on the rip. The key point on the rip is to stay as close to the blocker's body as possible, stepping on the back of his heel on the backside.
- Slip (both)—You want to make it as tight to his body as possible. Again, on the read rush, this is off a pull on the low shoulder, or it is off the near shoulder on the speed rush. We are trying to rub paint with his body. We are going to be tight on the man.
- Bull (read)—If we get a man off balance so he can't get back on a power position, we will run him back to the quarterback. We will try to make the tackle with the blocker. It is a bull rush. We want to turn loose and go all out.
- Olé (read)—This is a move of the bull-rush move. It is a read situation. We are trying to take the momentum that the man is giving us and use it to get by him. We want to throw our elbow into our body tightly, spin on our foot, and pull him around. We want to pull the elbow into our body, so we have separation with him, and then redirect. We will finish with a rip move on the backside.
- Swat and hop (both)—This is a move we got from the Raiders. It is similar to the olé move. They are making a swat with the hand and a hop on the move. They are hopping into the line of scrimmage and going with an arm rip to the quarterback.

It is a good speed move. Most kids can execute it without any problems. You can install this when they are in shorts and T-shirts.

I have given you five moves. Most players will only use one or two moves. We do not practice some moves for some players.

Next, I want to discuss some countermoves for the read and speed rush. We have a Reggie move that we got from Reggie White of the Eagles. That is when you are stuck on a rip move. The off hand is very important. We want to take his momentum in the direction that he is taking us. I withdraw the rip move, get the inside hand on his hip, and widen the rush lane. It is a countermove off the rip move.

The whirling dervish is a spin move. I do not like the spin moves because you lose the sight of the quarterback. Most of the time, you give back the ground that you have already won when you spin. Some players can do it well. A lot of kids will spin back one way or the other naturally. If they are stuck on a rip move, they want to come back on a spin move. They want to sink the butt as quick as possible. They want to get the backside leg into the line of scrimmage as quickly as they can and as far as they can.

I want to quickly cover a couple of escape moves that we teach. The biggest thing we like to counteract is the arm clamp. We use the limp-arm slip. I will just call it limp arm over. Don't fight it any more, turn it limp, and then go to the slip on the backside. I like to use the rip move. Also, we like to use the lift-off move and the under/over moves.

Quick Hands

We use some drills with our hands. It is all of that kung fu stuff. All I am trying to do is to teach them to use their hands. They work well on the speed move. This is what we do against hands extended.

- Double club over—The blocker has his hands extended. We take the hands, go over the blocker's hands, and break his shoulders down. You have to get the hands to a slip move.
- Double club under—This is the same thing. Now, we bring the hands underneath the blocker's extended hands. Then, we do our rip move.
- Side club (left or right)—We club to the right or left side. We must step to the side we use the club on.
- Cross club (left or right)—This is a cross-over-the-body move. We cross over and step through. It is good move on the perimeter.

I want to close with some ideas on motivation. We have a slogan that we use to remind us that we need to motivate our players: "Push 'em, but pull 'em, too!" We give weekly awards and seasonal awards.

Motivation

- Get to the passer—Each week we have a get to the passer award. Also, we give this award to someone at the end of the year. It is a big deal for us.
- 50-sack board—We have a board that we use to keep track of the sacks. Our goal is to get 50 sacks. We keep this up to date and go over it every Monday in our meeting. It is a team award.
- Point systems (pressure pays)—We keep individual awards for the end of the year. There are some things you can do to reward the players. We get most of our information from the film.

Point System

- Sacks
- Hurries
- Pull-downs
- Flushes
- Tipped balls
- Caused interception
- Making a pass or run = no 1st down
- Caused a penalty (hold, clip, face mask, etc.)

We give them a point value for each of the goals. We value each of these goals before the start of the season. We assign one, two, or three points for each of the good plays. They can lose points if they make a bad play.

14

Defensive Line Techniques

Vince Okruch
Northwestern University
1996

What I would like to do today is go through a format that will cover all the questions you might have. What I am going to do today is identical to what I do with our players each spring and fall.

The first thing I believe is you have to have some kind of philosophy. When I came to Northwestern, the respect we had there was minimal. They had gone through a number of losing seasons. Each year, we remind our players that there is a certain amount of respect that they have to earn from their opponents. Our guys had to force the teams in the Big Ten to respect them. We came up with a term called respect the hat. This was a motivational tool. We put a Northwestern helmet on the wall so that each day the players went to practice, they could see that hat and know there should be respect sent their way. In order to get the philosophy worked out, we thought there were five areas we had to improve in:

- Mental and physical toughness
- Physical shape and condition
- Intensity
- Pride
- Demanding as coaches

In order to do those things, we felt there were other things to consider. We felt we had to be in great physical condition. It is hard to be tough, intense, or demanding if you are not in shape.

The first thing we did was to start our off-season conditioning. If you are not physically ready to play, none of this other stuff will matter. I'm not talking about talent. If you looked around the Big Ten, you wouldn't find Northwestern at the top, as far as talent. Talent has nothing to do with physical condition.

There has to be a great desire to play. I want our defensive linemen to play like their hair is on fire. I don't care whether it is four, eight, or 10 snaps. While they are on the field, I want them playing like they are crazy. The best way I found to achieve that is to play more than one guy at a spot. Which would you rather have in a critical situation, a first-teamer who has played 45 or 50 snaps or a fresh second-teamer? I don't think there is going to be a whole lot of difference.

The other thing we had to change was the attitude. That is the most demanding thing we had to do. There is an old saying that goes, "Whether you think you can or can't, you're right." We inherited a program where there were a lot of bad thoughts. Everyone wanted to look behind. One of the first things Coach Barnett stressed from day one was we were going to look forward.

There are some things the coach and player can do to make this philosophy work. The coach has to be enthusiastic. If you are not happy with what you are doing, you can make a lot more money with the hours you spend doing something else. I can't wait each day to get on the field. I hate sitting in that meeting and film room. I just want to get on the field, get somebody to move the ball, and let things fall where they may. The coach has to transfer that to his players, especially those players who are playing in those trenches. It is tough in there, if you are not excited about it. How are they going to get excited about getting hit in the face 65 times in a game? I think the coach has to be demanding. We tell our players, if they will allow us, we are going to take them somewhere they couldn't take themselves. We will force them beyond their normal range of capabilities. The third thing the coach has to be is positive. That is the hardest thing for me. When the score is Notre Dame 45, Northwestern 3, it is hard to be positive. The players are not going out there and intentionally not doing what you ask them to do. If the coach stays positive, they'll do the best they can to stay positive.

As players, they have to do their job. We have a competitive chart. Anytime we do something competitive, we grade it. It doesn't matter whether it is practice, scrimmage, or game. That is how we measure whether the player is doing his job. I think everyone has had the guy that looks the part. He lifts the weights, runs great times, and looks like a football player. When he gets on the field, you find out he has played a whole game and made one tackle. Then, you've got this guy who is thirty pounds underweight, looks like he's never been close to a weight room, and looks bad. But, put him on the field, and something happens. We play the guys that make something happen. I don't have to answer another question when a guy comes in and wants to know why he is not playing more. All I do is pull out his competitive chart and show it to him. You can use this as an evaluation tool for yourself as well as the player.

We tell our players it is a team game. Up front, we are a reduction defense. This defense is as old as they come. We reduce one side or the other. Our defensive linemen try to make plays. But, their most important job is to make sure the linebackers can flow to the football. The coach has to convey to the defensive linemen, and they have to buy into it. We had a linebacker this year played nine games, won the award for the nation's best defensive player, and probably not a coach in here would have recruited him. He was our team captain, leader on defense, and does a great job. All we had to do in the defensive line was to make sure the guards and center could not get to the second level. If they don't get there, that linebacker would make the play. Sometimes, that meant the noseguard had to sacrifice himself in the double-team. Our defensive linemen have to know where they fit in with our scheme of defense. We are not like the Miami Hurricanes, who attack, flatten out, redirect, and make the play. We don't have those kinds of people. I know, if our tackles and noseguard will keep the offensive blocker on or around the line of scrimmage or consume two blocks, our linebacker will make plays.

The players have to be their own unique personality within the team system. I don't want a bunch of robots. About 90 percent of the guys are going to have an earring. That used to fry me. Now, if they want to wear an earring, that's okay with me. The new thing now is a tattoo. They wear them on their arms or legs. Who knows what they are going to have cut in their hair or how they are going to trim their face? I don't care. What they have to understand is their unique personality stops at the sideline. When they go onto the field, they are part of a team.

There are nine musts of defensive line play. We work in phases. My players must understand these things. Let me go through these with you, because this has been my format for teaching everywhere I've been. The first three are grouped together: one, alignment, two, assignment, three, get-off. These three musts are mental. The alignment is basic to any defense. Without proper alignment, the soundness of the defense goes out the window. The second thing is assignment. If we are not moving the defense on a stunt, then our assignment is a shade technique. We are going to play base defense about 85 percent of the time. Understanding the assignment is critical to the defense. The last thing that is mental is the get-off. Some guys try to tell me that somebody should have a faster get-off because he is faster. I don't buy that. I tell them there is a string from the end of their nose to the football. When the football moves, that should pull them forward. I believe, to be effective on defense, the defensive line has to get off on the snap and go full speed through their responsibility. I spend an awful lot of time on get-off drills. We do it on bags, air, sled, in the chute, moving left and right, and on the ball. I believe that once the ball moves we become an aggressive attacking defense. I don't think you can work it enough. When they start to move slowly, that is a mental thing. They have allowed something else to get into their head. They are tired or something else.

Those three factors should not determine who plays and who doesn't. Everyone in this room knows their right from their left. They know a 1 and 3 technique. They know what coming off the ball full speed is. When the ball moves, they move.

The next three musts are ability related: four, hand placement, five, face placement, six, read. These factors can be improved with practice and training. We work a tremendous amount of time on hands in the proper place. We want to work into the pectorals, with our thumbs up, and try to get full extension. I can guarantee, if you don't get either hand into the offensive blocker, you are done. If you get one hand in, the defender has a chance. If the defender can get both hands inside, he can control the blocker regardless of the size or strength of that blocker.

The next thing is face placement. When I talk about that, there is some athletic director getting nervous. I know everyone has heard that using the head is wrong because of the neck injuries. I think if you don't teach where to put the face, I think we are wrong as coaches. I have a great drill I'll show you later about face placement. I teach them where their face should fit. They have to keep their face up to see. With the face up, that is the safest position for the neck. When I say work this, we are talking about every day.

The third part is the read. This has a lot of ability tied into it. To teach the read, we try to give them as many repetitions as we can. We work key drill, half-line drills, and group run situations.

The last three are seven, escape, eight, pursuit, and, nine, tackling. We teach that those things are tied into effort. If the defender gets blocked and uses all the techniques he has been taught, there still comes a point in time when the defender has to get off the block and make something happen.

I believe that most of that is effort. I know you guys have coached players who are always around the ball. You are not quite sure how they get off the blocks, but they are always around the ball.

We grade our pursuit in every competitive phase of practice. When I grade pursuit, if one of the down linemen is not in the frame of film when the ball stops, he gets a minus. If he shows up in that frame somewhere, he gets a plus.

We have a tenth must we talk about. The bottom line is they, ten, have to find a way to win. All the other things will help them win and become a successful lineman, but the ultimate goal is to win the ball game.

Let me go through these nine musts in a little more detail. When we talk about alignment, we talk about stance. We are a three-point stance team. We play with our inside foot back and our inside hand down. If I am on the left side, I am in a right-handed stance with my right foot in a heel to toes stagger. We believe the strength of the defense is from the belly out. That is why we step with our inside foot and never get turned out. There is always a collision point, and we are moving the inside part of our body into whatever shade we have. If we can make you run left and right instead of north and south, we have a chance to run you down.

It is difficult for right-handed guys to play on the left side. We start our right-handed in four-point stances until they become comfortable in the left-handed stance. All our drill work is done from a right- and left-handed stance. We feel by doing that we give them the opportunity to play out of a left-handed stance.

Our technique alignment is numbered just like our gaps. The guard-center gap is called the 1 gap. A lot of people call it the A gap. The guard-tackle is the 3 gap. The techniques are 1, 3, or 5, left and right. That is all they have to know.

The next must is assignment. The 3 technique player is responsible for the 3 gap. The 5 technique player has the 5 gap, and the 1 technique player has the 1 gap. We play with a tilted noseguard. That seems to drive centers crazy. I have no idea why, but it does. The noseguard's aiming point is the ear hole of the center's helmet. He is trying to fit himself into the "V" of the center's neck. The one thing the noseguard has to do is make sure the center does not leave the line of scrimmage. If the center is trying to scoop the noseguard with the backside guard, that can't happen. The noseguard cannot allow the backside guard to take him over. If the backside guard comes off for the linebacker, we feel the linebacker can fight through that. But, if the center gets off the noseguard, he can wall the linebacker back. As the ball is snapped, the noseguard goes right through the center's ear hole. If the center tries to leave the line of scrimmage, the noseguard holds him there. If he has to, he grabs him. Most of those officials can't see that.

We do all our get-off on movement. Anytime you are working any drill, take a football with you. I've tried using an orange football to highlight the ball. I have used a football cut in half so I could keep it with me at all times. I've done lots of things. Use any method you can to get them to come off on the movement of the ball. As the movement of the get-off comes, they must start to read the offensive lineman's hat. I want them to see the ball and the snubber on the helmet. The snubber is that area of the helmet where the team name or the maker of the headgear goes. I want to know if the snubber came straight at him. Did it go inside like a veer release? Did it take my outside shoulder like a reach block, or did it come straight up like a pass block? Every time you do these drills, take a football with you. If you are going to ask them to move off of that during a game, do it in practice. Moving your foot or a cap is not the same thing.

In the attack phase of our technique, we step with the inside foot to avoid being turned out. It also helps us to maintain good leverage. I'll talk about the drills later. When we step and attack, we read on the run. We are moving on the ball and reading the hat of the offensive blocker as we get into our assignments.

On the hand placement, we want to get into the upper pecs of the offensive blocker. Even though the offensive blocker may have a longer reach, if the defender can get his hands inside first, he can control the blocker. It is that simple. Whoever gets the inside has control.

We talk about thumbs up. Our strength coaches tell us you have more strength with your thumbs in the turned up position. I fit them on the sled with their thumbs in proper position. We try to get the hand on the pecs, with the thumbs up, and grab cloth. By grabbing the cloth, the defender can steer the shoulders. If he can get the blocker's lead shoulder turned, there is no back in America who will try to outrun that. If he does, he is not going to gain much ground.

When we teach the face placement, we are thinking about safety. We want the face placed so that it is up. That is the safest position, and they can see. We have drills to teach the placement of the face. I'll show you those later.

The read phase requires a tremendous amount of drilling. There was a coach at Eastern Illinois about 15 years ago who did a study for his doctoral on skills. He went out to Stanford University to do these physiological studies. He found out that when a person does some physical skill, it takes 250,000 repetitions to become familiar with that skill. The shocking part about this is that to master or perfect a skill you must do that skill one million times. We tell our kids that, and they think they are going to hit the sled for months, nonstop. We are trying to tell them that there is no substitute for repetition. We are very fortunate to have the Chicago Bear headquarters very close to our campus. I have gone up there and watched their practices a number of times. I've watched Chris Zorich. When the first team is not involved in a team drill, he is hitting the sled. He does it over and over again. There is no substitute for repetition. We teach the read with repetition. We are trying to key the hat and tell which way it is going.

The purpose of the get-off, hand placement, head placement, and the read are to gain separation and get off a block. If the defender cannot separate himself from the offensive linemen, he can't make any tackles. Without separation, the defender cannot have success. The defender has to get off the block as quickly as he can. We want to escape and make the ball redirect as fast as possible. We like to use the terms shed and spill. When we spill, we are going across the ball. When we shed, we are going to the ball. It is terminology. If he shed, that means he maintained his shade and never crossed the blocker. If he spilled, he crossed the blocker. This only helps us in the movement of our linemen when we know what they did.

Pursuit is a want-to thing. The thing you can coach is a proper angle to the ball. We do pursuit drills every single day. We want to get all eleven hats to the football. I heard some coach say, "A defensive player's importance to his team was directly related to his distance from the ball." That is a very profound statement. That is in my meeting room. It is hard for big guys to do these pursuit drills. That is where the effort comes in.

When we talk about movement, we use the term rip. All of our movement involves a rip technique. A rip technique to us is a lateral step, dip, and rip. We want to give our people three ways to go. When we face an opponent, we want to be able to move our defenders to the outside or inside or play base. I don't believe you can play an entire football game in base defense and survive. As big as offensive linemen are, you have to move on them. If you don't move on them and keep them on their heels, you will have a long day. We move quite a bit, and it helps us. We don't do it with a slant technique. We do it with a lateral step. We try to maintain our shade technique. We dip our shoulders and rip up with the arm, just like a pass rush. We are working for penetration. When we take our lateral step, the defender wants to key the next offensive linemen. If I'm a 3 technique man, as I take my lateral step to the outside, I want to see the tackle. If the tackle is running away from the defender, he rips through the gap and goes for penetration. He knows the play is coming his way. If the defender takes the lateral step and the tackle is coming down on the scoop, he redirects and pursues the other way. We have a rip and redirect drill that we do about 10 to 15 minutes a day. We don't do this drill full go every day.

In our practice progression, there are three phases. The first phase is a teaching phase. We are in full pads. It is not an off period. It is not a joke-around time, but it is a teaching period. The second phase is a work phase. During this period, we hit the sled and do drill work, pursuit drills, and things like that. The intensity during this period goes up. The last phase is a competitive phase. During this period, we have scrimmages and high competitive drills. During these periods, we want to have a winner. Any competitive phase is filmed and graded. You can't go the whole practice with the teaching phase because it is too low key. You can't go the whole practice with the competitive phase because you would kill them. We work out a practice that is reasonable to accomplish what we want.

One of the things we do for tackling is a little drill with a bag. We use one of those hand-held bags. The dummy holds the bag in front of him to give the tackler a target.

The tackler comes toward him. This is not a full-speed drill. It is a half-speed drill to teach tackling. As the tackler gets about a step away from the player being tackled, the player drops the bag. The tackler has to dip, roll his hips, and squeeze that bag. What that does is eliminate the guys from throwing too quick. We were taught not to throw until you could step on his toes. This drill teaches us to get close before they throw. The guys we have to tackle are generally better athletes than the tackler. If we don't get that close, we don't have a chance to get a hold on him. We also do like everyone else. We teach the wrap-up, grab cloth, keep the feet moving, and follow through.

The last section of this outline deals with pass rush. We blended some of the 4-3 package into our scheme this year. Our pass rush was so poor we needed help. Poor is probably too nice a term. We were bad. In pass situations, we have gone to an even scheme and a nickel package.

In the pass rush, we believe there are two phases. There is the power or bull rush and the speed rush. We teach both kinds of rushes. If we are an outside rusher, about 90 percent of the time, we are trying to rush around the corner. We try to beat the fat tackle back to where the quarterback is going to set. We teach our inside guys the power or bull rush. We use a number of moves in their rush technique. We teach a, one, rip, two, quick rip, three, swim, four, quick swim, five, push/pull, six, club/counter, and, seven, spin/counter. We teach all these moves in training camp. But, I know, with a guy who is 5-11 and 280 pounds, chances of swimming are not good. He can't get his arm up high enough to make a difference. The same thing is true of a 6-7 guy. He probably can't use the rip move. After we teach all these things, we try to get them to focus in on one move. If you watch the great pass rushers on Sunday, you see them do the same thing over and over again. They do it so well that they believe the man blocking them can't block them. We want them to focus on one move and a counter for that move. Trying to do all these moves is not productive. They need to master one move and the counter to it. We also tell them in the pass rush the most important time when they are going to decide what move to use is when the secondary calls third-and-eight just as we break the defensive huddle. They can't wait until they get in their stance to decide what pass rush they are going to use. When they know it is a passing situation, they have to decide. If they wait until the snap of the ball, it's too late.

When you scout your opponents this year, put a clock on the quarterback. Find out how much time it takes him to throw the ball. We found out that if the rusher was going to affect the throw, he has to be in the area of the quarterback in 2.5 seconds. If they are not there in three seconds, they don't have a chance. If it takes longer than that, someone is going to come open. What I do each day when we go pass rush with the offensive linemen is take a pass rush. We put a center in the drill to actually snap the ball. When that ball moves, I start the clock. We record the time, so that when we watch the tape the next day, we will know if we are getting the job done. That does two things. It forces a sense of urgency. It makes them held accountable for what they are trying to do. What really helped me was the fact that a lot of guys don't realize it is taking them that long to get to the quarterback. They may think they are good pass rushers until you show them the time.

Let me put on a practice schedule and show you how we do this. The first thing we have is a specialty period. I am on the field, and our guys can come down and work on anything they want. We stretch for 10 minutes and then go to PATs. The next period is what we call a cat period. During that period, we do a strip drill for 10 minutes. I have one guy face another player. One player tackles the other, and the third guy comes in and strips the ball. After that, we come together as a defense and do the pursuit drill. The pursuit drill we did this day was the cone drill. We placed cones on the numbers, pitched the ball to one side or the other, and made the defense take proper pursuit angles to the sidelines. We come back in the first drill and do a key drill. The key drill for us is a half-line drill or an inside-3 drill. We take the center and two guards with two tackles and the middle linebacker or a half-line against the one side of the defense. We work good on good. The next thing we to is the butt and bench. That is the face and hand placement drill. We work on stunts and pass rush in the next two periods. The next period we work against the blocking scheme we are going to face. After that, we go to 10 minutes of group run. Next, we go to 10 minutes of pass rush. We follow that with work against the offensive line. There, we work full-line twists. After that, we have a team period, followed by a pup period. The pup stands for pass under pressure. We work all our blitzes against our offense. We go good on good. We finish up with the team in a scrimmage. That is pretty much how we run our practice.

Let me go through some of our drills. The first drill is our get-off drill. We take two guys and put them down in a tilt and 3 technique. I find out the cadence of our opponent that week. Most of the time, you can find that out. The defense is required to say a color when they come up and get down. We try and get a key out of the offensive linemen's stance. Our guys can tell sometimes whether a guy is going to pull by the amount of weight he has on his hand. We call red for run and green for pass. What is amazing is when the 3 technique gives a run call and the tilt gives a pass call. That means we probably are going to get a counter. After they give me the call, they have to go through the appropriate steps. I call the cadence and try to draw them offside by using a hard count. We change sides and tilts to make them get in both right- and left-handed stances. We also do this drill in the cage to keep them low.

To teach players to step with their inside foot, we put them on one knee on a sled. We give them movement and make them contact the sled. They can do it if they don't step with their inside foot. We make them contact the sled with their thumbs up into the pecs area. After we do the drill off one knee, we come back and do it full speed into the sled. They are still stepping with their inside foot and punching out with their hands.

The next drill is the butt and bench drill. The offense and defense are across from one another on their knees. The offense simply falls forward. The defense has to roll his hips and punch out with his hands. We are checking hand and head placement. Our guys hate to do this drill. All we are trying to do in the beginning is to get him used to headgear coming at him. As the drill goes on, the offense will fall to the left or right of the defense so the defense can see the helmet move as an inside block. This is the teaching phase of the drill. When the offense falls inside and outside, the defense tries to steer the shoulder of the offense. The end of the drill gets their attention. With the defensive man still on his knees, I put the offensive man in a three-point stance and get him to run over the defensive man. They give you a funny look the first time you do this. What it forces the guy on the ground to do is roll his hips and get full extension. If he doesn't, he gets run over.

We use a quick-hand drill. Sometimes, we do it at the start of practice and sometimes at the end. They are getting in a stance and getting their hands from the ground to the pads as quickly as possible. We don't coach hip rotation or punch. We coach quick hands.

Another drill we use to help with the pass rush is the hoop drill. You can make these hoops from electrical conduit or pool vacuum hoses. You need about 18 feet of hose. Make them into a circle. If you use the electrical stuff, you will need about three sections. You just lay them on the ground and have your guys run around them. You can make a game out of it. Make them go as fast as they can round the hoop. Make them run figure eights around two of them. What this does is let them practice the speed rush. At some point, the rusher has to get to the quarterback. If the offensive lineman backs up, he will run the rusher deep. At some point during the rush, the defender has to turn the corner and get to the quarterback. This drill helps him master the turn at the end of the speed rush.

15

Defensive End Play

Charlie Partridge
University of Pittsburgh
2005

It is an honor to get to talk to you. As I go to more and more clinics, I realize the things I hear only reaffirm what I am coaching.

We play with a 6-technique defensive end. He is head up the tight end and is a C-gap player. The 5 technique starts to vary as we align in different calls. The 5-technique player's toe is shaded on the offensive lineman's near toe.

The 3-technique player is toe-to-toe on the offensive guard. The nose is in a toe-to-toe alignment on the opposite guard or inside shade in a 2i. I want to give names to alignments or stunts that have recall value for the players. We have a technique called a "slope 5 technique." This is a slightly tilted technique on the offensive tackle. It is an alignment to get the defender to his pressure key. He aligns his hand five inches outside the foot of the offensive tackle. We should be able to draw a straight line from the defenders tail pad straight through his spine to that outside point of the offensive tackle.

We adjust all the techniques from their straight alignments. We have a slope, closed, and a tight 5 technique. That gets us beyond the simple 5 technique in the outside shade.

In our pre-snap progression, we want the players to know down and distance. We want them to know the personnel and formation in the game. We try to read the stance of offensive linemen.

When the defense is aligning and getting ready for the play, the defenders call out colors to each other. If the defender sees two linemen aligned with their weight back in their stance, they call "blue." That alerts everyone that it could be a pass play. If the defender reads a heavy stance by the linemen, they call "red." That is the alert call for run. The "yellow" call alerts a pull technique for the guard. That is when we read heavy alignment to one side and light to the other. The colors are based on the offensive linemen's alignment and body language.

We have a key progression. The first thing we key is the ball. Our next key depends on where we align. The defender has a primary and a secondary offensive lineman key. If he is a 6-technique player, his first key is the ball. Once the ball is snapped, he transfers his eyes from the ball to the inside plate of the tight end. The inside plate is the inside half of the player. He does that as he steps upfield. His primary key is the inside plate of the tight end and his secondary key has to be the offensive tackle. The tight end is his pressure key and he should be able to feel him. If the tight end and offensive tackle are working a combination block on the 6-technique, he feels the pressure from the end and sees the offensive tackle.

If there is no pressure from the primary key, the 6 technique's eyes should focus to the inside. The hands are another set of eyes. The third element of the key progression is the scheme used by the offensive blockers.

I need to back up a bit and talk about stance. The stance of the defensive linemen affects the get-off and his steps as he comes off the ball. A lineman with a narrow stance steps out on the first step instead of up the field. If his stance is too narrow, widen him so he can get off the ball and get up the field. We want them in a shoulder-width stance with a toe to mid-foot stagger. We want them in a shoulder-width stance so they do not take big steps coming out of the stance.

The down hand in the stance is in front of the back foot. If he puts his hand down in the center of his body, the stance is twisted. Putting the down hand in front of the back foot squares the stance. Do not create a tripod with the down hand. Reach out with the hand so that 75-percent of the weight is on the hand. That helps the defenders get off the ball.

The defensive linemen want to take two short steps coming off the ball. The first step is a direction step and the second step is a set step. We want to get both steps back on the ground as quickly as possible. They do not react to the scheme until the third step. If a defensive lineman takes long steps, he gets reached. The third step is the reaction step and is based on blocking scheme.

Instead of talking gap responsibility, we talk lines and plates. I teach the 6-technique end he has the inside plate of the tight end. That is how I begin to teach responsibility. The end is not worried about a gap; he is thinking inside plate of the tight end.

The 5-technique end on the open side of the set spills any blocker that comes at him. The problem is when the defender gets too far upfield and has to turn to get under blocks coming at him. The way we avoid getting upfield is by "chasing plates." His pressure key is the outside plate of the offensive tackle. If the offensive tackle blocks to the inside, the defensive end chases the plate to the inside. That puts him under all blocks coming at him. He has to work on the bootleg coming his way but we teach running straight lines and chasing plates as his get-off technique.

When we talk to our defensive end about pass rush, we talk about straight lines to the quarterback. We do not want them to arc and get off the straight-line attack. I know when they use pass rushing techniques such as spins, they get off the straight-line concept, but they must try to rush in lines.

The next fundamental we work on is the hands. The punch with the hands has to be an eye level punch. When players first start to punch, their mistake is punching too low. The elbows are in and the thumbs are up in the punch. When you punch, do not expose the chest. The weight room is a great aid for the hand punches. We have a great strength coach. Everything he does in the weight room is truly football-oriented.

Instead of bench press, he does dumbbell presses. He does one arm at a time and turns the weight at the end to simulate the punch. He uses a medicine ball punch drill to work on the linemen's punch. Two players partner-up and use the medicine ball drill. They sit on benches opposite each other and throw the medicine ball at one another. One player chest passes the ball to the other player. As the ball comes to him, he uses his punch on the ball. The strength coach does all kinds of drills that carry over to the football field. They are simple drills but make sense. He also does some position pattern running designed for particular groups. Everything he does in the weight room tries to build good habits and ingrain skills.

I have some drills that you can do in the off-season. This first one looks like a linebackers drill, but it works on the hand punch (Figure 15-1). We set up four tube dummies and put a defensive end on one side and a simulator with a hand dummy on the other side.

The dummy holder and end start in a two-point stance. They enter the first chute and approach one another. The end delivers a punch with both hands locks out and drives the dummy holder out of the chute. They retreat into a backpedal and enter the second chute and do the same thing. He slides to the third chute and repeats the drill. The emphasis in the drill is hand explosion and knee bend. We want the elbows in and

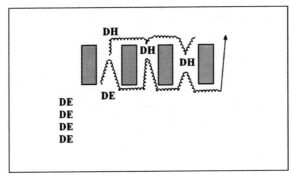

Figure 15-1. Punch drill

the thumbs up in the hand explosion. The defensive end bends at the knees and not the waist.

We do board drills to help the defender focus on keeping his base. We do the drill like a board drill with a dummy holder on one end of the board and a defender on the other end. They move onto the board and the defensive end punches the dummy, locks out, and drives the dummy off the board. The punch is the same as the in the punch drill. The emphasis in this drill is to keep the base wide so you maintain stability. This helps us in playing blocks. When blocks start to move, this helps keep our base and not cross over in our footwork.

We do the same drill in a partner drill. We fit the defender on the offensive player. He places his hands on the chest of the offensive blocker. On a command, the defensive player snaps his hips and locks out on the offensive lineman. He moves him back five yards in the locked out position. They switch roles and go the other way. We do the drill twice looking for the full body snap.

To teach punch, we use a punch progression drill to emphasize what we expect. We can start players on their own by aligning them around the wall in a weight room or workout room. The players get down on their knees and punch out into the wall. This is nothing but an upper body shoulder punch. That gets them ready for the explosion drill by working the punch part from their knees. The next part of the progression is to get the defender into a six-point stance against a dummy.

To start the drill, we lift the toes off the ground and snap just the hips exploding into the dummy. From there we ground out the toes and do the six-point explosion drill. When they explode, they do not rock back on their heels and come forward. They sink their hips and explode with the hips behind the shoulders. From that position, we get into a three-point stance and explode with one step.

After the player goes through the progression with the repetitions he needs at each position, he begins to see where his power comes from. From the one-step explosion, we get them into a two-step punch on a wall.

Another drill we use is a ball drill. When a defensive player plays in a game, he is not punching a wall; he is punching a moving target (Figure 15-2). This drill works on that concept. The players get into a three-point stance aligned on a ball on a stick. The ball on the stick is for the get-off. The medicine ball is for the punch. This helps the players train their eyes to hit a moving target. The eyes take his hands to the target. As soon as the ball on the stick moves, the medicine ball is rolled at the defender. The defender gets out of his stance and punches the ball. If the ball is rolled inside that is where he attacks the ball.

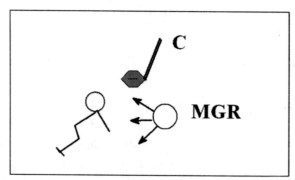

Figure 15-2. Medicine ball punch

The next drill is the "sumo drill." This is a drill that emphasizes hand battles. This is a partner drill. We have two defensive linemen facing one another. They get in a good bent-kneed position with their heads back. One player gets his hand inside on the other player's chest. The opponent has his hands outside the other player's hands. On the command "go," the players try to get the inside hand position and push the other player backward. We do not want the drill to turn. We want it to go straight back as the players work for inside hand position while moving their feet.

This is a competitive drill and best done with the headgear off. If you take the helmet off, the players are less likely to use their heads to butt the other player.

The next drill is a "get-off bag carry drill." In this drill, we have someone hold an agility bag opposite the defensive player. As the defensive player gets off, he punches and makes contact with the agility bag. He grabs the bag and carries it five yards up the field. The focus is getting off the ball and shooting his hands. If the bag were not in the drill, it becomes a five-yard get-off drill. We want concentration on hand placement. We make sure when we work get-off that we get something in front of them to work their hands and feet.

You can do the next drill any number of ways. You can use an old mattress, a high-jump pad, or a stack of tumbling mats. Have the defender take one or two steps and lunge forward on the landing pad. That gives the player a complete extension of his legs, through his hips, and behind his shoulders.

We have a simple "get-off and react drill." The defender aligns on the line of scrimmage with the get-off ball. I stand five yards away from the defender. As the ball moves, the defender charges off the ball and attacks toward the coach. I give him a right, left, screen, or draw call and he reacts accordingly to the command.

Make sure you show your players how the skills they work on in drills apply to game situations. Use game films to illustrate the skills they work on in drills. If you do not, they will not work hard in drill work. They have to know what they are doing can be used in a game.

We do all kinds of drill in the chutes. You can invent anything that has an application to game situations. We work our line stunt games through the chute. We do straight get-off drills. We line a defensive lineman on the pole of the chute and let him cross face an offensive blocker. That keeps him low and attacking with his shoulders forward. In all the drills you do in the chute, the theme is the same. You want them to work with their pad level down low.

Another drill we do is "closed-eye pressure drill." We do the drill as a one-on-one or two-on-one drill. We tell the players they have two sets of eyes. They have a set of eyes in their head and a set of eyes in their hands. In the 6 technique on the snap of the ball, the defender steps with his inside foot. He gets his hands on the inside plate of the tight end and feel the pressure coming from the tight end. The hands on the tight end are his first set of eyes.

He feels the pressure from the pressure key and turns his eyes inside to see if the tackle is coming out to try to overtake the end's block. He feels the pressure and sees the blocker. If the tight end releases, the defender focuses inside on the tackle. He reads the tackle in the pass-blocking mode and gets into his pass rush.

In the "closed-eye drill," the defender gets into a fit position with the blocker. On a "go" command, the offensive blocker simulates a block, release, or some kind of line maneuver. The defender has his eyes closed, plays the pressure key, and fights the resistance. When he feels the pressure of the block, the defender pushes and pulls to escape the block. We do this every day.

We work the "hoops" with a wrinkle in the drill. We put a simulator in the middle of the hoops with a hand dummy. The hoops are five to six yards in diameter (Figure 15-3). We want the defender to try to cut the circle off, but the simulator will not let them. He is banging the hoops runner as he goes around the hoop. The simulator has to work hard in the drill to make the defender work hard. The defender gets in his stance and gets-off. He gets his hands into the simulators dummy and works his charge. If the defender can turn early, he will. The hoop is there to give him a mental concept of what we are doing. If he can turn the simulator and run right through the middle of the hoop, we consider that a great job by the defender.

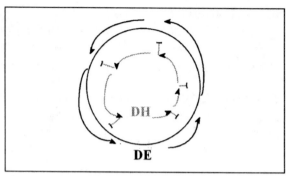

Figure 15-3. Hoops drill

This drill is the "catch drill." It teaches the defender to get off on the movement of the offensive lineman and catch him as quickly as possible. The offensive lineman has a defender about one-yard-and-half in front of him. We have a shirt five yards behind the offensive lineman. The offensive lineman retreats in his pass set. The defender gets off the ball and has to catch the offensive lineman before he gets to the five-yard cutoff point.

We tell the defender where his shade is on the offensive lineman so he can make contact with the proper plate on the lineman's body. When the defender gets to the plate, he has to execute some kind of escape move on the offensive lineman. He can use a push, pull, rip, or whatever you have taught him to escape the pass block.

I want to get into some pass-rush drills. We start with a "one hand mover." The defender puts one hand behind his back. As he gets into the offensive blocker, the blocker starts to fire random hand shots with one hand at a time to the body of the defender. The defender uses his one hand to knock off as many of the offensive blocker punches as he can while working around the corner of the blocker.

We continue the drill except the defender uses both hands to ward off the punches of the blocker as he works around to the outside. The next part of the drill is similar, except the offensive block shoots both hands at the defender. The defender tries to grab the wrist of the offensive block and gain control of the blocker's wrist.

From the wrist control, we teach them a move called "airplane." These are individual moves. The players can work on them all the time. In the airplane move, the defender grabs the wrists of the offensive blocker. He splits the hands by pushing his outside hand high and his inside hand low. He forms the wings of the airplane. He gets his body on the offensive lineman's body and releases the inside hand as he steps with his outside foot. When he releases the inside wrist he gets back on the line to the quarterback.

Another move is the "heart pick." The defender attacks the blocker and attempts to grab the wrists. He gets the outside wrist but misses the inside wrist. With the inside hand, he punches the offensive blocker in the chest and pulls with the outside hand so he can step through to the outside. When the offensive lineman pulls his hand back, he opens his hips and gives the defender a great line to the quarterback. Even if you cannot gain control of both wrists, as the offensive lineman start to panic, he opens the gate for the defender.

Once you teach the players a few moves, put them in a "gauntlet drill" (Figure 15-4). You do not need to teach ten moves to every player. They cannot use them all and will not be able to do some of them effectively. They pick two to three moves and prefect them. Once your players learn and become good at a couple of moves, it is all they need. I like to use people holding dummies instead of just dummies. Have the defenders work through three dummies using a different pass-rush move on each dummy. At the end of the gauntlet drill, we make them perform a form tackle on a simulator as the quarterback.

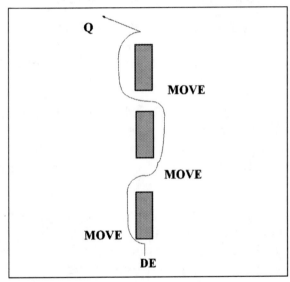

Figure 15-4. Gauntlet drill

When I first learned these moves, I thought there would be no way our players would pick them up. I did not think they would be able to execute these moves, but I was wrong. When we taught these moves to our players, they started to understand a concept of how they could control the body of an offensive lineman. The first move is the "samurai rip." As the offensive lineman starts to punch the defender, the defender grabs the blocker's outside elbow two feet in front of his torso with his outside hand.

The offensive blocker will try to pull the arm back. The defender wants to hold on to the elbow and rip with his inside arm. The blocker's body will start to turn and open the defender to the quarterback. When the defender gets his inside triceps on the blocker's outside triceps, the deal is over.

The "samurai swim" is the same concept. The defender grabs the blocker's elbow two feet in front of his torso. The blocker's upper body goes down as the defender gains control of the elbow. The defender takes the inside arm and swims over the blocker's outside shoulder and gets on the line to the quarterback.

On the "samurai bull," the defender tries to grab both elbows. When he gets control of the elbows, he tries to drive them back into the shoulder blades. The same thing can happen with a combination punch. If he only gets one elbow, he uses a heart pick, and tries to throw the elbow over the blocker's helmet. If you get body position and control of the blocker's upper body, you can do anything you want to him. It is not a matter of strength.

In our pass rush, we take what the offensive linemen give us. If they let us get into their upper plate, we bull rush through the blocker. If they try to punch, we use whatever works for us. Some players work on the wrists and others work on elbows.

If the blocker gives the defender his head by leaning forward to butt the defender, he uses that momentum to pull him forward. He grabs his jersey or wrists and reaches for his back plates. He opens his hips, pulls the blocker forward, and goes around him.

The defensive linemen read all different types of pass sets. If the blocker sets in a short pass set, it is one of two things. It is either a hot or quick pass, or a draw play. We want to squeeze the blocker into our gap and get our hands up if the play is a pass. If the play is a draw play, we do not want to run up the field on a short set. That is what the offense wants us to do. If we get the short set, we squeeze then respond to the play.

If the blocker short sets and releases, we play the wide receiver screen or a short screen to the back. If the blocker deep sets and tries to cut the defender late, bend the knees and play off the block. Retrace your steps back to the line of scrimmage because the play is some type of slip screen or wide receiver screen.

We practice under moves all the time. We want to use the under move at the same depth of the quarterback. If you are not at the depth of the quarterback, do not take the under move. When the offensive lineman turns his shoulder parallel to the sideline, he is in trouble. As long as the lineman has his butt to the quarterback, it is hard to get under because he is in control. When he turns his butt to the sideline, the defender takes one more step upfield and works under the blocker. We use the "hump move." Reggie White made that move famous. It does not require tremendous strength. You use the momentum of the offensive lineman to keep him moving the way he is going. Use the inside hand, throw the blocker upfield, and rip underneath. You can use the heart pick and rip underneath. They both are the same concept.

Another move your player can use is an outside spin. The rusher plants on his outside foot, sinks the hips, throws the outside arm, and gets himself to the quarterback. However, do not use this move until the rusher is at the depth of the quarterback.

When we get into pass-rush scheme, we have to decide what types of protections the offense is using. Most teams slide the center one way and use man protection the other way with the back reading the linebackers for blitzes. We focus on which way the center turns before we decide which games we want to run. We chart the center's movement. We chart him to or away from the running back. He could go toward or away from a tight end set. The other two checks we make are to the field or to the passing strengths.

In our pass-rush games, if we read run the game is off. If we run the "me" game (Figure 15-5), the defensive end takes two steps up the field, plants on the outside foot, and drives underneath the offensive tackle. When you run stunts, you cannot have a selfish attitude. On this stunt, the end is trying to free up the tackle. As the defensive end comes underneath the offensive tackle, there could be separation between the guard and tackle, which means man-to-man blocking. If the guard and tackle come toward, they are blocking zone and will pass the stunt off from one to the other. If they come toward, the end grabs the tackle/guard, and holds on. We hope the defensive tackle gets around to the outside and gets the sack. If there is a hole and the tackle is chasing him inside, the end takes the gap and goes to the quarterback. The defensive tackle is in a heavy technique on the guard and releases outside.

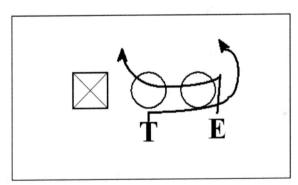

Figure 15-5. Me game

The "you" game (Figure 15-6), is the opposite stunt. On this stunt, the defensive tackle has a technique we call CTB. That means he charges through the B gap and works for containment to the outside. The end is the second defender coming inside over the offensive guard. We tell the end to expect one of two things as he comes inside. He could see the guard trying to pan back into position to pick him up. The end can use that momentum against the guard to try to get to the quarterback. He could see the center sitting and waiting for him. If that is the case, the defensive end has two to three yards of momentum built up and blasts the center.

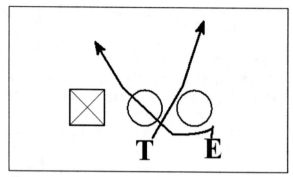

Figure 15-6. You game

We have a "coast" call (Figure 15-7), which is a "me" game on one side and a "you" game on the other. We base the stunt on which way the running back sets or what the game plan shows. If the center turns away from the running back, we know the "coast" is available in our stunt package. With the center sliding right, we run the "me" game to the right and the "you" game to the left. The defensive tackle to the "you" side does everything he possibly can to draw the guard out so the defensive end hit frees up the middle. We want to run the "you" call to the side of the running back.

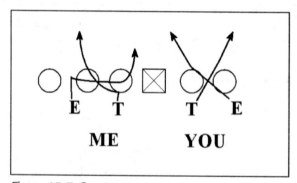

Figure 15-7. Coast

Another stunt we use is "Falcon" (Figure 15-8). This is a four-man game based on our scouting report and film study. We rushed the defensive end to the side of the slide into the man-to-man side of the protection. The defensive tackle to his side has a CTB technique and rushes hard to the outside for contain.

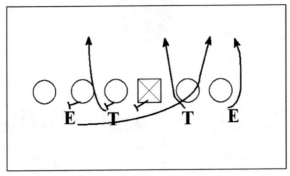

Figure 15-8. Falcon

The defensive end to the man-blocking side is a true containment man. He has to stay on the outside and cannot go underneath the blocker. Even if the under move is there, he cannot take that move. This stunt was good for us a couple of times this year. In all these games, if the read is a running play, the stunts are off.

I want to go to the film and show some of the things I talked about in the lecture. I hope you got something out of this. If there is anything I can help you with, please let me know and I will be happy to visit with you.

16

Defensive Line Drills and Techniques

Rick Petri
University of Kentucky
2009

Thank you. It is a pleasure being here. It is an honor to represent the University of Kentucky, Coach Brooks, and his staff. We have an excellent staff, and we have some good things going on at Kentucky. I have coached for 32 years—31 of them as a defensive line coach, and one as an offensive line coach.

I was sitting downstairs waiting for this session, and I began to wonder if I had ever been in the hotel before. It dawned on me that four years ago I was here in the lobby, waiting for an interview. I had been fired at Ole Miss after six years. I was nervous as hell then, and I am nervous as hell now. I guess it is the hotel.

For a defensive line coach to talk for an hour and 15 minutes is tough. How many defensive linemen are there who can sit around and listen to something for an hour and 15 minutes? Twenty minutes is about all I can stand. If you start to see me drift toward a chair in 20 minutes, you will know it is from the training of being a defensive line coach.

You always hear that defensive linemen are not as smart as offensive linemen. I did have the privilege to coach offensive line for one year, and it helped me tremendously. You get to understand scheme and things on the other side of the ball. I was the assistant offensive line coach. The head offensive line coach told me I was going to work with the nub side of the line. I had been coaching three years, but I was not familiar with what the nub side of the line was. He told me it was the linemen to the openside of the formation. I asked him why they call it the "nub side." He said because the nub tackle plays on that side. The tackle held up his hand and was missing several fingers.

I asked him how that happened. He told me he was cutting grass and the mower got clogged. He reached under the mower to clear the clog without turning it off. That is an example of a smart offensive tackle. I relate the fallacy that defensive linemen are dumb to this story. I do not go for that thought, and I do not coach that way. I expect a lot of my players, both physically and mentally. On the football field, in this day and time, there are so many things that challenge players mentally.

I have been fortunate to work with a lot of good coaches. I worked 10 years for a coach by the name of Larry Lacewell. He was an excellent and demanding football coach. One thing you learned when you worked for him is to be challenged. He challenged you to learn. We played many different concepts. You remember different things from coaches along the way. The thing I learned from him was not to talk too much and spend your time repping what we did.

My players learn through repetition. We do it over and over. To play defense, you have to react. That comes from reps. Offensive linemen can look at a sheet and know they have to block a certain defender. Defensive linemen have to react to what they see. They cannot think what technique they will use until it happens.

At Kentucky, we have three distinct modes of play in the defensive line. We play a *man-key* concept. We are not a ball-key concept. It is different. I have done the two-gap and read concepts. We are a read-and-react team. Before you get in your mind that we play a passive technique, I do not teach it that way. It has a lot of the same principles I taught in the ball attack get-off scheme.

We are reading and mirror stepping, but we are not catching or giving ground. We are extending and working off the ball in attack mode. We work with our hands and gain ground.

The second mode we play is *stunt/blitz* concept with on the ball key. When we do that, we cheat our stance, but I will talk about that later. We move the up foot or back foot, whatever the case may be. It is a gap concept. When we are in this mode, we are penetrating a gap. We have a *pass mode*, which is a ball-key reaction. Many people call it a jet movement. We are expanding and keying the ball when we expect pass.

10 PRINCIPLES OF RUN PLAY

Knowledge

- Stance

- Alignment/assignment
- Pre-snap keys

Technique

- Get-off—play mode called
- Hands, hips, feet
- Separation—vision through separation
- Key progress
  ✓Man on
  ✓Near back
  ✓Off guard

Effort

- Escape—wipe/shrug/rip
- Pursuit
- Tackle

KNOWLEDGE

There some things I want to get across quickly to our players. There are a lot of pre-snap things that the players have to be aware of. Our stance is slightly different than other people. We are slightly wider than shoulders width and the stagger is less than a heel-to-toe relationship.

We want our toes turned in and up the field. Nothing bothers me more than feet that turn out. I am a believer that everything works from the feet up and the head down. If I open my foot, hip, or shoulder, I am done. I do not know anyone playing the game that wants to have a soft shoulder on the run. If the lineman turns his head, the shoulder, hip, and feet follow. When we get down we want our forearms on our thighs with the hips down. I want the hips balanced between the feet with the down hand in front of the eye. We want to be in as good position to extend off the ball and lead with our hands. If we are moving we may cheat the stance.

Alignment is different for the inside defender than the outside defenders. The inside defender aligns his hand inside the foot of the man on which he is aligned. The 3-technique's hand is inside the outside foot of the offensive guard. He is square and crowding the ball. The shade nose has a little play in his alignment because of the bow in the offensive line. If they have problems with the read, they can back off the ball. The base rule for the defensive end is inside hand outside the foot of the offensive lineman. The end has to see so much more than the tackles. The end has to see the ball on or off the line and whether they have option responsibility.

From there we go to a pre-snap read. I want them to read splits and depth of the offensive linemen. They must know what the backfield set is. I expect them to know whether the back is far or near in their alignment. I want them to know if there are one or two backs, or an offset back. If they do not know the set, the scouting report is no good to them. They have to know what plays come from what set.

We want to know those things so we can address our alignment. If I know the split that the offensive linemen use when they combo block, I want to readjust my stance. I want to take the post man down the middle. I do not want to play a combo block with a blocker on each shoulder. I want to get into the post man and dominate him. If they are trying to power slip him, he wants to get into the post man, press the inside arm, gain ground, and get physical with him. If he is on the edge, they will man up to him and kick his butt.

TECHNIQUE

You have to get off the ball. If I am on a man-key and the man moves, I move as quickly as I can. I am not reading him so I can be slow. If he moves, I explode, get into him, and dominate him. I want to be quick, explosive, and violent.

We lead with our hands. The hands come first and are punched inside on the offensive blocker. The hands come at the level of the block. If the block is from the waist up, we want our elbows in and the thumbs up. I want to play with the hands at eye level. I do not know anyone in the world that plays with their hands at eye level that is playing high. They are playing high when the hands are down. I want my hips behind my pads and my feet behind my hips. Always play with body lean. I used to use the term roll the hips. I want them to extend off the football with a flat back. I want them to shoot their hands into the landmark and extend.

Once we get our hand through we want to get separation. You have to get vision through separation. We can control gaps three ways. You can control gaps with your body, the blocker's body, or with your eyes. If I get reached I work my body into the gap. If the blocker over-reaches, I use his body to fill the gap. If he over-reaches, I strike him in the ear hole, drive him up, and into the gap. I do not know anyone in the world that can generate any power from a high position. I can drive him into the gap with no trouble.

If I get a block and I control my gap, I use my eyes to control another gap. I squeeze my gap knowing the ball is inside. I can see the ball and know where it is. I can help people in other gaps because I can see where the ball is going and fall back to help once the ball gets level to my position. That is using the eyes to control gaps.

The key progression is man-on, near back, and off guard (Figure 16-1). I want them to know what their key is. I want to know what their eyes are doing and where they are looking. The defensive end has to see those things and more. He has to read hats and whether the ball is on or off the line of scrimmage. If the ball is on the line of scrimmage, he has a run key. If the ball is off the line of scrimmage, he may play pass.

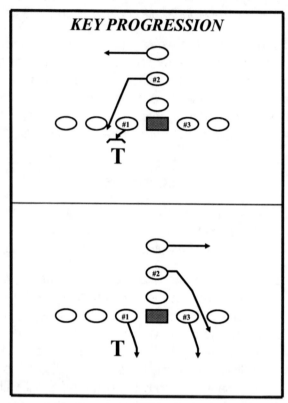

Figure 16-1. Key progression—read one to two

The defensive tackle is keying one to two. He keys the reach by the guard and the path of the fullback. He goes #1 to #2. There is no reason to go anywhere else with his read. There is no reason to go to his off-guard read. In the second drawing, he has the guard block with the fullback going opposite. When he has that read, he had better peek and see what is coming back. That happens with the defensive end or 5-technique defender. If he sees the back go away, he has to see what is coming back.

The same thing happens on a pass set (Figure 16-2). If the guard sets for a pass, the defensive tackle has to be aware of a draw. He has to see the same thing. He reads the guard and reads the back. He sees the guard in a pass set and the fullback on an isolation path to the other side and must react to what he sees. He has to go to his third progression, which is the offside guard. In the second drawing, you can see the pulling guard coming back. He has to see all those things happening. He has to read his keys and go through the progression.

Figure 16-2. Key progression—draw play

The defensive end has to see ball on or ball off the line of scrimmage. The end squeezes to the inside if he is playing a 5-technique (Figure 16-3). As he squeezes to the inside, he wants to splatter the dive back on the dive option. We do not want to come across the tackle because we want to bounce the ball to the outside. The technique terminology is splatter and hammer instead of spill and box.

We used to use the term spill. However, defenders were giving themselves up and not helping on the tackle. They went inside and got logged inside. That is not what we want them to do. We changed the terminology to splatter. We still want to get on the inside half of the blocker, but we get our hands on them and try to get upfield. We are not simply running under the block. If we cannot get up to the ballcarrier, we force him to bubble and go outside. The problem is the defender may get too far outside, and the ball cuts inside of him. That is bad because everyone is fitting outside of him.

If the defender is going to rip inside and splatter the play, he has to get up the field. The last situation is the power-O and the bootleg that comes off of it (Figure 16-4). The 9-technique defensive end has to squeeze and key what is coming inside. His man

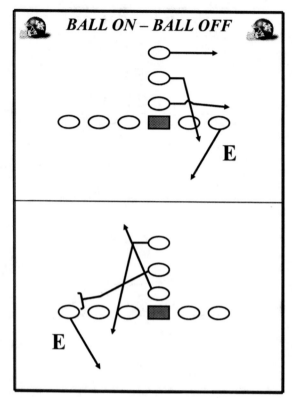

Figure 16-3. Ball on, ball off

goes inside; his next key is the near back, who is going to the opposite side. He reads his next key, which is coming down the line of scrimmage. He takes on the inside half of the pulling guard. After the contact, he climbs upfield, trying to pick off the pulling tackle coming behind the guard

On the bootleg, the defensive end reads his man-on as a down block. The near back is coming toward him. He collisions, taking the inside half and looking for the third key. He finds the pulling guard trying to hook him. He sees the ball off the line and gets upfield to contain it.

There is so much in the game that has changed with the blocking scheme. The tight end can be on the other side and is trapping to the other side. If the tight shifts off the line of scrimmage or aligns up off the line of scrimmage, the defensive end yells "Y off." That alerts the defensive end on the other side to be aware of the tight end kick-out on him. The defensive end has to find those blockers. It may be a fullback or the third tight end.

Before I talk about that, I will give you an overview of playing the run.

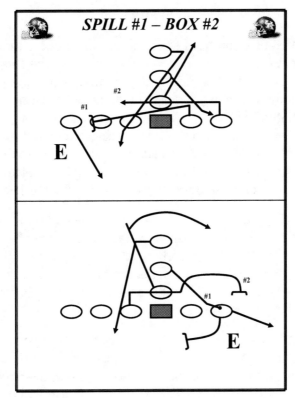

Figure 16-4. Spill and box

PLAYING THE RUN

- Three points of contact—hat and hands.
  - ✓Must have inside hands.
  - ✓Thumbs up, elbows tight at side.
  - ✓Speed of hands is critical, not power of stab; hands are merely levers.
- Focus on V of neck.
- Attack with flat back and hands at eye level.
- Hit on the rise; extend hips.
- Run feet.
- Knock blocker back; separate and twist.
  - ✓Blocker's shoulders to lock out upfield.
  - ✓Arm (power arm/trail arm, push/pull).
- Keep body lean at all times. Do not run your hips under your shoulders (keep hips behind your pads, feet behind your hips).
- Play on offensive side of line of scrimmage.
- Release and chase ball with full effort and intelligent pursuit angles.

EFFORT

To make plays on defense, you have to get off blocks. In our escape mode, we teach wipe, shrug, and rip. We work the most on wipe and shrug. The shrug is a swim move. We only rip on rare occasions. I do not want them to rip when trying to escape from a block. We rip only if the ball is in a pass-flow scheme. If the blocker is trying to cut the defender off or trying to block him, we want to wipe or shrug. If the defender tries to escape using a rip technique, the offensive blocker latches onto the defender's arm and rides him out of the play. We do pursuit tackling. We have three types of tackling drills we work. We work release tackling, sweep tackling, and roll tackling. I have some film to show those. Two of those three require the defender to release from a block.

In playing a blocker, there are three points of contact. We want to use our hat and hands to contact the blocker. The hands must be inside on the blocker's breastplate or target area. We want the thumbs up and the elbows tight to the side, except when we play a low block. In that case, they must get the hands down and the feet back. The speed of the hands is critical. It is not the power of the stab because the hands are levers to keep the blocker off the defenders body.

We tell them to focus on the V of the neck, but that is a general location and will change. I have players who read feet or the number on the shoulder pad. We do not overcoach that point. It is what works best for the player. We attack with a flat back, and the hands must be at eye level. We want to hit on the rise and extend the hips. The most important thing is to keep the feet moving at all times.

We want to knock the blocker back. As we lock out and go into our separation move, we want to twist the blocker's shoulders. We push or pull the shoulders of the blockers to execute the escape. We want a body lean at all times. We do not want them to run their feet under their pads. The hips should be behind the shoulders and the feet behind the hips. When they snap the ball, we want to play on their side of the line of scrimmage. When we release from the block, we want to chase the ball, using intelligent angles. It takes maximum effort to pursue the football.

I have some tips on pass-rushing techniques.

TEN PRINCIPLES OF PASS RUSH

Knowledge

- Stance and alignment.
- Have a plan. Know your opponent. Predetermine move and counter, if needed.
- Pre-snap keys.

Technique

- Get off—explode on snap. Every step to quarterback.
  ✓Have great body lean.
- Rush a half man.
- Be quick and decisive on initial move. Be violent.
- Hands
  ✓Quick and hand (vice-like).
  ✓Break blocker's arms down.
  ✓Coordinate hands with feet.
- Take advantage of blocker's momentum and mistakes.
  ✓Power rush soft setter.
  ✓Use finesse moves on short setter.
  ✓Take advantage of what blocker gives you—counter.

Effort

- Accelerate off moves.
- Get hands up; break on ball. Effort tackles.

If we get a jet or go call, we change our stance and alignment. We narrow and extend our stance. We want to get as close to the ball as possible. If I am a contain rusher, I may be up to three feet outside the offensive tackle. If the rusher is outside a tight end, he gets no wider than one foot. I tell them to widen to ensure an inside release of the tight end. If the defensive end gets any wider, he spreads himself away from their rush lane.

When the defensive lineman comes off the ball, he should have a plan of how to attack the blocker and rise to the occasion. When we have one-on-one pass rush in practice, I want to know their plan. When I ask them and they do not know, it makes no sense to me. If they do not have a plan in practice, what will it be like in a game when it is third-and-10 and they are hot and tired?

You must have a plan, and you must know what the opponent is going to do. You have to predetermine the move you are going to use and have a counter move to break down the blocker. Our tackles this past year did a great job of understanding slide protection. We get a pre-snap read on the blocking back. We define some of our stunts and twists off the alignment of the back.

Question: What moves do you teach?

I teach them a battery of moves, and they develop and perfect the move they do the best. They also develop a counter off that move. If they are not effective with that move, we let the lineman develop an additional move that he feels confidence in doing.

The defensive lineman must have a plan that ties into the back's set. If we get two backs in the backfield either in the I formation or the offset I, we have to know where the protections are going. I tell the tackle, if he reads heavy hands from the offensive blocker, that is probably a run, even though we are in a jet alignment. When we say "heavy hands," that means the offensive lineman has weight on his hand. If the weight is not on his hand, he is going to pass set or pull. We do not want the lineman using a double move where he fakes inside and comes outside because he might be coming out into a double-team block.

The defensive tackles communicate and talk in the pre-snap read. If one defender calls a heavy call and the other gives a light call, it is probably a run with one side pulling. The defensive end needs to know if there are four receivers to the same side. If the defensive end sees trips and a near back his way, it almost guarantees a sprint-out his way or something moving toward him.

The defensive lineman has to get off the ball, and every step he takes has to be toward the quarterback. We may be working a move, but always gain ground toward the quarterback. When you rush the quarterback, always attack half the blocker. We want to get to his shoulder. The only time we rush the full torso is the bull rush. Even with the bull rush, you landmark the outside shoulder initially and go to the bull rush later. The offensive blocker would rather the rush come straight to him and try to bull rush. If he has to move his feet to respect the outside move, it makes it harder for him to get set to take on the bull rush.

When the rusher makes the first move, it has to be quick and decisive. He has to be violent in his approach with his hands. We want to knock the blockers' hands down and get them off our bodies. We use three blocks with the hands as our primary move. We use a sweep move, which is over the top. If I am an outside rusher and the blocker extends his outside arm, I use my outside hand to sweep his hand down and swim over the top. Our defensive ends use a Miyagi move. That comes from the movie The Karate Kid. It is the "wax-on, wax-off" move with the hands. It is a circular-rotation karate move performed with the hands.

When you rush the passer, you have to coordinate the hands with the feet. If he works with his right hand, he has to step with his right foot. We want to take what the offensive blocker gives us. We have to study film to understand the tendencies of the blocker. If he sets soft, we want to use more power on him. If he sets short, we want to shake him and get inside. We want to take advantage of what he gives us.

Whatever move you use, you have to accelerate off the move. That is hard to do in practice because all the emphasis is on "do not hit the quarterback, and stay away from him." When it comes game time, the emphasis is: get the quarterback. You have to find something in practice to teach acceleration off the move to the quarterback.

Do not rush the quarterback with your hands up. We want to get the hands up only when the ball is shown. We do not want to leave the ground unless the ball is out of the hand. After the ball is released, we want the defender to break on the ball and tackle with maximum effort.

If the pass rusher comes off the line and the blocker stays square to the line, the rusher should beat him to the corner. The pass rusher wants the blocker to turn his hips so he can get on the edge and get his hips pass the blocker. If we have a blocker who crowds the line of scrimmage, we can get off on him before he gets his outside foot down on the ground and force him to turn his hips. The defensive end can force the blocker to open his hips by width and alignment. If we can get the shoulders turned, we can use our pass-rush techniques.

I am always teaching our players different moves. The moves they use depend on the type of personnel you have. The defensive tackle has a smaller area to work. We do an "in-out-in" and an "out-in-out" move on the inside. Those stunts are head-and-shoulder movement. I do not want to fake with my feet. I want to move the head and shoulder to the outside, to the inside, and charge back to the outside. He keeps his feet under his pads and fakes with his shoulders.

I give a picture sheet of a particular offensive set to our players every week. I pull it off the computer, and it shows what they do from this particular set. In the example, the set is a gun-near set. From this set, our opponent ran the formation 89 times. Seventy-five percent of the time they threw the ball. On the sheet, I show them the variety of plays they ran and into what areas of the field. They should know when they see this set, they think pass. This chart lists what to expect from this set. It has the common runs and tips of what to look for.

I also give them a pass breakdown chart (Chart #1). It lists the passes for first, second, and third downs and the scrambles of the quarterback. If they play two quarterbacks, I use dotted lines for one of the quarterbacks. You can see in this chart that the quarterback scrambled all over the place. Sometimes, you can find scramble patterns for a particular quarterback. Sometimes, we find a quarterback who only scrambles to his left. If that is the case, we want to plan our blitzes and line movement to match those tendencies.

This chart (Chart #2) is something we started this year, but I did it a long time ago. We have our own goal board. The first goal is to win. The second is to hold teams to 3.2 yards per carry. We want to cause a turnover or recover a fumble. This year, we scored two touchdowns by defensive linemen returning a fumble. We want to sack the quarterback on one out of eight passes. We want to total 24 tackles. We want to pressure the quarterback on one out of three passes. We want hustle tackles where we tackle a wide receiver or running back downfield. That includes hustling out and making a tackle in the screen game. We get a production grade for each lineman. We take the number of plays and divide it by the number of points he amasses for things done in the game. The last thing we post is the production leader.

Across the top of the chart, you put the teams you play and keep a running total of what you did throughout the season. To come up with a production grade, we use a production chart for the defensive team. To find out how productive our team is, we evaluate the player's performance. The production grades come from comparing the points they accumulated to the number of plays they play.

We assign points to plays in a game. We give points for tackles and assisted tackles. We give points for fumbles recovered and caused. We give points for interceptions and scores. We have other categories for which we award positive points. We also give negative points for mistakes and loafs. We add up the total points and divide by the number of plays they participated in to come up with the player's productivity. That goes on the chart. Players who have the highest number of points in the fewest plays are your most productive players.

We want them to produce, have fun, and take pride in what they are doing. Thank you very much.

17

Defensive Line Drills
and Techniques

Joe Sarra
Penn State University
1997

One of the most important things in football is to get the team ready. You have to teach and motivate for a team to perform. The key is to get players to play at the highest level of their ability. We have to push our kids to the point where they don't think they can do it any more. These players don't know what their highest level is because they haven't been pushed that hard. They have to learn to fall down and get back up.

If a player has feet and courage, that is what it takes to be a good defensive player. I ran into one of our players up in the hall before I came down here. He was our manager. We were getting ready to play Notre Dame, and our long snapper got hurt. This manager lined up and long-snapped the ball against Notre Dame for us.

If a kid has courage, you can teach him to be a big hitter. You can make him the best tackler on the team. If you have courage to hit somebody and feet to get to the ball, that's all defense is. If a kid has those talents, it is hard to keep him on the bench.

This next point is important in football but is also important in life's critical situations. You have to *control what you can control*. You can determine whether your team out hustles people. You can determine their getting to the ball. You determine whether your team is in shape. You determine whether your team is in condition. We play two halves of football. The first-half score means nothing. The final score is what counts. You determine whether your team out hits the opponent. We can control the fact that we out prepare people.

We control conditioning. In the winter program, if they won't pay the price and condition, they will get you beat on the goal line. They will lose on the goal line. We rate our players in several areas. We consider conditioning, the weight room, academics, and other areas.

When I have a meeting with my players, I put on the blackboard, "Today is today. Make it count." However, it's more than that. It is the moment that counts. Any one of us could walk out of here and drop dead. Any tragedy could happen to any of us. You have to cherish the moment.

Here are some things that you build your defense around. You have to be a productive defense. We talk all the time about forcing turnover. Coach Paterno will come into our meeting and tell us that we need more interceptions and fumble recoveries. We have to force turnovers. The defense must have pride. They have to dominate and defend their area. They have to feel as if no one can run the ball at them. They will defend their area, and no one can run into their area.

We have a saying that is on the board in the linebackers' meeting room: pay the toll. That is the linebacker area. It is just like the Pennsylvania Turnpike. To use it, you have to pay a toll. Anyone who comes into the linebacker area gets his head knocked off. If a guy crosses the linebacker's face, if he doesn't deck him, he gets a -3 on the grading scale. They are to dominate and control their area.

You have to play smart, with poise and pride. They have to have confidence in themselves. There may be a guy with less ability who can play because he is confident that no one can beat him. Toughness is what wins the game. You have to think team, be committed, and be unselfish. Those are things that a lot of people don't have today.

You have to do whatever it takes to win. If you want to win, you have to work harder. People can say that they want to win. That is easy. They have to prepare to win through hard work. You can out hustle people, but execution wins.

This next point is a big one. Coach Paterno does this great. We meet every morning. We look at our personnel board. We move people up and down that board. Who should be moved up a number? Who should we move down? You have to get the proper people in the proper positions. We have moved guys from defense to offense. We had a kid who came to Penn State as a linebacker. Now, he is a running back. If you get the proper people in the right positions, they make the plays.

You have to talk to your team. They have to understand your goals and what they are working for. We as coaches are going to work hard but smart. We are working to win. Some people work hard, but they don't work smart.

You have to punish people. You won't win games unless you punish people. You have to get your kids ready to punch somebody in the mouth. You have to get people on the run and, when you get them down, put them away. This is a physical game. We want to beat our opponent physically. How fast you get to the ball only matters if you punish people when you get there. You control gang tackling. It is not how fast you are; it is how physical you are. When the running back is getting pounded, he starts asking the coach to spread the ball around a little.

What are the qualities we look for in the defensive line? The number one thing is toughness. I never recommend a guy for our coaches to look at if he is not tough. When I say tough, I mean the tougher the challenge, the better he plays. We want a kid who is a competitor. You won't see size on our list. You can't worry about size. In the line, it is a street fight. You don't talk about weight classes in a street fight. It is the same way with the defensive line. You can't tell the guy that you can't fight him because he is out of your weight class. You can work harder than anybody else to get better. You can go to the weight room and work on your strength. You can work on your hand and foot quickness. The game of football is played with the hands. If you have a guy with quick hands and feet, he can play. We work with martial arts to increase the speed of the hands.

A defensive lineman has to be aware of what is going on around him. He has to shed blockers. He has to be able to change direction effectively. That is important in defensive football. The lineman must stay focused. He has to be able to get off a block. He has to be just downright mean.

In the defensive linemen's meeting room on the left-hand side of the bulletin board is, "Loyalty and trust." It never comes off the board. We trust each other, and we are very loyal. We never criticize our teammates or talk about them. If I can't trust a player, he is not going in the game. When all the guys are working together, they share that trust in one another. You can't talk out of both sides of your mouth. You have to talk straight.

We evaluate our players. We have a sheet that we use to evaluate them. The strength coach evaluates the players. The trainers and coaches evaluate them. Their academic advisors evaluate them also. We give them a 5, 4, 3, 2, or 1 grade. We want to get the winners on the field. These guys control the tempo of the game. They are the ones who can make big plays and turn the game around. If you have a horse, make sure he gets in the race. Make sure the good back gets his hands on the ball. I'm not talking about some prima donna. I'm talking about guys with character who won't get you beat.

There are three types of guys. There are players who are winners, players who won't get you beat, and players who will get you beat. Forget about potential and get them to execute. If you have an excuse player, don't play him. He always has an excuse for why he made a mistake. Don't play him. He'll get you beat.

I give our kids a checklist. Defense is our game, and winning is our aim. That is a catch phase for the defensive linemen. I give them a form. On the form are things that we are going to grade and work on all year long. I have the kids grade themselves. I grade them and write down comments for them.

I give them drills to do over the summer to improve on. It is a job description for them. Included on the sheet are the following: change of direction, stance, alignment, assignment, delivery of a blow, shed, pursuit, tackling, and a good base. We also include backpedal, opposite reaction, explosion, read keys, mental alertness, and second effort. I grade the players every night after practice and give them the sheet the next day.

Next are fundamentals. A player has to move and control his feet. He has to shed the high and low blocks. If a person can shed, he can make plays. Some guys can't get off a block. The tackles have to pass rush, make tackles, pass react, pursue, and be tough.

I'm going to talk about stance. We use a three-point stance in the defensive line. If I am teaching a young player a stance, I'll put him in a four-point stance. A four-point stance keeps the lineman down. You can't play with your shoulders turned. You want your pads square and your feet under you. A four-point stance helps the kid to do that. We get into a three-point stance, but 98 percent of our weight is on the ground. We have a slight stagger.

In our alignment, we play head up, shade inside and outside, nose up, wide or loose alignment, and gap. We key the ball or anything that moves. If anything moves, we are going.

Our responsibility is whatever defensive technique we are in. I'll cover that later. The reaction is to what the defensive lineman sees. He has to see blocking schemes. He must understand his pass-rush lane.

Let's go back to the mechanics of the stance. We don't use a wide base. That will get you in trouble. We want our feet under our hips. I don't say anything about shoulder width. Every kid thinks his shoulders are wider than they are. Good backs run with their feet under the hips. They don't get their feet outside the body. They are skaters. They work within the framework of their hips. When we start to get down, we put our hands on our knees. If I get in a right-handed stance, my right foot is back, and it is my push foot. If I get in a left-handed stance, it is just the opposite. My knees are bent, and I have some weight on my hands: not too much, but just enough. The off hand is close to the ground. We get in the four-point stance and then pick up the other hand. We are a takeoff team. We read on the run. When the ball is snapped, we take off. In our bent-knee position, we get the power angles we want. We step and explode off the ball.

The first thing we tell our linemen is not to get knocked off the ball. If they get knocked off the ball and back into the linebacker, we can't move. If the lineman is in an outside shade on a guard, his inside hand is down. He steps with the inside foot. By stepping with the inside foot, the lineman can keep his outside leg free. If the stagger is too much, it causes the lineman to rise up. It also doesn't allow him to get into the blocker as quickly as having a shorter stagger. We want to get to the blocker quickly, make contact, punch with the opposite hand, and get off the block.

When the offensive blocker rises up to block, we don't rise up. We strike through him. We learn how to use both right- and left-handed stances. We have to play some techniques that require using the opposite hand down. Make your players line up straight. Your feet determine where the lineman lines up.

When we run drills, we film them. We watch the footwork of the linemen. If they don't step with the proper foot, they get a -3. That is discipline. We do it one way. I never stand behind the defense when we are practicing. I stand behind the offense. I want to see the defensive linemen's eyes. I want to see what they are seeing.

I want his toes to be straight ahead. I may say, "Feet!" That means they are too wide or too narrow. I could say, "Stagger!" That means his stagger is too big or not big enough. If I say, "Tilt," that means their footwork will cause them to get reached.

We do something differently than a lot of people do. I have done this both ways. It doesn't matter what you call techniques, as long as your players know what you are talking about. We letter our gaps. The center-guard gap is the A gap. The guard-tackle gap is the B gap. The tackle-end gap is the C gap. Outside the tight end is the D gap. Head-up the guard would be B. If we want our lineman on the inside eye, that is a B minus. If we want him to straddle the inside leg, that is called tight B. The B plus is the outside eye of the guard. If we get into the B gap, that is called wide B.

We work hard on responsibility. I quiz my players on their assignments. You would be surprised at the number of kids who leave the huddle and don't know the defense or what the snap count is. They don't pay attention in the huddle.

Here is another thing we could talk about anytime. I'm not here to show you alignments, but we'll talk about them. They have to know the alignment, assignment, and reaction. Those things are more important. Never try to tell a kid that the defense will win a game. A scheme is only as good as the players playing it. Execution wins games. The front does not win games.

People ask us about flip-flopping people. We have done both at Penn State. If you don't flip your people, the guy playing on the right gets to play the trap the same way all the time. He uses the same steps and footwork all the time. But, if you flip the guy playing the trap, he has to learn both ways, and it adds to the assignments he has to learn. If you flip your people, you have to worry about jumps. If they are flipping, they have to get set in their alignment. If you don't flip, all they have to do is get ready to play. We don't flip our people anymore.

We run a drill about three times a week called early work. We take our inside people. We work best on best and run traps, reach, scoops, and cutoff blocks. We do this drill before practice. After we work on those things, we put the offense and defense together and work 7-on-7.

Let's get into the practice schedule and what we do on the field. Nothing fancy goes on out there. The first thing we do is stretch. I work with the snappers and kickers, but they do their stretching on their own. We work on our flexibility. The guys may be big, but the game is played with bent knees. I think we take too much time from practice to stretch. I tell them to get stretched out. I don't care when they do it, walking across campus on the way to practice or coming out to practice, but I'm not going to take practice time for them to stretch. You hope they don't do this, but it could happen. A guy gets into a fight. He can't say, "Hey, John, wait five minutes; I've got to stretch and get loose." We get loose during our drill work.

The first drill we do is a bag drill. They step over the bags and stretch. At the end of the bags, I have them do some kind of football-related finish. The first time, I may have them recover a fumble. The second time, I may roll the ball, and they have to pick it up and score. The third time, I may throw the ball to them. The fourth time, they have to tip it to someone else. Then, I may have someone there to form tackle. There are all kinds of things that you can do during the warm-up period.

There are ways to recover a fumble. If you are not getting done what you want to get done, keep your players after practice and make them do it right. When you are trying to recover a fumble, never get on your back. Grab the ball, lock it down with the arms, and pull up the knees and hips. When they come in on the ball, if they don't bend their knees, they'll kick the ball. We work on this every day.

You can make your players bend their knees and run quickly over the bags. To teach our kids to bend their knees, we do a drill called hand-touch knee bends. The player gets his butt down and face up, bends his knees, and puts his hands on the ground. We run three or four players at a time. We start them out with their feet straight up the field. You can't push off and have good acceleration and power with your feet out to the side. We start them running. When I yell, "Touch," they touch their hands to the ground then. They don't run two or three steps and then touch. In a game, your reaction is not when you want it. It is when it occurs. On defense, you have to gain ground on every move. After the touch, they come out low, hard, and accelerating. When a player comes out high, he is not gaining ground. Whatever drill you do, make sure they are gaining ground on the first step. I don't tell them to go. They touch and go.

Every day, we do stance-and-starts. We put them in their stance and make them come out low and hard. We tell them which foot to move first. We emphasize elbows in tight and pumping. We are looking for explosion.

We do a grass drill to teach players how to fall. If you feel yourself fall, what do you do? You put your hands down to break your fall. If you fall and want to get up quickly, you use your and hands and feet. We teach our kids how to fall. You have to get up on the way down. We do this drill. They start to chop their feet. I say, "Hit." They hit the ground, get their hands and feet under them, and come up running. Make them get up and down two to three times and make them tackle to finish the drill. This is the second-effort drill. How many times have you seen guys come off the ground to make tackles, sacks, or recover fumbles? I've seen it lots. If a guy can't give us a second move, he can't play for us.

We use this drill for linebackers and down linemen. The first way we teach this drill is in an up position. We teach them how to slide and change directions. You have to be able to defeat the low block. If you can defeat the low block, you can beat the high block. If you are playing the high block and the low block comes, you can't beat the low block because your legs are split. You cannot shed the low blocker. The feet have to stay under the hips at all times. If the feet get outside the hips, the player can't make a second move. If he keeps his feet under his hips, he can go right, left, forward, or backward. The knees have to be bent, and the back foot must be active in the slide.

In the change-of-direction drill, the toes have to remain straight ahead. If the toes turn, the shoulders turn. We want the pads parallel. We have three guys in the drill. There are six guys behind them in what we call the bullpen. They are practicing the drill. They are moving their arms and practicing. I say, "Switch," and the second line becomes the first line and continues the drill. The third line moves up and practices while they wait for the next switch call. You don't become a better player by standing around.

The next drill is the lateral run. We don't slide our feet, we cross over. We don't want a big, wide step. It is a short movement like a carioca step. We keep our toes straight up the field as we cross our feet. My butt is low, and my knees are bent. If we turn our feet, the shoulders turn also. We can't shed anybody or change directions if our shoulders and feet are turned. Don't let them rise up when they change directions. If you do, you will get beat. When your eyes see something, they don't tell you to rise up.

This next drill is not a good drill—it is a great drill. We do it every day. We have two long, flat dummies. We have two guys facing each other. One guy is going to his right, and one is going left. They have their hands on the dummies. They slide up and down the dummies. While they are sliding up and down the dummies, they can't take their hands off that bag. When they get to the end of the dummies. They turn and sprint. You can do the same thing with a board instead of a dummy. The main thing is to make them move laterally and keep their hands down.

We take the drill one step further. We have an offensive player and a defensive player. They do the same drill, but as they get to the end of the bag, the offensive player tries to cut the defensive player with a low block. The blocker is trying to get to the knees of the defensive player. The defensive player has to keep his hands down and shed the blocker. If the defensive player gets to the end of the dummy and rises up, he is blocked. We work on movement, shedding, and keeping down. We slide down with the toes straight and then cross over with the toes straight, always keeping our hands on the bags. It makes them bend their knees and stay down.

We look hard in our game films for guys who do these drills in actual game situations. This drill is one you can find all the time. That is why it is so good. We set up a series of bags and make the linemen step over the bags using the form they worked on in the hands-down drill. They step over the bags going right and left. At the end of the bags to the right and left, we have a tackling lane with a ballcarrier. We go through movement, change direction, see the ballcarrier, explode up into the lane, and make the tackle.

This next drill is a million-dollar drill that you can get on credit. Go down to the hardware store. Buy some rubber tubing and make a circle. Even when you pass rush, you have to maintain good body position. We put two guys across the circle from one another, one in a right-handed stance and one in a left-handed stance. On movement, they run around the circle. They have to keep the hands down on the tubing. They have to lean to stay on the circle. The head is up, and the knees bent. When they get all the way around, they change directions and go the other way. This gives them the idea about coming around the horn in the pass rush. It teaches them to lean in and make the play on the quarterback instead of running past him.

18

Defensive Line Run and Pass-Rush Techniques

Sal Sunseri
Carolina Panthers
2005

I am excited to be here. I know a lot of the coaches here today. I am going to take you through our program as if you were a rookie coming to training camp.

The first thing I teach the rookie is sound fundamental football. Everything we do in our practices we do quickly. When we move from one spot on the practice field to another, we go quickly. To have success within the defensive line, you have to be good with your hands and feet. We play hard on every snap as if it is the most important play of the game.

When we practice, we play as if we are in a game. We take what we do on the field in practice and apply it into game situations. If you think Julius Pepper is a good football player when he plays, he practices that way. The defensive line coach has to demand his players play that way.

We pursue to the ball. We do not care where the ball is on the field; we are going to run to it. The distance from the football at the end of a play measures the desire of a defensive lineman.

The defensive line sets the tempo for each game with physical play. We create contact on every single play. We tackle using good techniques. During my lecture, you will hear me talking about near foot, leg, and shoulder. To tackle an individual, you need to use the near leg and near shoulder to tackle. That gives you power to knock the ballcarrier back. If you tackle across the bow, you open up your base and have no power.

We have great team defense at the Carolina Panthers. The reason we have a great team defense is we install every thing as a team. When you install things with the team everyone is on the same page. Players have to understand the concepts of what you are trying to do. Players will learn their assignments. The coach has to make the player understand the concept of the defense and what you want to get done. If you do not teach the concept of the defense, the player will know what he is doing but not know the weakness of the defense.

If the player understands the concept of the defense, he will not come on an inside blitz. He knows if he comes inside he loses containment and that is one of the weaknesses of the defense. We do not teach anything that is illegal, but we use our hands to get off blocks and make plays.

This next piece of information I learned from Mike Trgovac, who is our defensive coordinator. He told me the number one thing a defensive line coach had to do was perfect the art of getting off the ball. In every aspect of the game, whether it is running or passing, the defensive linemen have to get off the ball.

In every drill you do, you should have a ball in the drill because defensive linemen are coached to move on the ball. They move on movement of the ball or individual movement by some player. A defensive line coach has to have a stick-football to use as part of every drill. Every thing the defensive linemen do is predicated on the stance. The linemen have to perfect the first step they take from their stance.

The first step is a six-inch power step with the back foot. It thrushes through the upper body to get into the neutral zone. From that six-inch step, we want the player to explode. He brings his hands and hat into the explosion and keeps the feet moving. When the contact occurs, the feet have to motor so the defender can push the offensive lineman backward.

The next technique we teach is hand placement. Do not let any one kid you about hand placement. That is the most important thing you can do in playing a defensive technique. If you get your hands in the right placement and strike them properly, you can control the line of scrimmage and get off blocks. The hand placement must be on the blocker's breastplate, with the defender's hands inside the blockers. The thumbs are up in the placement with the elbows tight. The player who gets his hands inside always wins the battle.

The defensive linemen have to play with leverage. The defender's helmet must be under the blocker's helmet to win the battle of the heads. I am evaluating tape right now on our team. If you find a player playing with a flat back, you have a chance to win. If you have a player playing with his chest, you have no chance to win.

When you evaluate players, you look for flexibility in the hips, knees, and ankles. The defensive lineman playing with his chest has stiffness either in his knees or ankles. Some players are naturally loose in the ankles and knees. However, some things can be done for players with stiff joints. Every drill you do should be predicated on bending the knees and ankles and striking a blow.

The next phase for defensive linemen is the knock-back. After contact, the defensive lineman becomes the blocker and tries to squeeze the offensive lineman into the hole. We teach the defensive lineman to sink his hips and drive the blocker into his gap of responsibility. His feet must penetrate the neutral zone. He regains leverage with his head if he lost that battle on the get off, or re-establishes his knee bend if he got over extended.

To get off a block, the defensive lineman must achieve separation from the offensive blocker. When he shoots his hands, he gets into a locked position with his hands and arms. He wants to keep his hands active to prevent the blocker for holding him. You must have separation to escape.

There is a tremendous amount of power in a six-inch punch if delivered with a snap of the hips. When the defensive linemen hit the blockers with both hands and snap the hips, they can create a tremendous amount of separation between the defender and blocker. You teach this by explaining to the players that they do not want to give up what they already have gained. If they let the momentum, which they established on the initial punch, go back to their bodies, they are at a disadvantage. When they punch the blocker and lock out, they have to continue the momentum and get separation at that time. They want to identify the play and get off the block right then. They can do it by ripping or swimming. By using quickness, the defender can stun a blocker with a short open palm punch. That pushes the blocker off so the defender can use the swim or rip to disengage and get off the block.

The defender wants to escape by shedding the blocker after he recognizes the scheme. He re-establishes the lockout with his arms and uses a technique called "post and pull." Keeping his outside leverage, the defender takes his inside hand, grabs the jersey, and pulls the inside shoulder down. He uses the outside leverage hand as the post. He pulls down with the inside hand and rips or swims to escape. We want to win with speed.

We want to play fast in the defensive line. To play fast the defender needs to be in his exact alignment and assume a good stance. The defender does not need to give the offense an advantage before the ball is snapped. If the defender knows his exact alignment and knows what to do, he will play fast.

Some coaches want to move defensive linemen after they line up. Once the defensive linemen get down and are ready to play, let them play. Communication is difficult once they get ready to play. What they can see is movement on the line and in the backfield. Teach the defensive line to recognize backfield sets and motion in the backfield. Teach them when a tight end moves in motion or trades from one side to the other, blocking angles change and will effect the way he plays. He understands leverage in the defense and knows if he does not adjust his position, he has lost leverage by alignment.

In playing technique, you have to give the defender a visual key. The visual key for most defensive linemen is the V of the offensive blockers neck. Wherever that key goes, the defensive lineman keeps his leverage and alignment relative to that key.

We use the butt technique to defeat the offensive lineman with a three-point hit. The three-point hit is with the hat and the hands. He leads with his hat and hits with his hands. They want to stay low, dig in, get their cleats in the ground, and manhandle the blocker. The punch to separate from the blocker has to be violent. The defender is not coming off and running up the field. He comes off hard and reads on the run. This is what we call "in-flight adjustments."

If the offensive guard attempts to reach a 3-technique player, his six-inch step may be too long. He has to get his foot on the ground so he can get out on the attempted reach. That is an in-flight adjustment.

In this situation, the offensive guard folds around the tackle and up on a linebacker. The tackle comes down on the 3-technique player to seal him inside. If the 3 technique tries to cross-face the tackle, the offense has won because that is what they want him to do. The 3 technique has to get off and get upfield on the guard. That makes the tackle come down flatter to pick off the 3 technique. That creates a big opening in the B gap. The backside 1 technique comes behind the play and makes the play on anything coming into that gap. The guard is forced deep and the tackle has to come flat. That is because the 3 technique got off the ball and up the field.

When you play defensive line, it is not precise. They have to make in-flight adjustments, move their feet, and know what is going on. We use all kinds of calls between the defensive tackles. Those calls come from reading the offensive lineman's body language and stance adjustments. We use the terms go, Rambo, and rabbit as three of them. The go call means the offensive linemen are sitting in a pass-set stance. If the backside tackle is calling "light," that means the guard is pulling on the power. We work on them in practice because if you do not hear them in practice, you sure will not hear them in a game.

Make sure the linebackers know if it is run or pass. I learned this years ago; if you know the play, let everyone know. Offensive linemen tip plays more than anyone does. If you think you know the play, tell everyone and we will read as we go.

In the defensive line, the defender has to do his job first. He has to react and cover his responsibility. He must have confidence in his teammates because together they can stop anything.

When you play in the defensive line, go all the way to complete the job. Punish the ballcarrier when he runs the ball. Pursue the ball until the whistle blows. The defensive linemen get hot and tired, but you cannot let them be late. The defensive line coach must make the linemen pursue the ball. When we have pursuit drill, those linemen's butts are flying to the football.

When you play in the defensive line you must have concentration and intensity. You have to be assassins on the field. They must be quick and decisive in their play. My players understand and recognize a triple or double set. They recognize an unbalanced set and they know where the play is going before it is run. That is why they are able to make plays.

This is important to me and it is critical. Show them exactly what you mean by alignment. When we draw our defensive alignment up for our defensive team, we go in numerical order (Figure 18-1). Head up the center is a zero technique and on the shoulder is a "shade." Inside shoulder of the guard is a 1 technique, head up is a 2 technique, and outside shoulder of the guard is a 3 technique. The inside shoulder of the tackle is a 4 technique, head up the tackle is a 5 technique, and outside shoulder of the tackle is a 6 technique. The inside shoulder of the tight end is a 7 technique, head up the tight end is an 8 technique, and his outside shoulder is a 9 technique.

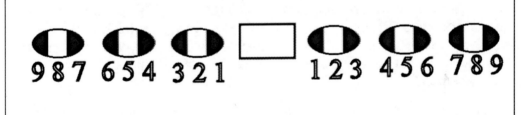

Figure 18-1. Technique alignments

I am sure everyone has used the numbering system for alignment for years. This is slightly different because John Fox, our head coach, said make it as easy as you can. We number in sequence from the inside to the outside on both sides.

If the defensive linemen are in a zero, 2, 5, or 8 technique, we are in a balanced stance on the nose of the center, guard, tackle, or tight end. When I say balanced stance, I mean the defensive linemen's feet align on the offensive linemen's feet. The defensive lineman's inside foot aligns on the offensive linemen's inside foot and the outside foot on the outside foot.

If the defensive lineman aligns in a 1 technique, his outside foot aligns in the middle of the offensive guard's crotch. If he goes to a 3, 6, or 9 technique, the defender takes his inside foot and splits the middle of the offensive linemen's crotch. We have a term we call "track." If we align in a "track 3 technique," the defender puts his outside foot slightly outside the outside foot of the offensive guard. The guard is not sure whether the 3 technique is on the shoulder or head up. If we play a track technique, we use the feet of the offensive linemen to align. If we play straight techniques, we use the crotch to align. If we play a "loose 3 technique," we align our inside foot six inches outside the outside foot of the linemen.

If anyone is playing any type of 46-defensive game, the key is the 3 technique. You play a zero technique on the center and two 3 techniques on the guards. Make sure the 3 techniques are in loose alignments and they can get up the field.

This is exactly how we teach alignment. All I am telling you is make it simple, make it accurate, and demand they get their alignment.

There are two main responsibilities for playing in the defensive line. They have to assist in stopping the run. That means the defensive line cannot be selfish. There are times when they have to spill blockers and grab offensive linemen. The job of the defensive line is to cause commotion and disruption at the line of scrimmage. When they cause commotion, they knock blocker off so that linebackers can make plays. If the defensive line does things properly, they have a chance to make plays.

The second main responsibility of the defensive line is to put pressure on the quarterback. Julius Peppers has to have 13 sacks every year. This year Mike Rucker went from 13 sacks the year before to four-and-a-half this past year. Our season went that way. We do not want to hear excuses because, in a nutshell, you have to pressure the quarterback.

When we teach pass rush, we start out by stopping the run on the way to the quarterback. In the defensive line, you may get a run call and the play is a play-action pass. The defensive linemen have to convert themselves from run stoppers into pass rushers.

In their running play rules, the defensive linemen must hit their target with bent knees, fly to the ball, and swarm. In the pass rush rules, the defensive linemen must explode, play technique, close, and defend the quarterback. When we attack, we explode through the blockers, attack, and react to the offensive linemen. We play with our feet on their side of the line of scrimmage. We will hit hard and are violent on every snap. Every move that we perform on run or pass will be of a violent nature. We will never allow our opponents to get their hands on us first.

That last statement is probably the most critical thing a defensive lineman must do. The most important drill you can do at any level for the defensive football player is using the hands against an opponent. It does not matter what type of drill it is. In a pass rush drill, the defender has to get his hands on the opponent first. If a defensive back is playing press coverage or re-routing a receiver, he has to get his hands on the opponent. If the linebacker is playing a block, he has to get his hands on an opponent. It does not matter whether it is high school, college, or pro football; in defensive football, that skill is crucial. If the defensive player cannot get his hands on the offensive player, he does not have a chance in hell of winning.

If you take your players to camp, that is a time for learning as well as practice. We let our players know what to expect in a meeting. They must be on time and bring a notebook. We take notes on everything we do. If a player shows up without a notebook and nothing to write with, throw his butt out of the meeting. He is not ready to play or anything else.

In preparation for our next opponent, I draw every offensive play they run and highlight the blocking scheme from each of their runs and formations. If we are in an under front with a bubble, our players know there will be a down block, with the center blocking back, and a guard pulling through the bubble. The 3 technique knows if we get the I-formation, he gets the double-team. They know what to expect.

I want to talk a little about pass rush. When the defensive lineman goes into a pass rush, he has to change his stance. In our normal stance, most of our pressure is on our outside foot. Our feet are slightly wider than our shoulders. The stagger is a toe-to-instep relationship.

Once the lineman reads pass, he changes his stance into a sprinter stance. The most important thing is the get-off. We look in at the ball and get-off on the movement of the ball. The defensive end picks a spot three yards behind the offensive tackle's alignment. He wants to beat the offensive tackle to that spot.

Pass rushers have to get off and knock the offensive lineman backward. Sometimes the offensive tackle opens up from the get-go. If the pass rusher can get to the blockers outside wrist, he generally can beat the blocker.

Players who also wrestle know how to use leverage in the pass rush. The simplest move is the "wiper" move. Wrestlers use the move when they wrestle. If someone tries to grab them they wipe the hand off the wrist or wherever. When the offensive lineman attempts to punch the pass rusher, he grabs the elbow and pushes it inside across the chest of the blocker. After the defender pushes the elbow inside, he steps with his inside foot across to the outside. The step with the inside foot clears the hip and allows the defender to flip his hip around to the outside. Some people describe the hip flip like a reverse carioca step.

You can anticipate pass based on the game situation and formation. They have to understand what formations the pass generally comes from. The defender must respond immediately to the pass set by the offensive linemen. He wants to have no wasted movement and be quick and deceptive on the initial move. The pass rusher wants to keep his movement toward the passer. Some pass rushers in their attempt to avoid the blocker end up working away from the passer and aiding the blocker.

The quickest way to the quarterback is a straight line. I tilt the defensive end at an angle to get to the quarterback as quickly as possible. He does not know what type of set the quarterback will take. If the drop is a three-step drop, the defensive end will not get there. He has to get his hands up and try to knock the ball down. The pass rusher wants to keep his movement toward the quarterback and make him change his set.

The worst thing the pass rusher can do is being predictable. If the rusher beats the blocker with a speed rush constantly, the blocker will figure out how to block him. Change up on the blocker and keep him guessing. Every good pass rusher has one counter off his initial move. One counter move for a soft pass setter is a "single arm bar." On that move, all you do is take the inside hand and grab the outside arm of the blocker, and lower the hips.

Use the natural agility of your players. They can use head movements and fakes to make the blocker miss the rusher. Quick feet and speed are deadly in the pass rush. Quick head and shoulder movements freeze the feet of offensive linemen. If you can do that, you can use rip and flip moves on him. If he soft sets, you can thrust speed into power and push him back into the quarterback.

The pass rusher cannot give up on his initial move too quickly. He has to give it a chance to work.

The spin move is a popular move of the pass rusher, especially as a counter move. You have to get up the field before you can use the spin. If you plan on spinning to the inside, make sure you have all your weight on the inside foot. He throws his outside elbow, extends his arm, and slaps the blocker on the butt to pull himself through.

The movement games are critical for the run and the pass. We run a game called "combo" (Figure 18-2). If we are in a 4-3 over defense, we put Julius Peppers in a 7 technique on the tight end. We have a 3 technique on the guard. We play a backside shade on the center with the other defensive tackle. We create a bubble to the weakside by playing the defensive end in a 6 technique.

We tell the shade tackle to jam the center hard and get across the slant by the defensive end and to the outside. We have two linebackers up on the outside if anything bounces. When you are a defensive line coach, you have to know what the offense is thinking. Show them the bubble and then disrupt it.

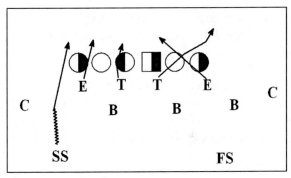

Figure 18-2. Combo game

What you do is take the same kind of running game stunt into the pass rush game. The nose tackle will probably draw a double-team from the guard and center. The defensive end makes his move upfield and comes under the offensive tackle. He is going to knock the guard off the shade tackle and let the tackle come free to the outside. They cannot be selfish. The defensive end gives him up to free the tackle for an outside rush.

You have to take advantage of weakness of offensive blockers. If you find a slow setter, use the speed rush on him. Make him so conscious of the outside that he becomes susceptible to the under move. If the tackle false steps, we want to get to his set side arm immediately.

Speed rushers need to work on the hoops as much as they can. I put a player with a pad inside the hoop and jam the hoop runner as he goes around. That makes the hoop runner fight resistance, lean, and keep his balance as he goes around the arc. The offensive lineman can feel a rusher that is leaning too far. If they feel that, they will bury him quickly. That is why balance is important when he runs the hoops. It gives him a realistic situation.

I do not do any drills that have no carry-over value for a game situation. I try to involve some kind of contact in every drill. Very seldom does a defensive lineman get a free run at anyone.

If the linemen get into three-point stances, take advantage of that. If the defensive end is in a 7 technique on the tight end and gets a "go" call from the inside, he adjusts his alignment. The offensive linemen, once they get into the three-point stance, cannot move. The defensive end can adjust his alignment, get extremely wide, and make it doubly tough on the offensive tackle to get him.

Pass rushers make mistakes all the time. Some of them have nothing pre-planned in their mind for a pass rush and no pass rush move at all. The first move should be the speed rush. After the speed rush, we use the wiper move. If you are having success with either of those outside moves, the next move should be the inside rip. A mistake a pass rusher has is too many moves. He should find two or three at the most and make them effective.

If the defensive end gets a "go," he watches the quarterback if he is under the center. Just before the quarterback takes the snap, he steps out or sinks his tail. When the end sees the sink, he is off. You have to remind your players that during the course of a game the offense probably will adjust their cadence to draw our defense offside.

The hardest thing the defensive lineman has to do is make the transition from rushing the passer head on to some kind of play-action or sprint-out pass. I work a three on one key drill (Figure 18-3) to help the defensive linemen adjust to the play-action pass. I align a 3 technique on the guard. The guard has three things he can do. He can fire out in a double-team block. He can quick set the guard or he turns out as in slide protection. The defensive linemen when double-teamed play the play like a run. If the guard quick sets, the tackle takes a step upfield and comes inside on the guard. If the guard set outside, the tackle beats the center with his speed.

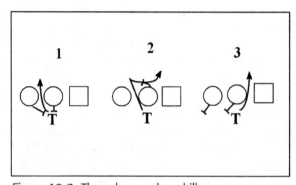

Figure 18-3. Three-by-one key drill

If we read the three-step drop, the defensive lineman does not put his hands up until he sees the ball coming out. This is a simple drill to run. It is effective in making the defense read different situations.

The next thing I want to talk about is the tackle set line. That is the imaginary line drawn behind the offensive tackle to a point three to four yards behind him. This is the point at which the defensive end thinks he can beat the tackle. The point will be different from game to game depending on personnel. The defensive end has to race the tackle to the point he has chosen. At that point, the defensive end has to make a decision on which move he will use if the tackle gets to the point first.

You have to know how the tackle is going to set. If he drops straight to the point, the defensive end may have to get wider in his alignment to make his move more effective and make the tackle widen his retreat line. If the defensive end can get the offensive tackle to open up and use a cross over step, he has won the battle. When the offensive tackle does that, he loses his power in his legs. The defensive end bull rushes over the top of him.

If the tackle is retreating straight back to beat the defensive end to the spot, the defender takes an inside move to slow his drop. If the tackle is beating the end to the spot, his weight has to be backward because of the speed he is moving. The defender uses his inside hand to push the tackle outside and uses an inside rip to get to the quarterback.

The critical thing is to put your players in a position where they are not square to the line of scrimmage. The defensive end to the open side of the set gets wider and tilts at an angle to the inside. That gives him good vision on everything inside and he can see the ball. That lets him get off the ball and do what he wants to do. We work on those little things in practice.

We have talked about the pass rush fundamentals. Now let us talk about the running game from the shade technique. You have to explain the different blocks the shade player is going to face. The first thing the shade player must understand is he will have an easier time getting his hands on the center because the center has to snap the ball before he can block. That means one of the center's hands is between his legs when the defender gets off the ball. The defender should knock the center off the line of scrimmage.

The shade player has a visual key, which is the V of the center's neck. He also has a pressure key. If his visual key tells him the center is working toward him and the pressure key tells him the guard is blocking down on him, he has to flip his hips and make himself skinny. He wants to take away a surface and make himself flat. The entry level of the pad of the defensive lineman is critical. If the defensive lineman's head is under his opponent and his hands are inside with his hips flipped to the guard, he is in good shape. He has leverage on the center and is in good shape with the guard.

If the center is trying to block back on the shade technique, the tackle wants to get off with his pad entry level lower than the center. He knocks the center back and keeps his gap side arm free. The center is the pressure key and he has vision on the guard. The running back is reading the movement of the shade tackle and running off it. If he beats the center and gets off into the backfield, he can create a lot of havoc.

If the center and guard try to combo block on the shade tackle with the guard climbing to the next level, the tackle has to beat the center. The center takes a drop step to get a better angle on the nose tackle. The tackle has to reach and grab the outside pad of the center. He will feel the guard coming down on his hip. If the shade tackle can grab the outside pad of the center and get hold of his outside triceps, the center will pull him through the block as the guard climbs for the linebacker.

If the center tries to reach, the nose tackle wants to do anything to keep his linebacker free. He grabs the center and keeps him from getting to the linebacker. If the nose tackle gets any kind of near back set, he does not step into the center. He steps into the guard. He has to anticipate reach, down block, and power. The shade tackle has to know the most popular scheme used on him is some kind of scoop or combo block. He will have two players working on him. He has to do anything he can to keep one of them from getting up to the linebacker.

The hard scoop is a popular scheme when running away from a 3 technique. The guard releases hard inside the 3 technique trying to get off on a linebacker. The offensive tackle comes down hard on the legs and ankles of the 3 technique. We drill this situation with a big ball drill. The 3 technique aligns on the guard. The guard moves hard inside. The 3 technique wants to get his hands on the guard. As the defensive lineman gets off and reaches for the guard, a manager rolls the ball at the feet of the 3 technique. The 3 technique takes his backside hand and punches the ball to get it away from his legs. That is a good drill to work on this situation.

When we teach the defensive line to get off the way we do, the defenders have to understand the angles of departure of the offensive linemen. There are two angles for the offensive linemen. There is the angle that keeps him on the line of scrimmage and the angle that lets him climb to the next level. The angle that keeps them on the line of scrimmage goes with the zone play. The offensive line tries to get the defensive line to move with the flow so they can use that momentum to wash them down the line and create a cut back lane for the running back. Because the scheme happens so fast, the defensive line is exposed. As the defensive line is working upfield, I tell them to get down and play low. Ideally, we would like to fit inside their blocks, but if we can create a pile, we have done our job. If the offensive turns someone and creates a hole, we have won the battle.

To be a good coach, you have to coach your players on recognizing the draw play. The offensive lineman takes a short drop one step off the line of scrimmage. On his next step, he screws his inside foot into the ground. The technique the offensive lineman uses is a slap technique. He invites the defender upfield and uses the momentum of the defender to push him further upfield. The offensive lineman slaps the defender on the inside pectoral muscle and pushes him upfield. As the defender feels the slap draw, he grabs the offensive lineman inside biceps. When he does that, he prevents the punch to the pecs and he can use the hold on the biceps to pull himself back to the line of scrimmage and into position. He can walk around the offensive lineman and get back inside.

Most times our defensive end plays in a track 7 technique. Playing that technique is critical for us in a running situation. I do not like to play a straight 7 technique.

If we play a straight 7 technique, we do not see the inside tackle. If he looks inside, the tight end will kick his butt every time. When we align in a 7 technique, the tight end is his basic key and we are going to beat him first.

Most tight ends concentrate on catching passes and could care less about run blocking. When the defensive end gets his hands inside, the tight end does not have a chance. He must be aware of a couple of blocking schemes. In the 7 technique the defensive end has C-gap responsibility. We can play a shade technique with the defensive end, which puts him on the outside shade of the tight end. From this position, he still has C-gap responsibility. People want to know how he can possibly be responsibility for a gap when he is one gap wider.

In this situation, two things are going to happen. He does not have to worry about the reach block. If the tight end tries to reach the defensive end, the end knocks him back off the line of scrimmage. When defender knocks the tight end back, the ball has to come inside of the tight end. If the defensive end gets a zone-blocking scheme to his inside, he takes the tight end and closes the hole with the tight ends body. If it is a pass play and the tight end releases, the defensive end has a better angle from which to attack.

If the tackle wants to combo block with the tight end, he has to bail off the line of scrimmage to get to the outside 9 technique. That lets the 3 technique get off the ball and press the hip of the offensive tackle. The 9 technique is a tight alignment on the tight end because of the run responsibility.

The reaction by the 7 technique on the drive block by the tight end is the same. His hands go inside. He steps with his inside foot to the tight end and wins the battle. On the arc block, the defensive end gets into the tight end with his hat and hands, and stays on him. Do not let the tight end get off the line. When the defensive end works on the tight end, he does not want to get flat with him. If you push the tight end back upfield, the zone play will not get off. If the defensive end lets the tight end arc to the next defender, the tackle will get his hands on him and they win the battle.

The blocking scheme that is tough on us is the scheme that New England runs. They base the defensive end with the tight end and bring the tackle on his hip trying to get his butt up inside. We tell our defensive end whoever initiates contact is the primary key. The defensive end turns on that player and kicks his butt. If the tackle gets the initial contact, the defensive end leans inside on the tackle. If the tight end initiates the contact, the defensive end destroys him.

I have to tell you a couple of theories. If we have a 9 technique end in a 4-3 defense, or if we have an outside linebacker in the 3-4 defensive set, they have to play against the counter off-tackle play. The defensive coordinator wants the end to read the backside pull of the offensive lineman. If the tight end blocks down, the defensive end squeezes down the line. He reads the pull of the backside offensive lineman. If the backside lineman is deeper than the frontside offensive lineman is, we want the end to take out both blockers. He wants the defensive end to spill the shallow pulling lineman.

The way we play our defensive end technique is to spill everything coming at us. When we see the double pull, we are not coming so flat that we hit the inside thigh pad and exchange one lineman for one defender. We use a technique called a "cheek" move. We get inside the shallow lineman. As the defensive end makes contact he strikes up into the inside breastplate of the pulling lineman. The defensive end wants to turn up on the pulling guard and try to push him up the field into the high pulling lineman.

Offenses run the bootleg or waggle pass off this action. The ends technique is a good technique to play against the play-action pass. We spill all backside-pulling linemen and cheek all tight ends, running backs, and frontside offensive linemen. In the cheek technique, the defensive end is not giving himself up to the pulling lineman. He is staying on his feet and forcing people deeper.

I hoped I helped you with some defensive-line play. Thank you very much.

19

Defensive Line Techniques

Jim Tanara
Eastern Kentucky University
1995

I want to teach you a little about the defensive front and how we do things at Eastern Kentucky University. I coached the old 50 defense until about 1991. That is when I switched over to the 4-3 defense. That was hard for me because I was the type of defensive coach that kept all the linebackers free. I taught stepping with the inside foot and squeezing down. Now, that I have gone to the 4-3 concept, all we do is line up and get after people's rear end. The first year I taught that, it was horrendous. The more I'm around the scheme, the more I like it.

We take speed and athletic ability over size all the time. That is within reason. I know you can't play with a 145-pound defensive tackle. Some of the things I'm going to talk about will be a natural for guys with athletic ability. For someone who doesn't have athletic ability, they have to be technique perfect.

Never ask your players to do something they can't do. If you want a two-gap player to line head up, whip the offense, and then play the gaps right and left, you better have a big physical guy. That is one of the reasons we went away from the 50 defense. We couldn't find those guys. When you get in a shade technique, I can talk to my guys about whipping half the man. That is what I like about the one-gap scheme. Basically, we see the same blocking schemes all the time regardless of what we play. In high school where you have to play anybody that shows up, you should consider this scheme. If you line your guys up and send them to the right or left, that is about the same thing. But, if you are making that guy read, whip the man in front of him and play two gaps, you may be asking him to do something he can't. If you have an athlete with skill, put him in an alignment where he can be successful.

One other thing I try to get across to kids is to be physically tough. Mike Tyson said it the best. They told him Michael Spinks had a game plan for him. He was going to keep him away with his jab and keep moving. Mike said, "Everyone has a game plan until they get hit." That is about the truth. You have to win the physical battle up front. If you can win the battle up front, you have a chance to win the game. We have a player on our team right now that doesn't have a whole lot of athletic ability. But, he was a hitter and would get after you. We won a lot of games because of him. It wasn't his ability, but he was technique perfect.

When I was trying to decide what I was going to talk about and how I was going to present it, I got confused. There are so many schemes that I didn't know how to present the material. But, all defenses come down to the basic point of whipping a guy and making a play. Those fundamentals are the same regardless of the scheme you use. That is what I want to talk about.

What I teach my kids, talk to them about, and drill them on came down to three areas. Those areas were *stance, playing with your hands*, and *footwork*. If our kids got blocked or were not successful, it was usually related to one of those areas or all of the areas. That is why I coach from the very first day to the last day about stance, hands and footwork.

Stance is a difficult thing to talk to a kid about where they think it is important to them. We line up as close to the offensive man as we can get. There is no margin for error. If I am a linebacker or defensive back, I can make some adjustments before I have to make contact. When the defensive lineman aligns, he better start off right. I've seen a lot of players get whipped before the ball was even snapped because they were aligned so poorly in the stance. They got blocked because their stance was so bad he couldn't get out of it. A lot of times, it is hard to get young kids to understand that. What I try to sell them on is the closer you get to the line of scrimmage, the more important your stance becomes.

I think it is easier to get in a good three-point stance than it is to get in a good four-point stance. In a four-point stance, everything on both sides of your body has to line up. Some of these guys can't physically get in a four-point stance. It takes a good athlete to get in a good four-point stance. I coached the four-point stance up until 1991, but I had the luxury of recruiting some athletes where you don't. If I were coaching a high school, I would put my defensive line in a three-point stance. I know I can start them out right because I can get them in a good three-point stance.

When I start talking to my kids about stance, I line everything straight down the field. Their shoulders, hips, feet, and everything else is straight down the field. If my left hand goes down, my left foot goes back. The left hand comes straight down. Here are some common mistakes your kids will make getting into a stance. Rather than drop the hand straight down, they put it in the middle. That throws their body and footwork off. That is the first thing you look at. We don't want a wide base. We want the feet up underneath in the stance. Not even as wide as shoulders width. We want the shoulders square. I always let the opposite arm hang. I don't want the shoulders tilted. By hanging the arm, that brings the shoulders square. Don't ask a kid to raise his head to look at the offensive linemen. If he does, then his tail will go down. If he wants to look at something, he turns his head. He does not raise it back. That is important because, if the head is up, his first step is going to be straight up. I have to make that correction all the time. From day one to the last day, I am still working on head position. The stagger of the feet depends on the body build of the guys.

The only way a defensive lineman can escape from a block is by using his hands. He has to play with his hands. When we line up in our 4-3 alignment, we are not lined on half a man. We are wider than that. We are on the tip of the offensive lineman. The reason we do that is to make it almost impossible for the linemen to reach block our people. Playing with our hands is extremely important. Every thing we do is with our hands. All offensive linemen cheat. They are going to hold. We never use that as an excuse for not doing the job. We keep our outside hand free at all times. The inside hand goes to the offensive lineman's breast. The head of the defensive player goes for the "V" in the neck looking over his shoulder. We are looking over the collarbone. The coaching point is to look your hands onto the blocker. If they do that, they are looking at the blocker. We want to take first things first. They have to whip the blocker first, then go make the play. The first thing high school kids want to do is raise up and find the ball.

After the defender gets his hands on the blocker, he has to get separation. The description we use is don't get alligator arms. That means real short arms. Get extension in the arm. Don't let the offensive blocker get his hands on you. If your kids are having a hard time playing with their hands, here is what you do. You line up with no gear except the headgear and play full speed. I guarantee that makes them play with their hands. Days we are out in shorts and headgears, I have full speed blocking drills. We don't get anybody hurt. We may get a bruise or so, but no one gets hurt. You will be surprised with what happens with your kids if you do this.

In our scheme of defense, the first step we take is straight up the field. The second step adjusts to the blocking scheme. Straight up the field means straight. There are no angles in the first step. The shade hand should be down on the ground. That means the first step is with the foot that is back. The right-side players play with their left hand down. If you have a guy who is making all kinds of plays, it doesn't matter which hand he puts down. As long as he makes plays, I could care less. You will be surprised that some kids can do a good job with either hand down. But, if a guy is getting into a bad stance, let him put down either hand to get into the good stance.

One thing I want to do on all blocks is to attack the blocker. That means get off the ball. All you guys have heard that old expression that, "Low man wins." That is exactly the truth. I don't care whether it is in junior high school or the NFL. If the defense gets off the football and is low, they win most of the time. Look at your film. Guys that set on the line of scrimmage get blocked all the time. My coaching point is to attack the outside half of the blocker with your eyes, hands, and feet. I like for our guys to look in for the ball so they get off on the ball. The first step is a power step to balance the defender. His second step adjusts to the blocking scheme. If the blocker goes down, the defender squeezes to the inside and spills any trap block coming.

When you get into the shade defense, you only see certain blocks. The blocks that you see are double-team, reach, turn out, spill, and scoop. The spill to me is a trap block.

We do not see a lot of true double-teams. What we see is two guys trying to knock us back into linebackers and one coming off for the linebacker. We see two guys trying to get one guy down the line of scrimmage with one coming off for a linebacker. We don't see a true double-team where two guys are blocking one man. The only time I see that is in short yardage and goal line. When we get this scheme, the first step is always the same. Straight up the field and attack the offensive blocker hard. I don't want the outside man to knock me back or down the line. When I see the outside man coming on me, I drop my head and outside shoulder to the ground. I look like an ostrich. After that, I take the shoulder and take out the outside blocker's inside leg. When I do that, I crawl a yard deep in the backfield. If I get the true double-team, I want to do two things. I don't want to get knocked off the ball, and I want to occupy two guys. If he can do that, he has done a hell of a job. If that guy can somehow get penetration, he can make the tackle. Most teams coach to run over the double-team.

What we see, I call chip and slip block. The guard and tackle come off together and engage the defensive tackle. The guard is the primary blocker with the tackle coming off for the linebacker. That is what I call a chip block. If the opposite thing occurs with the tackle as the primary blocker on the defensive tackle and the guard coming off for the linebacker, that is the slip block. We use the same technique on both blocks. The first step is a straight attack step up the field. When the tackle sees the offensive tackle coming down on him, he drops his outside shoulder underneath the blocker and drives into him. The important thing is to get under the blocker. We want the down block to go over the top of the defense. If the tackle releases and goes for the linebacker, the defensive tackle can make the play.

Figure 19-1

The success of that block has a lot to do with the Mike linebacker. If the Mike linebacker fills and attacks the line of scrimmage, the tackle or guard doesn't have the time to double on the tackle. One of them has to release, or they will never get the linebacker. If the Mike linebacker doesn't react, the offensive tackle will stay on the defensive tackle longer and make it tougher. We find that most teams don't do a good job of jamming the defensive tackle with the outside block anyway. The blocker's eyes are on the linebacker because that is his block. He is in a hurry to get off to get to the linebacker. For that reason, we don't go down on the ground like we would in the true double-team. In fact, if the tackle chips up to the linebacker and the defensive tackle doesn't make the play, that is a minus for him on the grading system.

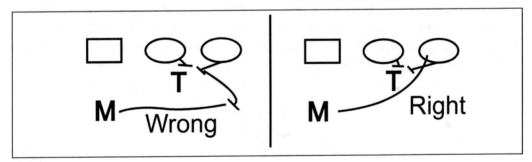

Figure 19-2

The next block is the turn out block. A turn out block to me is when the blocker puts his head inside on the defensive man. I know right now, if the blocker's head is inside, so is the ball. All we want to do on the turn out is to get up field and restrict the inside running lane. The good thing about getting up field is the back can't bounce the ball outside. If the end sets on the line of scrimmage and gets the turn out block, the back can bounce the ball and run right by the end. We want our players getting a yard to two yards up the field. If the ball stays inside, the end turns, retraces his steps, and makes the play. He only does that after the threat of the bounce and cut back are gone.

Figure 19-3

The reach block is the common block people depend on. The first thing I tell my guys is, if that ever happens to them, they are not going to heaven. It should never happen, but it does. If a man gets reached, it's usually the defensive man not looking his hands on the blocker or he is stepping inside. If he looks his hand on the man that is blocking him and steps straight up field, he should never be reached. The offensive blocker to reach has to open up. When he does that, he loses all his power and we run right through it. If the offense does gain leverage, we don't retreat or give ground. We are going to press the block and continue to try to run through it. If he retreats, he cuts off the linebacker. I grade my guys every play. If one of them gets reached, that is a double minus. We try to get across to our guys, if one guy blocks them, they are in the wrong business. To block us, we want the offense to have to double-team.

We get a lot of scoop blocking schemes. Teams usually try to scoop our defensive tackles. The technique we use is to get between the blocker and press on the scoop man. We want to get our feet to the next nearest lineman. If the center is leading on the shade tackle with the backside guard coming for the scoop, the tackle gets between the center and guard and presses on the guard. He wants to get his feet to the onside guard. We don't worry about the center because he is trying to get off for the backside linebacker. We see this all the time, and I work on it all the time. The tackles spend 70 percent of their drill work time on the scoop scheme.

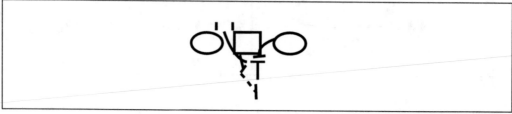

Figure 19-4

The spill block, to me, is no different than a trap block. All kick out blocks are spilled to the outside with a wrong arm technique. I like that because it kicks the play outside and our linebacker can make the play. When we spill, it is the only time we turn our shoulders to the line of scrimmage. The rest of the time, we want to play with our shoulders square to the line. The defense is coached to know if the offensive man goes inside someone is going to trap his butt. That is the first thing he thinks about. The first step straight up the field doesn't put us in very good position to play a trap.

The second step has got to be down the line. The way we teach it is to punch the hip. That means, when the blocker goes down, the defender takes his outside hand and tries to punch him in the hip. He can't do it, but it turns his hips and shoulder in to play the trap. The end probably sees the fullback while the tackle sees the guard. When we spill, we want it deep in the backfield. We don't want to sit on the line of scrimmage and spill anyone. The thing that is hard is the offense slams the defensive end with the tight end. The tight end slams and releases for the linebacker. The fullback comes and kicks out on the end. That is hard to play. The way we play this is to attack the tight end so he has a hard time getting off to block anyone. Instead of the tight end slamming our defensive end, the defensive end slams the tight end. When we spill, we want to attack the trapper. Don't stop and wait for the trapper.

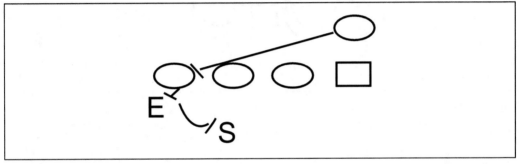

Figure 19-5

The play that can hurt the 4-3 defense is the buck trap middle. It hits so quick that all the 3 technique tackle can do once he feels the trap coming is throw his body back into the hole. The thing we do to help is bring the backside tackle to a backside shade on the center. That helps squeeze the play. The man responsible for the trap middle is the Mike linebacker. All the tackles can do to help is keep the hole as tight as possible.

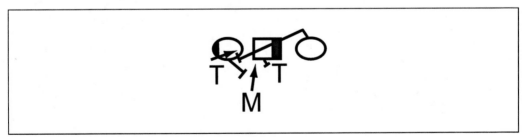

Figure 19-6

There are three techniques that your kids have to learn as defensive linemen. The have to learn the skin, rip, and quick more. They need to learn these things because that is what they do so many times. A skin technique, to me, is a directional technique. When you line a kid up and slant him right or left is a skin technique. From the shade technique, we back up off the ball six inches. That is to get the defense across the face of the blocker. If you are in a head-up position, don't back up. If I am going left, I mentally shift my weight to my right foot. The first step is a flat step to the line of scrimmage, and the right shoulder dips. The second step is up the field, and the right arm rips through the face of the blocker. The reason we take the flat step is to keep us from getting pushed down the line of scrimmage. The skin move is used to beat a reach or turn out block. If the defensive man takes his lateral step and the blocker blocks down, he lets him go and comes right off his butt to the inside.

Figure 19-7

20

Defensive Line Play

Bill Young
The Ohio State University
1992

My objective is to share with you specific techniques and strategies of the defensive line at Ohio State University. I've been the defensive coordinator and defensive line coach at OSU for the past four years. Two years ago, we changed our defensive line play from a flat-footed, read-and-react form of play (or mirror the offensive lineman) to a very aggressive, attack and read-on-the-run style of play. Of the different changes we've made with our defense, I believe this was the single most important one.

Basically, we want to be complex but not complicated. Communication is a cornerstone for our defense. We stress it in everything we do. We name every defensive position. Naming enables every player to know exactly who we are talking to when making corrections in meetings, at practice, and during games. We number each technique and letter every gap on the offensive front. We use key words in our defensive calls to alert the significant players of their involvement in a stunt or change-up in technique. For example, our base defense is eagle, a change-up defense is eagle T. The "T" alerts the defensive tackle to play a 2 technique as opposed to a 3 technique in eagle.

Another example is eagle Ed. That is a change-up for the End. The end now plays a 3 technique, as opposed to a 5 in the eagle defense. We want to be as complex as possible, giving our opponents different looks to block, yet keeping things simple. Defense is a game of reaction. The less our players have to think, the more effective they become.

We teach and demand our players to give great effort, to hit, to line up right, and to take great pursuit angles. Our players study film of our opponents. In fact, we've gone as far as making personal video tapes for players to take with them to study, along with very involved scouting reports.

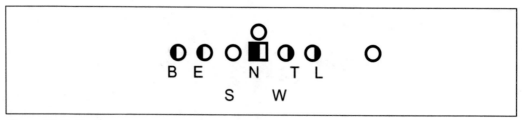

Figure 20-1. Eagle

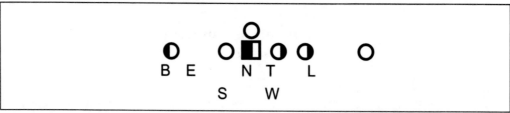

Figure 20-2. Eagle T

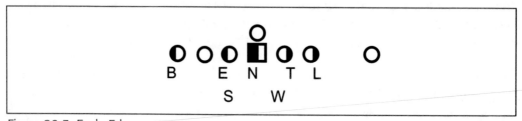

Figure 20-3. Eagle Ed

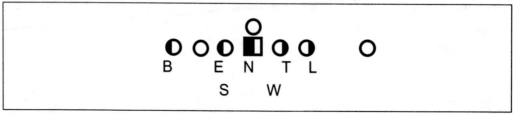

Figure 20-4

We believe our opponents' offense will tell us a lot if we will just listen. Areas of special importance to our defensive players, especially our defensive linemen, are what we call presnap reads:

- Time on clock
- Score
- Personnel
- Down and distance
- Vertical field position
- Horizontal field position
- Formation
- Line splits/receiver splits
- Stances

The time left in the game, or the half, will dictate a lot toward the tempo and play selection of the opponent. Obviously, the score will have a great influence in the play selection and what to anticipate from the opposition. The personnel in the game is key to the type of plays to expect. When a team gets into a one-back offense and the remaining back is a fullback, it's generally going to be a pass. However, if the remaining back is a tailback, it'll be a run, because he is a better runner than blocker. We really stress the down and distance tendency of each team we play. We use a computer to break down our opponents' film and pass this information to our players so they will anticipate plays in certain situations. The vertical field position is also important in knowing what to expect from opponents. Backed up to their own goal line, most teams are conservative, not wanting to give up a turnover. With the ball between the 30s, however, most teams will really open up their offense. We call this the alumni zone. Alumni always get excited about trick plays, reverses, and such. Opponents generally become more conservative as they move into field-goal range.

Every team is different. Therefore, we keep a vertical field position by down and distance chart in our defensive meeting room. This chart becomes part of the scouting report we give our players. Horizontal field position is a strong key. We always want to defend the wide field and force the opposition into the boundary as our twelfth man. The offensive formations are a vital form of information to us. If a defensive end sees trips and a back offset to his side, he expects a sprint-out pass and aligns a little wider.

There is one team we play that on third-and-long, if they get into the I, your ends had better move in and get ready to squeeze the draw. If your ends stay out wide and rush upfield, this team will gash you. We played a team a couple of years ago that got into a halfback offset to twins. When the fullback aligned behind the tackle, it was a run, with the fullback being the lead blocker. If the tailback was offset, it was a sure pass. The tailback would release and run a pass route, and the fullback would be a blocker. It seems the more formations a team runs, the more solid its tendencies become.

It's imperative that defensive linemen are alert to line splits. As a general rule, teams pack it in tight to run outside or pass. If they take big splits, they tend to run up inside. Often, teams will oversplit the middle or guard center gap to run the trap and oversplit one tackle to run the cutback.

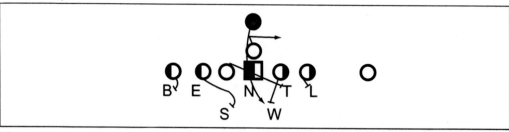

Figure 20-5

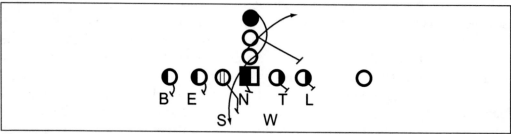

Figure 20-6

Tight wide receiver splits tell you to be alert for the reverse or crackback. A defensive back should be thinking about the possibility of an outcut. Probably the biggest tip-offs of all are the stances of the offensive linemen.

It seems each year the offensive linemen get bigger and bigger. It used to be rare for a team to have a 300-pound tackle. Today, not only are both tackles that big, but several of the guards are, too. Because of their size, they really cheat their stances. If their weight is back on their haunches, we think pass or pull. If their weight is forward, we think run. We work hard to communicate this to our defensive front. If both sides are showing pass, we anticipate pass or draw. If one side shows pass and the other shows run, there is a great chance they are running the counter sweep to the run stances side and pulling the other side.

The center's feet are another good solid key for us. I can't tell you how many teams we played that have had their center up on his toes on running plays and flat-footed on passes. Even more telling, have his offhand down in a four-point stance on runs and his hand on his knee on pass plays.

In coaching the defensive line, everything starts with the stance. We use four basic types: a take-charge stance, a move stance, a rush stance, and a short-yardage stance (or goal-line stance). The take-charge stance is used on normal downs in our base defenses. It is a three-point stance with the free hand hanging and ready to deliver a blow. We want our feet armpit wide with 40 percent of our weight on the balls of our feet and the remaining 60 percent of our weight on the down hand. We used to teach it shoulders' width apart, but our players had a misconception of just how broad their shoulders were. It's better to be too tight than too wide. The down hand should be four to six inches out in front of the headgear, with the hips a little higher than the head and the elbow flexed. The whole body is coiled, ready to explode and attack.

The move stance is used on defenses which require defensive linemen to slant, angle, rip, or jump around on the snap. This stance looks exactly like the take-charge stance, except the lineman must shift his weight to 40 percent on his down hand and 60 percent on the balls of the feet. Mentally, the majority of the weight should be on the foot opposite the direction of the move.

The rush stance is used in obvious passing downs. This requires not only a change in stance, but also in attitude. On a take-charge and move stance, we are thinking run first and react to the pass. However, on the rush stance, we are thinking pass first and then reacting to the run. We want a three-point stance, but we want to elongate it by moving the hand a little out in front of the head and increasing the distance, or stagger, between the feet to about one foot. We also want to move the width of the feet closer together, much like a sprinter in starting blocks. The fourth type of stance is our short-yardage or goal-line stance. We want to be in a low, four-point stance, with our weight shifted to 70 percent on our hands and 30 percent on our feet. Our hips are slightly higher than our head, our bodies are flexed, or coiled, ready to penetrate and create a new line of scrimmage.

We teach our defensive linemen to move on movement. We key the ball, the offensive linemen, and the quarterback's feet. We want to attack on movement. All of our drill work, even our after practice conditioning, is done on sight not sound. Before we changed from a flat-footed read of keeping the offensive linemen off the linebackers at-all-cost style to our present attack, read-on-the-run style of defense, we went so far as to grab the offside armpit of the center or guard on scoop blocks and tackled him to free up the linebackers.

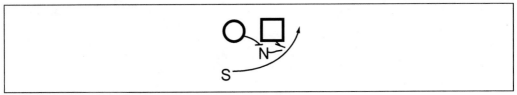

Figure 20-7. Old way: kept center off linebacker

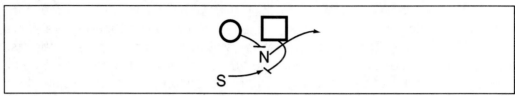

Figure 20-8. Now: we run off the center's butt and make the tackle

Becoming an attacking defensive line is the best thing we have done. Our sacks have doubled, and our tackles for losses have tripled. Although our linebackers occasionally get cut, we think it's worth the trade-off. We instruct our defensive linemen *to avoid being scooped*, if the man they are aligned on gets off on the linebacker, and to *make the play*.

In summation, defensively, we believe in good, sound fundamentals. We instruct our players to take care of the little things, teach them to analyze game film, and to study scouting reports. In short: *prepare to win*.

About the Editor

Earl Browning is a native of Logan, West Virginia. He currently serves as president of Telecoach, Inc.—an organization that conducts football clinics and produces the *Coach of the Year Clinics Football Manuals*. A 1958 graduate of Marshall University, he earned his M.Ed. and Rank I education certification from the University of Louisville. From 1958 to 1975, he coached football at various Louisville-area high schools. Among the honors he has been accorded are his appointments to the National Football Foundation and to the College Hall of Fame Advisory Committee on moving the museum to South Bend, Indiana. He was named to the Greater Louisville Football Coaches Association Hall of Legends in 1998. From 1992 to the present, he has served as a radio and television color analyst for Kentucky high school football games, including the Kentucky High School Athletic Association State Championship games.